23.99

CANADIAN
NUCLEAR
WEAPONS

CANADIAN NUCLEAR WEAPONS

The Untold Story of Canada's Cold War Arsenal

John Clearwater

DUNDURN PRESS
Toronto • Oxford
1998

Canadian Cataloguing in Publication Data

Clearwater, John
    Canadian nuclear weapons

Includes bibliographical references.
ISBN 1-55002-299-7

1. Nuclear weapons – Canada – History. I. Title.

U264.5.C3C53 1998   355.8'25119'0971   C97-931824-6

1   2   3   4   5   BJ   02   01   00   99   98

We acknowledge the support of the **Canada Council for the Arts** for our publishing program. We also acknowledge the support of the **Ontario Arts Council** and the **Book Publishing Industry Development Program** of the **Department of Canadian Heritage**.

Care has been taken to trace the ownership of copyright material used in this book. The author and the publisher welcome any information enabling them to rectify any references or credit in subsequent editions.

Printed and bound in Canada.

     Printed on recycled paper.

Dundurn Press
8 Market Street
Suite 200
Toronto, Ontario, Canada
M5E 1M6

Dundurn Press
73 Lime Walk
Headington, Oxford
England
OX3 7AD

Dundurn Press
250 Sonwil Drive
Buffalo, NY
U.S.A. 14225

TABLE OF CONTENTS

Acknowledgements   7
Acronyms   11
Introduction   15

Chapter 1
    Pearson's Cabinet and the Political Agreement to
    Acquire Nuclear Weapons for the Canadian Military   27
Chapter 2
    BOMARC: the Weapon and the Squadrons   55
Chapter 3
    Starfighter: the Weapons   91
Chapter 4
    Starfighter: the Squadrons   117
Chapter 5
    Honest John: the Weapon and the Batteries   153
Chapter 6
    The CF-101B VooDoo and Genie Rocket   177
Chapter 7
    Anti-Submarine Warfare   217

Concluding Thoughts   239

Appendix   241
    • The 1963 Agreement and the Service-to-Service
    Technical Arrangements
    • Commanding Officers
    • Bibliographic Notes, Sources,
    Files, Archives, Libraries, and Agencies

Endnotes   297

For:

Archie, Spider, Tanner, Kiwi,

Mika, Roger, Minah, Smokey, and Mittens.

ACKNOWLEDGEMENTS

Firstly, and most importantly, I would like to thank the staff of the Government Archives Division of the National Archives of Canada, and the Access to Information staff at the Archives for the superb support they have provided. The staff in the Reading Room at the Archives has also been terrific in putting up with a myriad of requests.

Secondly, I thank the staff of the National Defence Directorate of History (DHist) in Ottawa for allowing me access to their superb collection of squadron and unit histories. I am also grateful for the number of requests which Isabelle Campbell handled on an informal basis.

The Department of Foreign Affairs, formerly External Affairs, provided me with excellent support. I was accepted into their Academic Access Programme, and after they were assured that I was a qualified academic, I was given access to departmental files on nuclear weapons discussions and acquisition. These files had been cleared for academic viewing, but the contents remain closed until a declassifier reviews each page. Although this book is now in print, there are still outstanding requests from this process more than a year and a half later.

The Access to Information section in the Prime Minister's Office and Privy Council Office provided a great deal of help to this project. Ciuineas Boyle and her staff were able to give me all of the minutes of both full Cabinet meetings and of Cabinet Defence Committee meetings at which nuclear weapons were discussed. They have never been anything but completely forthcoming with aid and information.

The National Defence Photo Unit in Ottawa was also especially helpful in the completion of this work. I thank all of the staff in the Central Negative Library, and Cpl. Steve Sauve.

In the United States I received assistance from three vastly different sources. The US National Archives and Records Administration was able to provide State Department records for the 1961–1963 period, while the non-governmental National Security Archive in Washington allowed me to browse through their files on their upcoming nuclear weapons history project. The US Air Force was also helpful in that the staff at the USAF Historical Research Agency in Montgomery, Alabama, showed me files on USAF nuclear support units and fed me great bar-b-q. Although this was a long train ride on Amtrak from Montreal to Montgomery, it was worth it.

Back in Canada, the most curious research location was at Shilo, Manitoba. This training site for the R.C. Artillery hosted an Honest John battery, and is also an archival site. The CFB Shilo Artillery Museum has retained some files on both 1 SSM Bty and 2 SSM Tg Bty. Although it was a long drive from Winnipeg, it too was worth the trip.

COPYRIGHT ACKNOWLEDGEMENT

It is the position of the Government of Canada that all materials generated by persons in their employ, even if those materials are top secret memos between two persons, are covered by Crown Copyright and are the intellectual property of the Government of Canada for 50 years after their publication. While I disagree with this position, preferring to think that items paid for by the taxpayers are public domain, I am legally bound to acknowledge this policy. To this end, I would like to acknowledge the kindness of the Minister of Public Works and Government Services; the Minister of National Defence; the Secretary of State for External Affairs; and the Privy Council Office in the clearance and provision of these materials. All materials generated by a department appear courtesy of the Minister of that department. In addition, photographs appear courtesy of the Public Affairs office of National Defence Headquarters and National Defence Photo Unit (Ottawa). Lastly, I thank Paul Hellyer and the estate of Paul Martin for extending copyright clearance to this publication.

DISCLAIMER

ACRONYMS

ACM	Air Chief Marshal
ADC	Air Defence Command (RCAF or USAF)
AFB	Air Force Base (USAF)
ALCOP	Alternate Command Post
AM	Air Marshal
AOC	Air Officer Commanding
ASW	Anti-submarine warfare
ATAF	Allied Tactical Air Force
AVM	Air Vice Marshal
AW(F)	All Weather Fighter
B	Bomb type
BOMARC	Boeing & Michigan Aeronautical Research Centre
BUIC	Back-Up Interceptor Control
CAF	Canadian Armed Forces
CAG	Canadian Air Group
CAS	Chief of the Air Staff (RCAF)
CDC	Cabinet Defence Committee
CDS	Chief of Defence Staff
CEO	Canadian Eyes Only
CF	Canadian Forces
CFB	Canadian Forces Base
CFS	Canadian Forces Station
CGS	Chief of the General Staff
CHQ	Canadian/Command Headquarters
CI	Capability Inspection
CIBG	Canadian Infantry Brigade Germany
CINC	Commander-in-Chief
CNS	Chief of the Naval Staff
CONAD	Continental Air Defense (USAF)

DEFCON	Defense Condition
Det	Detachment (USAF)
DHist	Directorate of History
DND	Department of National Defence
DNW	Director of Nuclear Weapons (DND)
EOD	explosive ordnance disposal
FRG	Federal Republic of Germany
ICI	Initial Capability Inspection
kt	kiloton
Mk	Mark
Mt	megaton
MMG	Munitions Maintenance Group (USAF)
MMS	Munitions Maintenance Squadron (USAF)
MND	Minister of National Defence
Mod	Modification
MUNS	Munitions Maintenance Squadron (USAF)
MSS	Munitions Support Squadron (USAF)
NATO	North Atlantic Treaty Organization
NCC	NORAD Command Centre
NORAD	North American Air/Aerospace Defence Command
NSI	Nuclear Safety/Surety Inspection
PCO	Privy Council Office
PM	Prime Minister
PMO	Prime Ministers Office
QRA	Quick Reaction Alert
RCA	Royal Canadian Artillery (or)
	Royal Regiment of Canadian Artillery
RCAF	Royal Canadian Air Force
RCHA	Royal Canadian Horse Artillery
RCMP	Royal Canadian Mounted Police
SAC	Strategic Air Command (USAF)
SACEUR	Supreme Allied Commander Europe
SAGE	Semi-Automatic Ground Environment
SAM	Surface-to-Air Missile
SAS	Safe And Secure Storage
SAS	Special Ammunition Storage
SoD	Secretary of Defense (USA)
SSEA	Secretary of State for External Affairs
SSM	Surface-to-Surface Missile

Sqdn	Squadron
Stn	station
TAC	Tactical Air Command (USAF)
TRW	Tactical Reconnaissance Wing (USAF)
USAF	United States Air Force
USAFE	USAF Europe
USAREUR	United States Army Europe
USN	United States Navy
VCNS	Vice Chief of the Naval Staff
W	Warhead type

We are thus not only the first country in the world with the capability to produce nuclear weapons that chose not to do so, we are also the first nuclear-armed country to have chosen to divest itself of nuclear weapons.

Pierre E. Trudeau
Prime Minister of Canada

The United Nations
26 May 1978

INTRODUCTION

This book began in 1994 as a simple private research project undertaken to keep my mind active in Ottawa. My interest in the subject went back to the mid-1980s, about the time Canada gave up its final 54 nuclear weapons.

By the time Canada divested itself of its last atomic weapons in 1984, the country had been a direct participant for more than half of the nuclear-armed age. The country, with the help of the United States, had fielded the low-technology W25 and W40 warheads, as well as the newest Mark (Mk) 57 gravity bomb. Canada had nuclear warheads for missiles, rockets, and bombs. Only a naval component was missing.

The purpose of this book is to bring together information that was, until recently, secret about the nature of the nuclear arsenal in Canada, and combine it with known information about the systems in the US nuclear arsenal.

In this work the reader will view for the first time the minutes of the Pearson Cabinet and Cabinet Defence Committee meetings in which the acquisition of nuclear weapons was discussed. Also printed here for the first time is the 16 August 1963 agreement and subsidiary agreements made between Canada and the United States for the weapons Canada eventually deployed on four systems in the RCAF and Canadian Army.

The book then takes the reader through all four of the nuclear weapons systems deployed by Canada between 1963 and 1984: the BOMARC surface-to-air guided interceptor missile, the three nuclear gravity bombs carried by the CF-104 Starfighter, the Honest John short-range battlefield rocket, and the long-lived Genie air-to-air unguided rocket. Each section on a particular weapon includes information on the units which were trained and equipped to use that weapon. In the case of the Honest John rocket, only one battery was so equipped; but with the Starfighter, numerous squadrons were trained, classified, and operated as nuclear strike units, and were provided with various nuclear gravity bombs over the years of the commitment. For this reason, the Starfighter section is divided into two chapters: one on the four nuclear weapons, and one on the numerous nuclear strike squadrons deploying the bombs.

An important aspect of the study of nuclear weapons in the Canadian forces is their operational dates. Although each of the carrier systems, such as the Starfighter, was already operational (albeit without warheads) at the time of the agreement, there was a considerable time-lag between the signature of the final agreement and acquisition of the warheads. Therefore, a dedicated effort has been made to identify the dates of initial nuclear acquisition for each system.

The BOMARC was armed with nuclear warheads only four-and-a-half months after the agreement was reached, but the Genie did not reach operational status until early 1965. In the meantime, the Starfighter gained its first thermonuclear payload, and the Army had confirmation that the warheads for the Honest John rockets were in the storage igloos at Hemer, Federal Republic of Germany.

When they were eventually removed, the nuclear weapons used by the Canadian military did not leave in the order they arrived. Moreover, their departure failed to receive the press coverage lavished upon their arrival many years before. Only the BOMARC decommissioning would be publicly acknowledged, while the Honest John, Starfighter, and VooDoo/Genie commitments would simply fade away, long after they had disappeared from public consciousness. The final removal from Canadian bases has been documented here as much as possible.

Although history and data of the removal of the nuclear weapons from Canada and the Canadians in Europe is presented, little political background is provided. Due to the passage of years, the materials on the acquisition of the bomb by the Pearson Government are no longer considered military-sensitive documents. However, the newer material, all from the Trudeau period, is still too recent by Canadian secrecy standards to be released. Therefore, all the author could do was present the operational facets of the closing of the nuclear commitment in the four weapons systems.

One last, though crucial, aspect of the nuclear history of the Canadian military is the US Air Force and US Army participation in the nuclear weapons custodial role. The conditions of the Canada-United States Agreement of 16 August 1963 required that all US nuclear weapons remain in the custody of qualified US national personnel, and therefore with US military units so designated for this purpose. There was one such squadron for the BOMARC and Genie sites, and one each for the Starfighter and Honest John. Each squadron would be divided into "detachments," one of which would serve with each nuclear-capable base or station. The weapons system chapters also include an overview of the US military units utilized as custodians of the warheads.

The format chosen is one which relies heavily upon the original documents to help tell the story. None of the documents appear in their original form as all have been transcribed and edited for ease of reading. This was necessary as many of the original documents were barely legible, and would not have reproduced acceptably.

Many days, weeks, and months have been spent trying to have secret files opened for public examination. Fortunately for researchers, many of the files, some classified as high as "Secret — Canadian Eyes Only" have been opened by the National Archives. For this reason, the text of this work is based heavily on original wording of documents usually written in the 1960s. By using this technique, it is hoped that the feeling of the time in dealing with Canada's nuclear weapons will be accurately conveyed. Rather than presenting heavily-edited words, the book lets the authors and their papers speak for themselves in their *own* words.

Researchers wishing to continue this important work should find the documents and analyses presented in this work of great use. What they will also find appealing is that the final section, "Sources and Bibliographic Notes," is devoted to a discussion of the resources available and the location of those yet to be fully exploited.

Although some argue, correctly, that the story of nuclear weapons for the Canadian Forces began during the Diefenbaker years, this work concentrates exclusively on the post-Diefenbaker period. This is due to the simple fact that Diefenbaker never got the bomb, and Pearson did. Therefore, an operational history of nuclear weapons in Canadian military service must essentially ignore the years preceding 1963.

Nuclear weapons came to Canada as early as September 1950, when the USAF temporarily stationed eleven "Fat Man"-style atomic bombs at Goose Bay, Newfoundland.* From that point on the Canadian military longed for the weapon which separated the military haves from the have-nots. Although Diefenbaker initially supported this acquisition, his failure to carry the task through makes the history up to 1963 a moot point. I have, therefore, left this part of the story to other historians. My job as a military-strategic analyst is simply to show what happened when the will to acquire the nuclear warheads was finally mustered.

THE PHANTOM WARHEAD

It is now clearly provable that the Canadian military was not armed with nuclear weapons until New Year's Eve, 1963, yet this conclusion has not been universal. In his important 1993 book, Commander Peter Haydon (RCN retd) writes that "(t)here is good reason to believe that in late 1962 the RCAF had access to nuclear weapons."[1] He further asserts that "it is not impossible that some US nuclear weapons had been moved into Canada before the (Cuban missile) crisis under a secret agreement. There is evidence, albeit circumstantial, to indicate that nuclear weapons were present in Canada during the crisis."[2] Haydon then goes on to recount that the RCAF Air Council had put off consideration of sending BOMARC warhead components back to the USA in accordance with a USAF request.[3]

Haydon, formerly of the Royal Canadian Navy and now a scholar in the Dalhousie University Political Science Department, writes that the RCAF had access to nuclear weapons just before the Cuban missile crisis. He asserts that warheads were probably present at North Bay for 446 Surface-to-Air Missile (SAM) Squadron, but were withdrawn as the confrontation began. His only proof seems to be a cryptic reference in the minutes of the Air Council in October 1963, which appears to state that they were sending back some BOMARC warheads from North Bay to the United States.

This is indeed an incredible assertion, not least of all because if true it would mean that Diefenbaker *had* acquired at least a few

---

* This was a notable deployment because, as it left Newfoundland, the lead bomber dropped its Mk IV atomic bomb over the St. Lawrence River on 10 November 1950.

warheads. However, the operational evidence against this is more than overwhelming. The US Air Force does not simply give nuclear weapons to friendly countries. What the original uncensored document at the Department of National Defence Directorate of History (DHist) shows is that the Air Council agreed that "the request from the USAF for eight modified target-seeker heads for BOMARC-B missiles shall not be replied to until the Chief of the Air Staff discusses the matter with the Minister." The censor probably removed the words "eight modified target-seeker heads" and left Haydon with the impression that the item referred to the W40 nuclear warheads.

On the operational side, it is instructive to note that no unit could have access to nuclear weapons until it passed the Initial Capability Inspection (ICI) given by the US Air Force's Inspector General, and that no unit could keep nuclear weapons without passing an initial Operational Readiness Inspection (ORI). However, 446 SAM Squadron did pass an early ICI in February 1962, but it appears that this rating could not be kept if the weapons were not on site. Additionally, there is no evidence of an ORI being given prior to the Cuban Missile Crisis. Therefore, North Bay's 446 SAM Squadron had to pass another ICI on 07 November 1963,[4] and the first deliveries following that satisfactory inspection rating were on 31 December 1963.[5] The annual history even noted that "technical interest was generated by the delivery at Stn North Bay of the first warhead for 446 BOMARC Squadron, which was accepted on 31 December 1963, and convoyed to the BOMARC Site immediately on off-loading."

Later, the annual report of 446 Squadron would state that

> the year 1964 began very well indeed for 446 Sqdn since the first consignment of Nuclear Weapons arrived New Years Eve. This was a great boost to the morale of squadron personnel as they had been waiting for these packages since February 1962 when the unit passed its Initial Capability Inspection. Under normal circumstances satisfactory ICIs are followed by the installation of warheads.[6]

North Bay would then go through their full ORI in late February 1964.[7] The monthly report notes that

> on the 25th of February 1964 the biggest inspection team to date arrived at the unit for a four day Operational Readiness Inspection (ORI) of all phases of the squadron operations. On the completion of the inspection the team announced that the squadron had passed. This was the word that the squadron had been waiting for, for a period of 2 to 3 years. Now the squadron was officially and finally cleared to carry out its Primary role in the NORAD Defence System.[8]

All available evidence strongly suggests that this was their first ORI, and that these were their first nuclear weapons.

Another clue as to the nuclear status of North Bay is the date of the formation of the US Air Force Detachment responsible for custody of the warheads. No warhead would be present without a custodial agent and detachment. North Bay was supported by Detachment 1 of the 425th Munitions Maintenance Squadron, and the detachment commander, Captain W.D. Pickett, had initially arrived at North Bay in March or April 1962, but then left and did not return to organize the detachment until 15 September 1963.

North Bay was not the only BOMARC site, but it was the only one which, theoretically, could have handled nuclear weapons in the fall of 1962. La Macaza, the station in Quebec, would also eventually deploy BOMARCs and nuclear warheads. But the missile site, built under contract by Boeing, was not handed over to the RCAF until 15 October 1963, right in the middle of the Cuban Missile Crisis, and after the mysterious warheads were to have been returned. Further, La Macaza went through its first ICI during 13–15 November 1962, and then again during 8–13 December 1963. Delivery schedules then strongly suggest that their first nuclear warheads did not arrive until at least 01 January 1964, and that their ORI was then held on 2–6 March 1964.[9] Even then, it was clear that La Macaza was unfit to have nuclear weapons, as their ORI report rated them as only "Marginally Satisfactory."[10]

Lastly, and probably the most telling evidence against this idea, is the fact that the first BOMARC missile bodies and wings arrived from Boeing at North Bay on 19 October 1962, a date near the *end* of the Cuban Missile Crisis. If there were warheads already on site, the military obviously planned to throw them at Soviet bombers with their bare hands.

Therefore, we can conclude that there is no credible operational evidence that any BOMARC missile in Canada, either at North Bay or at La Macaza, was ever armed with a nuclear warhead prior to 31 December 1963, and certainly not as early at October 1962.

THE NUMBERS GAME

In any study of nuclear weapons, the bean-counters will raise their heads and cry out for numbers. While this is relatively easy for a system such as the BOMARC, it is considerably more difficult for the CF-104. However, some educated guesses can be made.

Let us start with the easiest system to count: the BOMARC. Canada deployed two squadrons of 28 BOMARC missiles each, and each BOMARC was armed with only one warhead. This leads us to the conclusion that there were 56 BOMARC W40 nuclear warheads (plus perhaps four spares) in Canada. At the outside end, we can surmise that a total of 60 W40 warheads were in Canada at any one time between 1964 and 1971.

Also relatively easy is the count for the Honest John rocket system used by the Army in Germany. There were four launcher vehicles, each of which was equipped to take four rockets into the field. Each primary rocket, and there were only 16 of these, had a single warhead which would accompany the convoy from the Special Ammunition Storage (SAS) site near Hemer. This would only be done in times of war, and once war had begun there was no more need for the SAS. It is therefore reasonable to conclude that the US Army provided 16 W31 nuclear warheads to 1 Surface-to-Surface Missile Battery.

Moving up the ladder of difficulty, we come to the CF-101 VooDoo/Genie deployment. The original deployment of 54 VooDoo aircraft to three nuclear bases would at first suggest that there were at least 108 W25 warheads for the Genie rocket in Canada. However, an anonymous source at National Defence Headquarters told the author in 1984 that the last 54 warheads had been withdrawn earlier that year.[11] We must, however, take account of the fact that Chatham, New Brunswick had lost their warheads in 1974, with some or all of the W25's being withdrawn to Bagotville, Quebec. In the end, it is possible that the warheads were simply moved about in Canada, and that a relatively stable number existed throughout the entire 20 years of the commitment. With a normal war load of two Genies on each aircraft, the 12 aircraft at Comox, British Columbia in 1984 would have to be provided with at least 24 nuclear warheads. If this number is doubled to take account of warheads for Bagotville and some spares for Chatham, the number indeed settles above 50 weapons. This leads us to the tentative conclusion that there were 54 W25 nuclear warheads at the end, but perhaps as many as 108 plus some spares in the early years of the Genie/W25 deployment in Canada.

Lastly, and without doubt the most difficult to assess, is the war load of the CF-104 commitment in Europe. In the beginning, there were six strike squadrons with some 90 committed aircraft. If each aircraft was guaranteed a Mk 28 thermonuclear weapon, there would have to have been at least 90 of this first deployed weapon. The addition of the Mk 57 in early 1966 could double the totals, or the weapon could have replaced the Mk 28 for certain bombing missions. It is not possible to know from the open sources whether the Mk 57 replaced any Mk 28 weapons, or whether all of both 3 and 4 Wing, two units based in West Germany, could have been equipped with both weapons. This would give us a number anywhere between 90 and 180.

To this we must add the number of Mk 43 weapons brought in to arm the two strike units at 4 Wing for a one-year period between 1968 and 1969. At most, with one weapon per strike aircraft, there could have been up to 30 Mk 43 weapons stored at Baden. If the weapon was just added to increase the super-heavy bombing capability, then it is possible that there was not one per aircraft, but rather a few for each squadron.

At the top end, and this is a truly extreme guess, there could have been an absolute maximum of 210 different nuclear weapons deployed for the Canadian strike commitment in Europe. At the lowest end, it is possible that there were as few as 90, even during the original deployment of 90 aircraft in the strike role. The most likely numbers are to be found mid-way, as there was no need to double-up on all the weapons deployed. This theory would see about 150 nuclear weapons deployed by the United States Air Force Europe (USAFE) for Canadian service. Of course, as the commitment drew to an end, there was only one strike squadron left. Even if armed to the teeth with two weapons per aircraft (a Mk 28 and a Mk 57 for each), the SAS would have held some 30 bombs, but the CF-104s could only have delivered some 15 weapons before the airfield was targetted and destroyed by the Soviet military.

Therefore, at the height of the Canadian nuclear deployments, the greatest number of weapons which could have been available to Canada would have been between 250 (low estimate) and 450 (high estimate). The number would drop precipitously between 1970 and 1972, leaving only the 48 to 54 warheads needed to arm the Genie rockets on the VooDoos.

THE FREE GIFT

The Canadian nuclear weapons system deployments were like a free gift to the US military. During the 1950s, the "Pentomic Era" in the United States, the Pentagon had become truly enamoured of all things nuclear, and warheads were mated to every conceivable system. It is therefore no surprise that the US government also extended the option of nuclear deployment to the allies during the late 1950s. This is when Canada decided to get on board.

Canadian deployments were little more than extensions of US military deployments and strategy. If the US had not thought a certain Canadian military acquisition was useful to them in some way, it is unlikely that they would have armed the Canadian military with nuclear weapons. So for the US military, Canadian deployments meant that there were just that many more nuclear carriers available to carry out US war plans in NORAD and NATO, but without the associated costs.

For example, the Canadian government paid the entire cost of producing the CF-104 at Canadair. However, the production of an additional $200-million worth of the aircraft for NATO European-nation use, and paid for mainly by the United States, reduced the overall production costs of making the aircraft in Montreal. Still, for this role the Canadian taxpayer was out of pocket. The government also directly purchased all of the Honest John rockets and associated launch equipment from the US manufacturer, Douglas Corporation, this time with nothing being produced in Canada.

Canada's CF-104 contribution, even after the 1967 cuts, amounted to twenty per cent of the all-weather nuclear bomber capability of 4 Allied Tactical Air Force (ATAF), NATO. This is a substantial share, and it cost the United States and NATO nothing. It has not been possible to make this comparison with the Honest John due to the secrecy surrounding ground forces deployments. However, it is reasonable to conclude that the 16 primary war-use Honest Johns of 1 SSM Battery in Germany were a tiny fraction of the nuclear artillery available in the region at that time. Still, within the British Army of the Rhine (BAOR), the Canadian contingent provided twenty-five percent of the nuclear-armed rocket force as the British fielded only 12 Honest John rocket launchers to Canada's four.* In the end, the Honest John had more to do with NATO alliance cohesion through multilateral cooperation than with militarily necessary fire-power.

In the case of the BOMARC, the costs were split. The USAF paid for the missiles, the launchers, and the specialized equipment: the Canadian Government paid for all of the facilities' construction and the annual operating and maintenance costs. The VooDoos came to Canada after the cancellation of the Avro Arrow and the realization by the United States that there would be no replacement fighter built in Canada. The US could scarcely afford to have their northern border protected by a country with no fighter-interceptors. In 1961 the US and Canadian governments signed an agreement by which the US Air Force would provide 66 VooDoos from the USAF inventory, on the understanding that the aircraft would be used only for NORAD duties and placed under NORAD operational control. In return, Canada took over the operation of 16 USAF Pinetree Line radar stations in Canada, and the government was able to state that the cost of the Pinetree operation over 10 years was equal to the cost of the VooDoos. While the aircraft were essentially free, their operating and maintenance costs over 25 years certainly drained away money from taxpayers.

Canada fielded 20 per cent of all BOMARC units in NORAD in 1964. By 1970 that number would be 33 per cent, as the USAF was closing sites. With the maximum US force of 242 missiles, Canada contributed support to 18.8 per cent of the entire NORAD deployment. This is substantial given that the United States has 10 times the resources, and routinely spends many times that on its massive superpower-status military.

---

* The British Army already relied heavily on US nuclear weapons. They fielded 100 of the W7 warheads for the Corporal missile between 1958 and 1967; 36 of the W33 eight-inch howitzer shells starting in 1960; and 36 of the W48 M109 155 mm howitzer shells starting in 1968. By the early 1970s, with the closure of 1 SSM Battery and the transfer of the rockets to the British, the British Army was fielding some 120 W31 warheads for Honest John rockets.

NORAD's primary concern was intercepting Soviet bombers making their way into North American airspace, and to do this they fielded hundreds of interceptors. Although the three Canadian squadrons seem puny, their numbers were important. By 1974, just before the nuclear weapons were withdrawn from Chatham, the Canadian VooDoos accounted for 26.6 per cent of the regular NORAD interceptor force. This number drops to 10.25 per cent if the US Air National Guard units are included. However, the fact remains that Canada contributed more than one-quarter of the regular interceptors within NORAD. This is also substantial, and was at little additional costs to the US taxpayer.

Back in 1963, when a dollar bought quite a lot, Minister of National Defence Paul Hellyer stated that the Canadian taxpayer was going to have to spend at least $7.6 million immediately, and at least $8 million in recurring annual operating costs for such things as parts, spares, pay, maintenance, fuel, training, construction, engineering, housing and other associated costs.[12]

In the end it must be concluded that the Canadian nuclear commitment was essentially a free-ride for the US. Though not responsible for producing the warheads, the Canadian taxpayer bought and supported nuclear weapons systems, fulfilling roles on behalf of the US Air Force in Canada and in Europe, and on behalf of the US Army in Europe.

REQUEST FOR INFORMATION

There remains a great deal of research to be done in this field, and the author is still seeking more information on the subject of nuclear weapons in Canada, whether deployed by the RCAF, the Canadian Army, the Royal Canadian Navy, or the Canadian Forces. If you were involved in any nuclear weapons duties and are willing to be interviewed on an attributable or non-attributable basis, please feel free to call or write. Also of continued interest is the history of US nuclear weapons deployed to Canada for the use of the US Air Force and US Navy, especially in Newfoundland, between 1950 and 1975. This is a virtual black hole of Canadian history, and much work needs to be done.

CHAPTER 1

PEARSON'S CABINET AND THE POLITICAL AGREEMENT TO ACQUIRE NUCLEAR WEAPONS FOR THE CANADIAN MILITARY

Nuclear weapons were acquired for the Canadian forces solely on the basis of action taken by the Pearson Government after it defeated the Diefenbaker Government in the spring of 1963. Immediately following the installation in Cabinet of Prime Minister Lester B. Pearson, Secretary of State for External Affairs Paul Martin, and Minister of National Defence Paul Hellyer, moves were made to re-open the negotiations with the US Department of State. It was the action of these three men which lead to Canada's securing the nuclear weapons necessary for the arming of the Army's Honest John, and the RCAF's CF-101, CF-104, and BOMARC.

In this chapter readers will see for themselves the words and debates of the Pearson Cabinet both preceding and following the agreement to provide nuclear weapons to Canada. There is no reference at any place in the Cabinet minutes of dissension over acquiring nuclear weapons, and all efforts were placed in working out the details of the acquisition. Likewise, the Cabinet Defence Committee took an even more mechanical view of the situation, and set to the task of formulating a proposal which would fulfil Pearson's promise to live up to the commitment which he said Diefenbaker had shunned.

Prior to becoming the governing party, the Liberal Party was in a period of policy upheaval. Having originally attacked the Diefenbaker Government for buying nuclear weapons carriers, the Liberals under

Pearson, Hellyer, and Martin turned that policy around. Paul Hellyer, soon to be the Minister of National Defence (MND), lobbied the party leader, Lester Pearson, to gain acceptance of the nuclear commitments.

DOCUMENT # 1

December 1962. Memo from Paul Hellyer to Lester Pearson, re: NATO/NORAD Nuclear Weapons.

MEMORANDUM TO THE HONOURABLE L.B. PEARSON

THE AIR DIVISION — In 1958, we (Canada) undertook to replace the eight (8) squadrons of F-86's with CF-104's and to undertake the strike attack role. This role consists of forward reconnaissance with atomic capability to deal with special targets. It is considered an essential role particularly for the next five years until the question of medium-range ballistic missiles and possible NATO control of such a force is decided and acted on. SACEUR feels that a strike capability adds greatly to the credibility of the defence and particularly in the case of a situation where reference to all-out war would not be taken seriously.

ARMAMENT — The CF-104 is designed to carry atomic bombs. The first squadron at No. 3 Wing (Zweibrucken) will be flying in December and ready to go active at the end of April. I am advised that it takes six months from the time a bi-lateral agreement is signed to work out the necessary details including supply of the weapons and training required to handle them. The military people at SHAPE are very concerned about the indecision of the Canadian government.

ALTERNATIVES — It was my opinion that the arming of the Honest John rocket while it is considered desirable is not absolutely essential in order for the brigade to continue to play an important role. The question of the air division is a different matter. If it is not armed with nuclear bombs, the consequences are far reaching. SACEUR is counting on this capacity. If we do not fulfil our commitment, there will be intense pressure on us to withdraw and turn the facilities over to others. Our influence in NATO will be reduced to negligible. There is no question but that we could have adopted a non-nuclear role four years ago and still have made a real contribution to the total effort. To make the choice now, however, for immediate implementation would involve a very great disruption and immediate expenditure of hundreds of millions of dollars on new equipment. It would be a decision of such a magnitude that I do not believe it practicable.

PROLIFERATION OF ATOMIC WEAPONS — The signing by Canada of a bilateral agreement with the United States and the acceptance by us of atomic devices is not, in fact, proliferation of control. The weapons would still be under the control of the United States and this is logical in view of the fact that they have the ultimate responsibility in any event. We would only be joining those of our allies who have already joined in similar arrangements. Italy, Greece, Turkey, Holland, England, Germany, Belgium, Denmark and Norway have already signed agreements. Not all of these countries actually have the weapons on their soil but the majority do.

NORAD — If we decide to fulfil those commitments which we have undertaken in NATO, I cannot see why we should not do the same in NORAD. The one agreement would permit both. I have not changed my opinion about the usefulness of the BOMARC missile, but if there is one thing that is more useless than an armed BOMARC it is an unarmed BOMARC. Similarly, I cannot see the logic of surveillance planes which, if they did discover an enemy attack, would be helpless except to warn the United States. Surely we have not withdrawn from collective responsibility to the point where we would only clutter up the skies and impede our friends in their task.

ECONOMIC CONSEQUENCES — These are inevitable. If we don't fulfil our agreements the Americans are almost certain to reduce or terminate their production sharing arrangements with us.

POLITICAL CONSEQUENCES — The great majority of the Canadian people would want their country to fulfil its obligations. We are on sound ground in the fact that we have consistently recommended a different course at a time when a different choice was feasible. Now, however, our choice is limited by the circumstances. Furthermore, we are not bound by the present circumstances for all time. If we wished to play a different role this could be negotiated and implemented over a period of years in a responsible way. Now, however, we must uphold the honour and dignity of our word as a nation.

RECOMMENDATION — In view of the circumstances, particularly the fact that we as a nation have undertaken, of our own free will, certain commitments which we are now expected to fulfil, and the implementation of which is now a critical necessity in the alliance of which we are a part, I recommend that the Liberal Party state categorically that Canada should sign a bi-lateral agreement with the United States and fulfil its commitments forthwith.

(signed)

Paul T. Hellyer [1]

Pearson accepted the ideas, and in January 1963 the Liberal Party reversed its position when Pearson announced that if elected he would finalize a nuclear weapons agreement with the United States and bring the warheads to Canada. This change in policy also caused Pierre Trudeau to temporarily leave the party in disgust. Later, the change of direction lead directly to the Cabinet and Cabinet Defence Committee discussions which produced the 16 August 1963 Agreement.

The only real debate in either the Cabinet or the Cabinet Defence Committee was a result of the Department of National Defence trying to add another weapon to the list of four. Supported by Hellyer, the military was trying to get airborne nuclear anti-submarine warfare weapons added to the four proposed systems. In this quest, Hellyer found himself virtually alone. Although at least one Cabinet member stated that such an addition was a prudent means of covering future contingencies, Pearson stated that there had been no record of any such commitment ever having been made. Further, Pearson and Martin, and certainly some other members, felt that to add another nuclear weapon to the list would stretch their credibility with the public.[2] Pearson recognized that his government held on with the slimmest of margins. In the end, Hellyer was defeated, and the original four nuclear weapons system commitments remained the only ones in the annex to the 16 August 1963 diplomatic note.*

Pearson was quite clear about Canada "acquiring" nuclear weapons, in that he stated Canada was *not* acquiring nuclear weapons.[3] This was a case of Mackenzie-King-like logic which professed "if necessary nuclear weapons for Canada, but not necessarily Canadian nuclear weapons." In what came to be a classic of political obfuscation, Pearson would tell the public that Canadian military units only had access to United States nuclear weapons which would always remain in the custody of US military units. In this way, he avoided the thorny problem of horizontal proliferation. Pearson also avoided problems with US laws which forbade the United States government or military from transferring nuclear weapons into the control of another country. So although the Canadian forces "acquired" a set of new weapons for their exclusive use, they were not "acquired" in the sense of being purchased and owned: they were simply on restricted loan. In defence of the Pearson stand, it must be pointed out that paragraphs 4 and 6 of the 16 August 1963 agreement (see Appendix) make it quite clear that these would not be Canadian nuclear warheads, and that they would at all times be in the exclusive custody of US forces.

In politics, timing is everything, and this was certainly the case with the signing and publicizing of the 16 August 1963 agreement. Both the Canadian and US sides realized that although the negotiations had been concluded by mid-July,** it would be impossible to sign the agreement right away.[4] The United States, the Soviet Union, and Great Britain had just completed the Partial Test Ban Treaty outlawing nuclear weapons tests in the atmosphere and under

---

* Please see Chapter 7 for a more complete explanation.

** The final wording of the agreement was set by 11 July 1963, and forwarded to the Governor General.

water in the hopes of reducing radioactive fallout. It would have been most impolitic to turn from the signing of what many considered an important arms control document, to the signing of an agreement which spread nuclear weapons to another (non-nuclear) country.*

Unlike the full Cabinet, the Cabinet Defence Committee (CDC) was made up of select ministers whose portfolios contained a security brief. During the nuclear debates, these included the Prime Minister, the Minister of National Defence and the Associate Minister of National Defence, the Secretary of State for External Affairs, the Minister of Justice, the Minister of Finance, and the Minister of Defence Production. At certain meetings, the military Chiefs of Staff would also be called upon to attend. It was this secretive Committee which approved, line-by-line, the final agreement to acquire nuclear weapons. They also received the direct reports of the Minister of National Defence and the Secretary of State for External Affairs on the situation regarding nuclear weapons. It was, therefore, mainly the work of Paul Martin and Paul Hellyer and their two staffs who pushed the agreement to a conclusion. Pearson clearly took the lead in these meetings, and although in favour of living up to what he saw as Canada's commitment to its closest ally, Pearson was wary about the true nature of the commitments. In the very first CDC meeting, he even questioned whether there was any firm commitment on the part of Canada to arm VooDoo aircraft with nuclear Genies.[5]

Paul Martin, then the Secretary of State for External Affairs, covered the discussions and disagreements in his autobiography. He wrote that, right after assuming office, US Ambassador to Canada Walt Butterworth told him that Kennedy "wanted to conclude early agreements authorizing the joint control of nuclear weapons deployed with the Canadian armed services. Thereafter, Butterworth was in and out of my office about this matter more times than I care to recall.... Kennedy said that it would not take long to ready temporary storage facilities for the BOMARC warheads, and that, within eighteen months, Canada would be able to arm all its weapons with nuclear devices. That summer, a committee of officials from both sides drew up a preparatory agreement; Ross Campbell was in charge of Canada's team."[6]

---

* While this decision was made exclusively on the basis of perceived public opinion, at least it was better than the rationale for the signing of the Intermediate Nuclear Forces Treaty. Mikhail Gorbachev and Ronald Reagan signed the INF Treaty on 08 December 1987 instead of on 07 December because Nancy Reagan's astrologer said that the original date was cosmically unfit.

The following extracts are all from minutes of Cabinet meetings and Cabinet Defence Committee meeting at which the Pearson Cabinet debated and discussed the acquisition of nuclear weapons for the Canadian military. The major players were Pearson himself, Paul Martin from External, and Paul Hellyer from Defence. Virtually all debate was between the two Pauls, with Pearson stepping in to settle disputes. The documents range from the very first Cabinet discussion of the nuclear question in the Pearson years, to the meeting held on the day the agreement was signed. Once agreement was reached, Canada then had the problem of calming relations with the Federal Republic of Germany, as the unique Canada-US nuclear agreement was one the US did not wish West Germany to have. The West Germans, like many other European NATO allies of the United States, did not have the same level of control afforded Canada in the Canada-US agreement. For this reason, the United States was unwilling to allow the Canadian government to show the agreement to the Bonn government. Information on this tricky bit of diplomacy has therefore been included.

THE MEETINGS

Three days after being sworn in as the government, the new Pearson Cabinet Defence Committee met for the first time to discuss the thorny nuclear weapons issue. Paul Hellyer was the first to speak, and he reviewed the history of the situation regarding the strike role in Europe, the Honest John rocket, the BOMARC and the CF-101B interceptor. He stated that "for lack of nuclear warheads, these forces were for all practical purposes ineffectual."[7]

Paul Martin, the new Secretary of State for External Affairs, then waded into the debate. His primary concern was Canada-US relations, which had been badly damaged by the Conservative government of John Diefenbaker. He stated that "early Canadian actions would do more than anything to improve relations with the United States and that the initiative clearly rested with the Canadian Government."

Pearson replied that he would be bringing the entire matter up with US President Kennedy at the earliest moment.* He went on to say that the commitments then being discussed should not be undertaken to the exclusion of the examination of future political and military policy changes.[8]

---

* This referred to the summit at Hyannis Port, Massachusetts in May 1963.

Pearson was already trying to escape from the nuclear grip of the military, and asked whether the BOMARC and CF-104 commitments were likely to be modified in the foreseeable future. The Chief of the Air Staff (CAS) replied that the US Secretary of Defense had said that the BOMARCs would be fielded until at least the end of 1966. The CAS then told the Prime Minister that the present strike role continued under NATO plans and force goals through 1966, and that the planning for 1969 still included all eight strike-reconnaissance squadrons.[9]

Pearson then tried to see if the VooDoo-Genie commitment could be minimized. He asked if the CF-101B interceptors actually required nuclear-tipped missiles,* and was told by the CAS that with high-explosive missiles the aircraft were less operationally effective. Pearson and Martin concluded that Canada "appeared to be committed to adopt nuclear weapons or warheads for the CF-104s, the Honest John artillery missiles and the BOMARC [but that] the requirements of the CF-101 interceptor were not clear."[10]

Moving to the purely political, Pearson asked whether any NATO countries had signed general agreements with the United States but failed to implement them. The military reported that two nations had signed general agreements but did not yet have specific requirements, and that many others with general agreements had not completed the negotiation of specific technical agreements.[11] No specific examples were provided.

At the end of the long session, the Cabinet Defence Committee agreed to form an interdepartmental committee which would review the means for acquiring nuclear weapons and propose various approaches to the US government on the Canadian requirements. It was then decided to immediately inform the US government that "action is being taken as a matter of urgency" to finalize the agreement.[12]

Two weeks later the Cabinet Defence Committee met again, no discussions having taken place in the full Cabinet. At this meeting the CDC got its first view of the draft agreement. Paul Martin had a copy of the original 15 October 1959 US draft, and of the redraft prepared by the interdepartmental committee. The first order of business was to fight over the title. As Pearson had said that Canada would not be acquiring nuclear weapons, the US-proposed title of "Acquisition of

---

* The Genie is actually a ROCKET and not a MISSILE.

Nuclear Warheads and/or Weapons for Canadian Forces" was impossible. The Committee therefore agreed to change it to read "Proposed Exchange of Notes Concerning Nuclear Warheads for the Canadian Forces."[13]

In discussing differences in the drafts, the SSEA noted that the US draft had a reference to "quantities" as well as locations, and that this was removed from the Canadian draft. When they came to the sections on financial responsibility, a report from the Deputy Minister of National Defence showed that capital costs to be borne by Canada were estimated at $15 million, of which about $5 million would be required in 1963. There would also be annual recurring costs of about $7 million, but these were personnel costs, and would be incurred only if service strengths were increased to meet the new requirement, which was estimated at about 1400 additional people. Responding to the costs, Pearson wondered why the taxpayer should have to pay for housing US personnel in view of the fact that their deployment was a US and not Canadian requirement.[14]

When the discussion moved on to the thorny question of custody and control, "the Prime Minister said that it was essential to distinguish between custody and control, and that it should be made clear that responsibility for custody of the stockpiles was entirely in the hands of the United States. It was noted that Canadians would have no access to the warheads themselves and, in this sense, would not share in their custody."[15] The Paul Martin told the Cabinet Defence Committee that the agreement would "in effect establish a joint responsibility for the custody of the warheads. The United States would be responsible for custody and internal security; [and] Canada would be charged with the external security encompassing protection against all hostile elements."[16]

From the discussion of custody the members moved on to the most difficult issue: consultation prior to the release of nuclear weapons. "Release" referred to the warhead being physically released by the US custodial unit to the Canadian operation unit which would use it in combat. The substantive sections of the records dealing with this discussion have been censored, and appeals for review have been unsuccessful. We do know, however, that the final agreement stated that release would be subject to prior inter-governmental consultation, where practical.

The Prime Minister said that he understood the principle of joint control to mean that both countries would have, in effect, a veto over the use of the nuclear weapons and the wording proposed in the Canadian redraft seemed to provide this. How the Canadian control over use was to be exercised would have to be worked out in the light of practical military necessity, but it seemed appropriate that the principle be stated in the general agreement.[17]

The Chairman, Chiefs of Staff said that because the reference to prior consultation before release could not be made binding, it was only a plea which might or might not be effective. The fact that use of weapons by Canadian forces must be authorized by the Canadian government was of purely Canadian concern and would be out of place in a stockpile agreement with the United States. The measures by which the Canadian government would control the use of the weapons by the Canadian forces had not yet been worked out.[18]

Paul Martin then pointed out to the CDC that the Canadian government's "authorization of use by its own forces was a separate matter from the presidential release. This was the essence of the "two key" principle of "dual control."*

The military was unhappy with the restrictions being considered by the politicians, and boldly stated that the "two key" concept was fine for offensive weapons, but "seemed less significant in relation to the short-range defensive and tactical weapons covered by the agreement; air defence weapons could only be used when enemy forces are overhead, at which time the greatest need would be to avoid unnecessary delay."[19]In the end, the dual key approach would be maintained, as Pearson was adamant that the "principle of dual control, including the requirement that the use of nuclear weapons by Canadian forces be authorized by the Canadian government, should be explicit in the agreement." Pearson knew that he would be asked in Parliament about the control procedures, and he would have to give assurances that the right of the Canadian government to authorize the

---

* See Chapter 2 for a description of the "two-key" system.

use of nuclear weapons by the Canadian military had been protected in the agreement. On this point Minister of National Defence Hellyer agreed with Pearson.

At the end of the day the CDC agreed to recommend that the draft agreement be approved by Cabinet, and that after Pearson visited Kennedy, the draft be sent to the US for response. After this a negotiating team would be established and talks initiated. Lastly, considering the possible short life of the BOMARC, Hellyer was directed to speak with US Secretary of Defense Robert McNamara and gain assurances that no action was to be taken by the US which might be construed as seriously discrediting any decision taken by the present government regarding the BOMARC deployment, and that any such action would be proceeded by consultation with the Canadian government.[20]

Two days later, on 09 May 1963, the Prime Minister reported the discussions of the Cabinet Defence Committee to the full Cabinet. In addition to outlining their conclusions and recommendations, Pearson told Cabinet that the "proposed agreements were designed to set out the general governing principles which were to govern the conditions under which stockpiles of U.S. weapons would be made available for use of Canadian forces and of U.S. forces in Canada." They were told that the agreement followed the form of agreements concluded between the US and other NATO countries, that it was based on a draft proposed by the US in October 1959 and incorporating Canadian changes, and that the actual implementation would require a separate service-to-service technical agreement for each weapon system.[21]

After discussing the possibility of the Minister of National Defence being embarrassed during a debate due to his previous stance on the BOMARC, and a short talk on the sale of Canadair Caribou II aircraft to the United States and possible withdrawal of US concessions on Canadian oil exports, the talk turned to secrecy. The Prime Minister stated that the agreement would remain a secret and would not be tabled in Parliament. Only a general discussion in the House of Commons would be allowed, as this would protect the national security.[22]

Perhaps the most important discussion that day dealt with the questions of custody and control of nuclear weapons in Canada and their use by Canadian forces. It was outlined that ownership and physical custody of the warheads would always remain wholly with the US. Cabinet was then told by Martin and Hellyer that under unspecified circumstances (war) "the warheads would be released from US custody by the President, and the proposed agreement would require, where practical, prior intergovernmental consultation." The ministers pointed out that even following US release, the "use of the warheads would be in accordance with procedures established by the appropriate Allied Commander or by the Canadian and U.S. military authorities, as applicable, but always subject to Canadian control." Cabinet was then assured that nuclear weapons deployed for the Canadian military, and they seem to have focused on the BOMARC at this point, could not be launched or fired or detonated by the US military, before or after warhead release.[23]

Cabinet was given the full five-item list for the annex which included the BOMARC, the CF-101, the CF-104, and the Honest John. It also included nuclear anti-submarine warfare weapons, and skittish Cabinet members called this new commitment into question.[24]

Based on the word of the Prime Minister, and on the work done by the Cabinet Defence Committee and working group, the Cabinet approved the draft agreement on nuclear warheads for the Canadian forces as a basis for negotiations. They also approved of Pearson telling Kennedy that Canada was now ready to negotiate the general agreement and then move on to technical arrangements for four weapons systems.[25]

Two weeks after becoming prime minister, Lester Pearson visited US president John Kennedy at the Kennedy retreat in Hyannis Port, Massachusetts, USA. Pearson told his Cabinet colleagues that defence questions topped his list of subjects for discussion with the pro-nuclear president, and that defence production sharing was second.[26] Upon his return it was revealed to Cabinet that military matters indeed had top priority at the talks.[27]

Pearson reported that he and Kennedy had settled on the four weapons systems, "the BOMARC, VooDoo, CF-104, and Honest John, as intended to be covered by this agreement." He also said that he told Kennedy that the need for full parliamentary discussion would mean it would be another three or four weeks before the bilateral agreement could be concluded.[28]

At the next meeting, the full Cabinet agreed to send the new Canadian draft agreement to US Ambassador Walt Butterworth on or about 17 May as a discussion document.[29] They then noted with approval five days later that this action had been taken by Paul Martin.[30]

In reality, the measure of support on the issue was slim. That week, after a debate on defence, the new Liberal Government would survive a vote of confidence by a mere eleven votes. Pearson knew he could not afford to anger those MPs whose constituents were unsteady on the nuclear issue, and he knew that inclusion of the never-before-specified nuclear ASW weapons commitment might push the balance against him.[31]

The US State Department, by now delighted that they had a partner interested in working out the agreement, moved into high gear. The document they received from Paul Martin through their ambassador in Ottawa on 20 May was reworked and returned to Canada a month later.* The new draft sought to ensure that the control procedures for NORAD forces were not too restrictive.

By 02 July the new US draft and commentary had been studied by an interdepartmental group of officials set up by the Cabinet Defence Committee in May. They concluded that the draft was acceptable if Canadian concerns about the BOMARC were dealt with in a letter of understanding between Hellyer and McNamara. This negotiations working group then met with the US team on 10 and 11 July, and agreed on the final text of the agreement, the draft letter of understanding, "and a further supplementary letter to be sent by the Minister of National Defence to the U.S. Secretary of Defense, requesting assurances that the BOMARC missile system would remain an integral part of both Canadian and U.S. elements of NORAD for a reasonable period of time."[32]

Not wanting Canadians to know that the agreement had already been accepted by the government, Secretary of State for External Affairs Paul Martin rose in the House when asked if Canada and the United States had "reached agreement in principle on a pact with respect to nuclear arms," and replied that it was not done and "progress is being made in this regard."[33]

Although the negotiations had gone well, there was still the issue of release and authorization with which to deal. Paul Martin reported to the CDC that the letter of understanding made two important points: firstly that "procedures and means for consultation of the two

---

* The redraft and informal commentary was presented to Ottawa on 25 June 1963.

governments preceding use of the weapons would have to be reviewed by the two governments and some new arrangements might have to be worked out," and secondly that to provide for meaningful and effective consultation, "Canada must be prepared to buy additional equipment and accept the nuisance of procedures which provide control on a 24-hour basis the year round."[34]

Pearson immediately backed Martin by saying that this move would allow the government to state that the "weapons could not be used without authorization by the Canadian government."

With these words in mind, Cabinet authorized Martin to sign an Exchange of Notes (the agreement) as soon as possible, and directed that the Letter of Understanding be forwarded to the State Department at the time of the signing. Then Cabinet did something odd: they said that only after all of these arrangements had been made would they have their team and the US negotiators review the procedures and means for consultation on and authorization for the operational use of NORAD and NATO US nuclear weapons by Canadian forces. Cabinet had bought the system, but still had no idea how it would be controlled.

Forever worried about the public impression being made as Cabinet readied the government and military to accept nuclear weapons, much time was devoted to preparing for a possible public-relations disaster. The Cabinet Defence Committee discussed possible press releases and contingency statements, and carefully vetted each and every word in the draft texts for public release. During the 16 July discussion, the sections of the text referring to the secret nature of the agreement and the fact that Canada was joining the nuclear weapons club were removed. Members worried that the agreement would be presented, albeit in secret, to the US congressional committee on atomic energy, and that "any similar disclosure to the House of Commons Special Committee on Defence in closed session would create a precedent which might be very awkward."[35] The government did not want to place itself in a position whereby it would have to reveal secret agreements, even in closed sessions of a Parliamentary committee: this would violate the British Parliamentary tradition of preserving the absolute secrecy of the Privy Council Office, even on matters concerning the entire nation.

Other problems of secrecy arose over the following weeks. The State Department had given External Affairs some sample questions they expected the press to ask, and provided draft answers. Paul Martin noted that two of the answers could prove difficult for the government due to the more obsessive nature of Canadian Parliamentary secrecy. In one case they proposed to say that the agreement did not require US Senate approval, but that "the Joint Committee on Atomic Energy of Congress has of course been kept currently and fully informed of these developments." The last thing Pearson wanted was for the Standing Committee on Defence to try to get a copy of the agreement, so Martin asked the State Department to limit their answers to single words such as "no".[36]

Later that same day the question of the proposed agreement came up at a full Cabinet meeting. The Prime Minister told Cabinet that the form and substance of the agreement, the letter of understanding and the letter concerning the future of the BOMARC, and the draft public announcement to be delivered in the House of Commons required the approval of the full Cabinet. Pearson said that the announcement could not be made that week, as it would lead to a debate, and the debate could not be held the next week, as the first part of the week was devoted to consideration of budgetary measures, and the end of the week saw the Prime Minister away at a Premiers' conference. It was agreed that the announcement would be tabled when the agreement was signed.[37]

A week later there was another problem. There was a strong possibility that the Partial Test Ban Treaty would be signed in the coming days, and it would be a public relations disaster for the Canadian government to announce that the agreement on nuclear weapons for Canada had been concluded. Pearson and the State Department agreed that it would be unwise to have the agreement concluded within a few days of the signing of the test ban.[38] At the 07 August Cabinet meeting, Paul Martin pointed out that the "lapse of about a week between signature by Canada of the test ban treaty and the announcement of nuclear weapons for the Canadian forces was probably desirable in any case for presentational reasons."[39]

A week earlier, on 29 July, the Prime Minister was asked in the House by Stanley Knowles if the signing of the agreement had been put off because of the Partial Test Ban Treaty. Pearson replied "No," and said that "negotiations are still proceeding." Knowles then wanted to know if the Prime Minister was referring to negotiations to put off the signing, or negotiations for the signing, Pearson again replied that negotiations were still underway leading to the signing of the agreement.[40] This was not exactly true, as the negotiations on the agreement had been successfully concluded in mid-July, and had been recognized as such during the Cabinet Defence Committee meeting of 16 July, when Paul Martin was authorized to sign the agreement. Pearson knew the agreement had been finalized, and yet deceived Parliament. Even newspapers in the United States were carrying articles about the finalization of the agreement, yet the Liberal Government would not make this simple admission.

Time was running out, and it seemed that it would not be possible to sign the agreement in time to make an announcement in the House of Commons, as the House was about to leave for the summer recess.[41] Although Cabinet had agreed to table an announcement concurrent with the signing of the agreement at a meeting two weeks previous,[42] this was not to happen. The House left for summer recess on 02 August and did not return until 30 September 1963. Parliamentarians would not have a chance to question the government about the agreement until nearly two months later.

In an aside to a regular Cabinet meeting, the members decided to meet again two days later to give final approval to the agreement, which would be signed on 16 August, and to the public announcement.[43] Two days later, Pearson told them that his staff had arranged a noon-time press conference at which the PM would reveal the public nature of the agreement.

However, it was felt that this might be a bad day, as earlier that morning the British government had announced that they were withdrawing from the agreement under which the United States provided nuclear weapons to the UK. It was feared that the British announcement might make the Canadian announcement look counter-productive.[44]

Walt Butterworth, the US ambassador to Canada, and a close friend of John Kennedy, would sign the agreement in the US Embassy that morning at 11:00 AM. Both Kennedy and Butterworth had made it clear that they now expected the Canadian government to move on the US request for an agreement to allow the nuclear arming of US Air Force units in Canada. Martin was told that this requirement would be of indefinite duration, but that the Genie rocket had a very low nuclear yield.[45]

In a last ditch effort, Paul Hellyer again requested that the nuclear Anti-Submarine Warfare (ASW) section be re-inserted into the annex. He pointed out that it "was almost a commitment comparable with the others," but other members noted that it had never been identified as such.[46] The ASW idea was finally dead, and the political agreement was signed. The full text of the 16 August 1963 agreement can be found in the Appendix of this book.

In the end, protest was muted, and the reaction of the press in Canada was favourable to the Liberal Party. In fact, even the opposition parties would only say that they "might attempt" to raise the matter when Parliament reconvened after the summer recess. An External Affairs telex to the Canadian Embassy in Bonn put it very well when the author wrote: "The public reaction in Canada was much as might be expected. There was no widespread opposition, although there were of course a certain number of individuals and organizations which voiced their objection. By and large Canadian press comment was favourable. Opposition party spokesmen indicated that they might attempt to raise the matter when Parliament reconvenes."[47]

On their first day back, 30 September 1963, NDP Member Tommy Douglas asked the Prime Minister to table the 16 August 1963 agreement in the House. Pearson said "No," because "there were military details in the Exchange of Notes which, in accordance with NATO practice and considerations of military security, could not be made public."[48] The final agreement, printed in the Appendix, clearly contains no military secrets, as it was simply the political agreement which would allow for the service-to-service technical arrangements which would bring the warheads to Canada.

Tommy Douglas did not believe Canada needed nuclear weapons, and he did not believe the Pearson Government should hide what they were doing from the people. Three days later Douglas again asked for the agreement to be tabled, noting that the even more secretive British government had tabled the 6 April 1964 "Polaris" agreement in the House. Douglas stated that "Indeed, the government has gone much further and has refused to allow Parliament to see the agreement upon which this commitment is based."[49]

The Pearson Government refused most questions, and quietly and secretively went about the business of bringing nuclear weapons into Canada and into Europe for Canadian forces.

INTERNATIONAL RELATIONS WITH GERMANY

Canada was to have a rather unique nuclear relationship with the United States, and it was one the US government was unwilling to share with the West Germans. Canada, as a NATO partner and tenant on German soil, was willing to show the text of the agreement to the German government as it requested permission to station nuclear weapons at the Canadian air bases and near the Canadian army camp inside the Federal Republic of Germany. The Germans were kept abreast of the progress of the negotiations,[50] and the Bonn government was clearly interested, but this put Canadian officials in a bind.[51] The US State Department objected, as their nuclear relationship with West Germany did not actually involve asking permission of the Bonn government for US nuclear weapons stationing or use. The provisions of the agreement with Canada dealing with authorization for use was something the US was unwilling to share with their German allies. The Canadian Embassy in Bonn was instructed not to speak with the German authorities about the details of the agreements, and that all of this would be dealt with by Ottawa.[52]

Recognizing the new reality of ultra-nationalism in France, the Canadian military planned to move their nuclear commitment to Germany. The Air Staff's proposal was that two aircraft from each of the four squadrons in France would stand their nuclear alerts at the RCAF's bases in Germany since this could not be done in France.[53]

CANADIAN AUTHORIZATION FOR
THE USE OF NUCLEAR WEAPONS

Only once nuclear weapons had been acquired for the Canadian forces did the Pearson Government give much thought to the idea that they may someday be called upon to control their use. With this in mind, Canadian and US negotiators set up a framework through which the prime minister and the US president could consult prior to the release of nuclear weapons, if time permitted. Because there was always the thought that time would not permit, Pearson signed a short memo passed, through the US ambassador, giving his prior permission for the unilateral US release of nuclear weapons in exceptional circumstances (read: war).

Both the Diefenbaker and Pearson Governments were aware that Canada had signed on to NATO theories of employment of nuclear weapons starting in the 1950s. It was the secretly stated position of NATO political and military authorities that "in the event of a war involving NATO it is militarily essential that NATO forces should be able to use atomic and thermonuclear weapons in their defence from the outset."[54] This made national consultation a privilege which could be taken away by the US commander of NATO forces.

Later the Pearson Government would sign on to the renewed NATO defence concept in 1968 which stated that in cases of Soviet nuclear attack, NATO would respond with nuclear weapons, but that "(t)he possibilities for consultation in this context are extremely limited."[55] NATO leaders also planned for the contingency of using nuclear forces against purely conventional attacks, but "anticipated that time will in this case permit consultation."[56] The only scenario in which nuclear use would definitely be subject to prior consultation was if the attack on NATO territory did not come in the form of direct nuclear or conventional attack. How this would happen was purposefully vague.

While it may be bothering that the Canadian government had given up some of its authority in regards the use of nuclear weapons by the Canadian forces, there is a second disturbing fact: there was no formal mechanism for consultation and authorization at all when Canada first acquired the weapons. Negotiations on the political control mechanism did not begin until late March 1964. Worse yet, the formal arrangement did not come into effect until the spring of 1965, more than a year after the first BOMARC was armed.

This said, it should be noted that there was a system in place from 1957 and 1959 which allowed for some consultation. The first agreement provided for consultation prior to instituting higher alert measures in North America. This 01 March 1957 and 10 November 1958 exchange of notes called for Canada-US consultation at the point either government determined a need for increased alert. The countries would consult on diplomatic and military levels, and such consultation would only be required for a full scale alert of the entire armed forces and the nation as a whole. Either country could raise the alert level unilaterally if impelled by time considerations. It was also determined that the agreement would not affect the freedom of either country to take whatever actions it considered appropriate for its own defence or for the defence of its partner.[57]

A week after the arrival of the BOMARC warheads on 31 December 1963, Paul Martin informed the Prime Minister that there would be no time in the immediate future to work out a political control mechanism, as Pearson was to meet with President Johnson within days.* Martin recognized that this was an important issue, and said that External Affairs and the Department of National Defence (DND) were already drafting a framework interim agreement which Pearson could show Johnson.[58]

Previous to this, and previous to the arrival of the BOMARC warheads, the Paul Hellyer had stood in the House and explained, for the first and only time this author has been able to find, the provisions for base security, storage, maintenance, safety, and inspection of the nuclear warheads. He went on to detail the release procedures for BOMARC launching. The statement in the House was based on detailed advice provided to Hellyer by his staff and which Hellyer would that same day provide to Martin.[59] It is noteworthy that the speech does not include a single reference to how political authorization would be gained, nor how the Commander-in-Chief NORAD (CINCNORAD) would get this authorization from the prime minister.

> First, the commander in chief, NORAD, must have been notified that the President of the United States has authorized the release of weapons from US custody for use by Canadian forces assigned to NORAD. Second the commander in chief, NORAD, must also have received authorization from the Prime Minister or his authorized representative to release weapons carriers for use by Canadian forces assigned to NORAD. Third, the US custodial officer on duty in the SAGE direction centre must have received properly authenticated evidence that US governmental release has been given. He would thereupon unlock the US release switch. Fourth, the designated Canadian officer on duty in the SAGE direction centre must also have received properly authenticated evidence that Canadian governmental release had been given. He would thereupon unlock the second release switch. Fifth, at this point the weapon would be available for firing but still would not be fired until

---

* The death of Kennedy in November 1963 left Lyndon Johnson in charge. It was Johnson who signed the order allowing the US military to ship warheads to Canada.

the SAGE sector commander had authorized the senior weapons director to commence using the BOMARCs against hostile targets.[60]

None of the consultation and authorization procedures had yet been formalized into a written agreement. The best current explanation for this curious order of action is that the United States was probably unwilling to discuss any lessening of their prerogative in the nuclear sphere until after Canada had signed the acquisition agreement. Only then could the Pearson Government negotiate a formal set of procedures, rather than simply relying on the oral agreements for consultation in place prior to the arrival of the weapons on 31 December 1963.

A few weeks later Paul Martin would again be troubled by nuclear release arrangements, this time in Europe. Negotiations with the USAF were taking a long time due to USAF officers not wanting to include references to Canadian authorization for use in the CF-104 technical arrangement document.[61] Internal US politics dictated that this was a troublesome point, especially in their relations with the Bonn government. The United States was anxious that the West German government not learn the specifics of the bilateral Canada-US agreements which gave Canada some say over the use of nuclear weapons by Canada or over Canada, as this would conflict with US policy in European NATO.

In his autobiography, Paul Martin wrote that the most sensitive parts of the agreements Canada would reach with the US would be the

> clauses spelling out the consultation and authorization procedures. The negotiations dealt with such matters as the procedures whereby the senior officer at NORAD headquarters would communicate with the Prime Minister, and at what point he might be expected to grant permission for the use of weapons based on Canadian soil, which were under joint control. Once the two governments had signed an agreement on 17 September 1965, our defence relations with Washington became steadier.[62]

Again, it is clear that relationship stability with the US was very important, and the question of control was secondary.[63]

Martin had told Pearson that the question of authorization was a difficult one, and that although the nuclear warheads had already arrived for the BOMARCs, the Canadian government was not yet in a position to discuss the question of release and use of nuclear weapons. Martin provided the Pearson with a draft covering items to be included in the final agreement, but stated that it would not be ready for full discussion at the Canada-US summit meeting two weeks later.[64] All Pearson would be able to tell Lyndon Johnson was that Canada was working on the matter.

The important item at the time, given that the warheads were already in Canada and mounted atop the BOMARCs, was the question of interim procedures. Ross Campbell had informed the Chairman of the Chiefs of Staff that since the warheads were in Canada, the question of the final agreement should be put on hold while they put an interim agreement in place.[65] Since the final agreement was not signed for almost another two years, it is fairly safe to conclude that all effort went into providing the governments with the necessary interim procedures.

The final draft and signed agreement on authorization are still unavailable for public review. It is suspected that the final agreement includes provisions for consultation based on the communication systems already in place; carriage of nuclear weapons in armed mode under DEFCON 1 or AIR DEFENCE EMERGENCY; and release of nuclear weapons without consultation in case of immediate need. This would be the same model as used in the Argentia arrangement in which the Prime Minister provided the US government with prior authorization in letter form.

In the public domain, however, a draft dated the same day as the initial warhead arrival sheds light on the structure and workings of the arrangements made in 1965. The Canadian government recognized that the White House had given prior authorization to various theatre commanders, and that this issue would have to be discussed so that the government in Ottawa could be prepared for the eventuality of Commander-in-Chief Continental Air Defence (CINCCONAD) or the United States Commander-in-Chief Europe (USCINCEUR) or Supreme Allied Commander Europe (SACEUR) releasing nuclear weapons to Canadian units without Canadian government approval.

The document would have been based on the premise that "consultation will precede the significant military measures, except in extreme circumstances," but war was an extreme circumstance, and the United States could hardly be expected to take into account the tiny voice of Canada as they geared up for a thermonuclear exchange.

DOCUMENT # 2

31 December 1963, External Affairs, Secret, Draft, *"Authorization for the Operational Use of Nuclear Weapons"*.

Proposed Passages for Canada-United States Consultation Arrangement.

1. The vital defence interests of Canada and the United States are intimately interrelated. Should either country be attacked, the attack would in all probability be directed against both simultaneously. The outbreak of major hostilities anywhere in the world, and particularly if they involved the forces of either country directly or the use by any country of nuclear weapons, would create a grave risk of escalation leading to a massive nuclear assault upon North America.

2. Recognizing these facts, the Governments of Canada and the United States have agreed to consult together on a continuing basis concerning developments in the world situation which might lead to the outbreak of major hostilities and more particularly to the use of nuclear weapons. Such consultation will take the following three forms:

a. Continuing consultation through normal diplomatic and military channels,

b. Occasional meetings between senior representatives of both Governments, either civil or military or both, called at the initiative of either Government, and

c. Consultation at a direct Government-to-Government level, i.e. with the participation of Ministers or Heads of Government, in circumstances indicated below.

3. It will be the object of consultations in the forms indicated under 2(a) and 2(b) above to arrive at a

common appreciation of situations which might lead to the outbreak of major hostilities, to exchange views about the courses of action to be followed in relation to such situations, and to have each Government inform the other of the particular developments arising from such situations which in its view might require it to resort to military action. In this way it would be possible, insofar as matters of national security are concerned, to achieve the objective agreed at Hyannis Port by President Kennedy and Prime Minister Pearson "that the intentions of each Government may be fully appreciated by the other and misunderstandings ... be avoided."

4. Developments may take place which give rise to an emergency situation, i.e. which lead either Government to conclude that the outbreak of major hostilities has become probable or imminent, or to consider in a period of international tension that significant military measures of a precautionary nature should be taken in view of an increasing risk of major hostilities. Such developments would include the receipt of information indicating a possible intention on the part of a third power to initiate major hostilities. They would also include any action by any power even if not of a direct military nature, which seemed likely to provoke or lead to major hostilities. Significant military measures of a precautionary nature which might be considered in a period of international tension in view of an increasing risk of major hostilities would include the institution of alert measures in the United States or Canada, action to increase the state of readiness of NORAD forces, or the release of nuclear warheads to meet operational requirements.

5. The two Governments hereby reaffirm the various existing agreements providing for consultation between them in periods of international tension, and agree that, in any emergency situation such as those indicated in the preceding paragraph, they will consult together as soon as possible in the manner indicated in

paragraph 2(b) above, and on a direct Government-to-Government basis as indicated in paragraph 2(c) above if the situation is sufficiently serious. Such consultations may be initiated by either Government, and will precede the institution of significant military measures, or other action which might increase the risk of war, except in the extreme circumstances indicated in the following paragraph.

6. Consultation in the circumstances and manner provided above shall precede significant military measures or other action which might increase the risk of war, except in the following circumstances and subject always to the proviso that the freedom of action of either Government to take appropriate measures for its own defence or that of its other treaty partners shall remain unaffected:

a. In the event of surprise attack, either upon its territory or upon its forces abroad, either Government will take appropriate action in its own defence on the understanding that it will inform and consult with the other Government as soon as possible.

b. If either Government considers an attack upon North America or upon its forces abroad to be imminent in a matter of hours rather than days, consultation might, of necessity, coincide with or even follow the institution of significant military measures of a precautionary nature. If either Government is compelled by the time factor to take such measures before initiating consultation, it will immediately inform the other Government of the action taken and will consult with it as soon as possible.

7. Consultations in an emergency situation, as discussed in paragraph 4, 5 and 6 above, shall have the following objectives:

a. To come to a common assessment of the situation in both its political and its military aspects;

b. To agree if possible upon a common course of action to be followed by both Governments;

c. In any case to coordinate the action to be taken

by the two Governments in such a way as to minimize the risk of general war and to facilitate as much as possible the achievement of agreed political objectives; and

    d. To ensure as far as possible that, before either Government shall resort to the use of nuclear weapons, there shall be agreement between them upon the necessity for this action.

In March 1965 the full Cabinet had accepted the submission by Paul Martin of the draft agreement. Martin stated that the agreement would not come into force until Pearson and Johnson had once again met and reached a renewed understanding on the issue of "timely authorization" for the use of nuclear weapons in NORAD.[66] The final agreement on the procedures to be followed for the authorization of the use of nuclear weapons in the NORAD theatre of military operations came in April 1965, when Cabinet accepted the text.[67] Then, on 17 September 1965, Canada's ambassador to the United States signed the final document, and almost two years after the nuclear weapons arrived, the formalized procedures for their control were in place. There is no public copy of the final signed document.

The United States custodial detachments caring for the weapons would receive authorization for the release of their weapons to Canadians through US military channels. A sample release order, though for ICBMs, gives a taste of the language which would have been used.*

> **THE NATIONAL COMMAND AUTHORITY HAS DIRECTED THE RELEASE OF NUCLEAR WEAPONS. UNLOCK VALUES ARE N O P A B Z.**
> **PLCA IS O.**

The receipt of this order, and its authentication, would constitute the authority necessary for the US detachment commander to release nuclear warheads to the applicable Canadian military unit.

---

* The release order for Minuteman III CIBMs was a gift of the Strategic Missile Wing Commander at Grand Forks AFB, North Dakota, in July 1993.

PRIOR AUTHORIZATION

There is very strong evidence to suggest that Canadian authorization for the use of nuclear weapons over Canadian territory was given to the United States in advance. In the case of the anti-submarine warfare forces stationed by the US Navy at Argentia, Newfoundland, Prime Minister Pearson had given prior approval for their operational use. On 27 July 1967 Secretary of State for External Affairs Paul Martin gave Pearson the text of the "timely authorization for the employment of the weapons" which Pearson could sign and forward to the US ambassador. The Martin wrote that the single page authorization had originally been given to the Prime Minister on 26 May 1967 and approved by Pearson at that time.[68] As this document was accepted by the Pearson Government, there is little reason to think that prior authorization could not have been granted for the use of nuclear weapons by the RCAF Air Defence Command in Canada should NORAD be fully generated for defence of North America.

Additionally, a memo from the summer of 1967 notes that "in an actual or indisputably imminent attack it has been agreed that the President and Prime Minister will grant the required authority to CINCNORAD without consultation."[69] Although the bulk of the document deals with the US Navy at Argentia, the reference to prior approval was clearly for NORAD air defence forces, as the US Navy in Argentia fell under the command of the US Navy North Atlantic command.

All together, there is clear evidence that the Canadian government had signed away the right to consult in an emergency, and it is hard to imagine an attack on North America which the US would not classify as an emergency.

DIRECTOR OF NUCLEAR WEAPONS

With the signatures on the service-to-service technical agreements, the military moved to ensure the smooth running of their nuclear operations. This task fell to the newly created Director of Nuclear Weapons (DNW).

Formed under the Chief of Aeronautical Engineering sub-division within the RCAF at National Defence Headquarters, the Director of Nuclear Weapons staff was created on 18 November 1963. This was barely a month before the first warheads would arrive for the BOMARCs at North Bay.

The staff were tasked with performing a liaison function between the Canadian military and the US offices responsible for nuclear weapons. This meant that DNW had to maintain a liaison office at Kirtland AFB, Albuquerque, New Mexico, to work with the USAF Director of Nuclear Safety (DNS), the Defense Nuclear Agency (DNA), and Sandia Laboratories. They also worked closely with the USAF Air Defence Command Inspector General at Ent AFB in Colorado, ensuring the smooth and efficient running of inspections and certifications.

In general, the DNW was most concerned with the safety of the weapons systems. It was not their task to plan for the wartime use of the weapons. Their files have been of particular use in the completion of this work.

TERMINATION OF THE 1963 AGREEMENT

Twenty-four years after it was signed, the 16 August 1963 agreement was terminated by joint agreement on 09 March 1987.[70] This is just less than three years after the final nuclear warhead left Canadian soil. In fact, at the time of termination, none of the weapons listed in the secret annex remained in the Canadian military arsenal.

Confusion was the cause of the final termination. By 1986 the new Progressive Conservative Government had found themselves deeply confused as to what arrangements Canada actually had with the increasingly nuclear-happy US government. The Privy Council Office ordered that a review of Canadian nuclear duties and responsibilities be done through the Management Coordinating Committee (MCC) on behalf of the Permanent Joint Board on Defence (PJBD). As a result of this comprehensive review of all Canada-US nuclear weapons arrangements, the 1963 agreement, no longer functional, was terminated. Canada terminated its side of the agreements in August 1986, but it took until March of the following year for the US State Department to take the action necessary for the US side of the agreements and arrangements to be terminated.

CHAPTER 2

BOMARC: THE WEAPON AND THE SQUADRONS

The BOMARC surface-to-air anti-bomber missile, used by both 446 SAM Squadron at North Bay, Ontario, and 447 SAM Squadron at La Macaza, Quebec, was the most visible symbol of Canada's nuclear commitment. When editorial cartoonists wanted to show either Diefenbaker or Pearson with the potent or impotent nuclear weapons, it was usually the BOMARC they chose to satirize.

Both squadrons were armed with 28 BOMARC nuclear-tipped aerodynamic anti-bomber missiles each, with 28 nuclear warheads in place on the missiles at all times. These were the first nuclear warheads to arrive in Canada.

The Service-to-Service Supplementary Arrangement for the BOMARC system was made in October 1963, concurrently with the Genie. Operational Status with the W40 warhead was reached in January 1964. This was the first fully operational nuclear weapons system in Canada.

Documents from the time show that the military and civilian authorities understood that the BOMARC CIM-10B (Coffin launched, Interceptor Missile #10, B model) would speed along at Mach 2.7 to a 21 km altitude for a distance of 600 km from the launcher. It would then destroy its target with a 10 kt nuclear warhead. Tests in 1966 showed that the BOMARC was capable of intercepting a bomber-like target. This was done by having the (Semi-Automatic Ground Environment computer (SAGE) order the BOMARC to switch on its target seeker and commence searching as it approached the area of the target. When the missile "sees" the enemy aircraft it locks on and guides itself to an interception. The interception is not necessarily by collision, and in fact normally is not, as the warhead is fused to detonate at the point where the missile comes closest to the target.[1]

The missile contained, from nose to tail: a target seeker under the fibreglass nose cone; the electronics package containing the brains of the missile including the inertial guidance system, command system, and proximity fuses; the space for the warhead; and the fuel tank containing JP4 jet fuel.[2] The following document demonstrates a typical BOMARC test mission undertaken off Florida:

DOCUMENT # 1
08 September 1966, USAF 4751st Air Defense Sqdn, DNW file #3311-20.

One CIM-10B launched under SAGE/MOADS control against a simulated SAGE target flying at 65,000 feet on an inbound heading of 320 degrees at 900 knots ground speed. With the missile 67 nautical miles downrange, recommit action will be taken by SAGE against a BQM-34A flying at 45,000 feet, on a heading of 205 degrees at 445 knots ground speed. Intercept to occur at 45,000 feet, 157 nautical miles downrange utilizing Profile II final turn tactic.

Because of the US desire to deploy more anti-bomber defences across North America, and because of the rationality of placing them as far north as possible, it was natural that Canada, the NORAD partner, become home to some BOMARCs. To this end the US Air Force would pay much of the initial BOMARC costs. However, as this included a lot of procurement in the United States, there was little economic spillover into Canada. The costs for Canadian and US taxpayers on this joint defence programme were broken down thusly:

60 BOMARC missiles	$29m	USAF pays
56 launcher shelters	$12m	USAF pays
special equipment	$19m	USAF pays
general construction	$14m	Canada pays
training of personnel	$2m	Canada pays
other costs	$5m	Canada pays
annual operating costs	$6m	Canada pays

| North Bay construction | $4m | Canada pays |
| La Macaza construction | $7m | Canada pays |

By 1971, the last full year of operations, it was reported that the military was spending about $4 million per year to operate the two BOMARC squadrons.[3]

One large cost, not included in the original estimates, would be the SAGE computer and command facilities and the massive and complex Semi-Automatic Ground Environment computers and directing terminals essential for BOMARC operations, but useless for any other system. The SAGE was essential as the BOMARC launcher sites at North Bay and La Macaza would have no control over the missiles whatsoever. Every step from the initiation of a launch sequence through to the final interception would be controlled from the SAGE site. Each SAGE had three nuclear-weapons-related critical components: these were components directly involved in the launching of an armed BOMARC, and therefore had to be under constant two-man observation, or emplaced in the authenticator bulk safe.

The first of the critical components were the two BOMARC Interlock Switch Keys, one held by each of the Canadian and US Combat Operations Centre duty officers. BOMARC release was accomplished by having the USAF custodian in the SAGE or BUIC III turn the USAF BOMARC Interlock key and the Canadian duty officer use his key at the same time. The second was the AN/FSQ-7 DCA Program Tapes which contained the BOMARC flight interception and detonation programmes, and the third was the AN/FSQ-7 Tape Drive Units (TDUs) which read the unique coded BOMARC tapes.

This was to be the first joint defence programme between Canada and the United States that involved a large weapons purchase and joint operations. The programme was joint in two ways: firstly the USAF had already deployed a number of BOMARC A and B units, and secondly, the US military would be financing much of the Canadian BOMARC acquisition programme, and supplying the warheads free of charge.

The Canadian government was worried about the possible life-span of the questionable missiles. Although there were eight BOMARC squadrons in the US, the Kennedy Administration, under the prodding of Robert McNamara, was considering closure of the units and the dismantling of the missiles. Pearson and Martin worried that the White House would pull the rug out from under them by withdrawing BOMARC support after Pearson had spent much political and economic capital on acquisition.

With this in mind, Paul Hellyer directly contacted Robert McNamara and told him that the BOMARC was a controversial weapon in Canada, and that there seemed to be some uncertainties surrounding its life expectancy in the US arsenal. Hellyer went on to state that "a difficult situation would be created if there were precipitate moves to abandon the BOMARC system."[4] Hellyer emphasized that the Canadian government wanted the BOMARC to have a life of about ten years, but that if the US decided against this, Canada should be fully informed and be a participant in the planning.

McNamara assured Martin that the missile would continue in limited service until at least 1970. Later, the Canadian Charge d'Affairs in Washington, Basil Robinson, reported that the US planned to phase-out all the BOMARC-Bs at the end of the 1960s, but that the Canadian BOMARCs were to stay in place longer due to their northern location.[5]

USAF BOMARC Units

6 ADMS Suffolk County	(closed 01 Dec 64)
30 ADMS Dow AFB	(closed 01 Dec 64)
35 ADMS Niagara Falls	(closed 31 Dec 69)
37 ADMS Kincheloe AFB Michigan	(closed 01 Jul 72)
74 ADMS Duluth Int'l Airport Minnesota	(closed 01 Apr 72)
26 ADMS Otis AFB Massachusetts	(closed 01 Apr 72)
22 ADMS Langely AFB Virginia	(date unknown)
46 ADMS McGuire AFB New Jersey	(closed 01 Oct 72)

RCAF/CAF BOMARC Units

446 SAM Sqdn CFS North Bay	(closed 01 Sept 72)
447 SAM Sqdn CFS La Macaza	(closed 01 Sept 72)

THE W40 NUCLEAR WARHEAD[6]

The W40 nuclear warhead was actually the boosted primary stage of the widely-used W28 weapon, and had an estimated yield of 7–10 kt. The weapon was chosen as the BOMARC warhead by the USAF in

December 1958. It was 0.804 m long, 0.455 m in diameter, and weighed about 159 kg complete. This was a Los Alamos design at its root, but the basic physics package was reworked as an air defence warhead by using only the primary stage of the B28 thermonuclear gravity bomb. Added to this were fuzes for proximity and time, the T-3019 arm-safe device, and a Boeing minimum altitude signal device to prevent detonation below 3000 m.

The first production unit was built in January 1959 with standard production starting in June 1959. However, a significant safety problem caused it to be withdrawn in August. It was re-released in September with a temporary fix built in. The W40 Mod 2 warhead retrofit was developed and sent out in December 1963 to solve the one-point safety problem discovered in 1960. About 340 W40/BOMARC warheads were built between September 1959 and May 1962. All W40/BOMARC warheads were retired by November 1972, as the USAF ADC BOMARCs had been retired, and the warheads used at Canadian sites had been returned to the USAF storage facilities.

The W40 warhead, at 7–10 kt expected yield, was lethal to a medium-bomber-type target up to 1000 m away. At the maximum range of lethality, it would be influence-fuze fired. At great altitudes the lethal range of radiation is greater than for lower altitudes, and it is likely that the Soviet bomber crews would suffer more than their aircraft from a detonation even beyond a distance of 1000 m.

Once installed on the missile, the W40 warhead would stay in place for 90 days prior to being off-loaded for periodic inspection and routine maintenance. The warhead would be removed from the BOMARC, trucked to the Ordnance (SAS) building, inspected, repaired if necessary, and then taken back to the launcher/shelter for re-installation.[7]

As with all US nuclear weapons, and especially those stationed outside of the United States, the "Two-Man Rule" was strictly applied. This meant that for any activity involving access to live nuclear weapons, or to a facility containing a live nuclear weapon, or to a facility containing critical launch components of a nuclear weapon, two or more qualified people must be present at all times. In effect, because of the dual-key arrangement, this meant that one of the people would have to be a US military official of any rank.

DOCUMENT # 2
30 September 1964, secret, SAFETY RULES FOR THE RCAF
CIM-10B (BOMARC B) WEAPON SYSTEM.

> 5. Two-Man Concept: During any operation affording access to a War Reserve Warhead or a missile with a War Reserve Warhead installed, a minimum of two authorized persons, each capable of detecting incorrect or unauthorized procedures with respect to the task to be performed and familiar with pertinent safety and security requirements will be present. The number of personnel authorized such access will be held to a minimum consistent with the operation to be performed.
>
> a. (S)(Gp 4) All storage functions in the USAF Maintenance and Storage Area will be performed under the direction and control of USAF personnel. RCAF armament personnel assigned as loading crew members may assist in handling and storing nuclear warheads only while under the direct supervision of USAF weapon custodians.

The Two-Man Rule also prevented unauthorized launches or detonations by dividing responsibilities between various personnel, and by ensuring that the BOMARC could not be launched without the insertion of two separate keys, each held by an officer from each country. All of the rules listed below applied equally to the Canadian battle staff officer on duty.

DOCUMENT # 3
30 September 1964, secret, SAFETY RULES FOR THE RCAF
CIM-10B (BOMARC B) WEAPON SYSTEM.

> a. There will be a designated US officer who will be physically present in the [Canadian] SAGE Direction Centre at all times. The US Officer will have exclusive custody and access to a single key which will operate the USAF BOMARC SAFETY INTERLOCK Switches. This key will be appropriately safeguarded at all times.
>
> b. The covers of the key-operated BOMARC

SAFETY INTERLOCK Switches will be safetied and sealed.

c. Until a condition of Air Defense Emergency, or Defense Emergency has been declared and appropriate national release has been received and authenticated, or until such time as an object has been declared or designated HOSTILE by proper authority in accordance with the applicable rules of engagement and appropriate US national release has been received and authenticated:

(1) The seals on the covers of the key-operated USAF BOMARC SAFETY INTERLOCK Switches will not be broken.

HOW TO LAUNCH A BOMARC

The command and control of the BOMARCs, including their launching, was not undertaken by the operational squadrons. All of this was accomplished by personnel in the SAGE or BUIC III centres. Canadian BOMARCs at 446 and 447 SAM Squadrons could only be launched by teams in Canadian NORAD facilities. Although SAGE centres in the United States could take over command and control of the missiles once airborne, US sites were unable to enact a launch sequence on the Canadian missiles.[8] Provided below are excerpts of the safety rules and procedures to be followed in the SAGE and BUIC III centres with the BOMARC launch keys and computers. This document gives us the clearest possible insight into the procedures used for a launch of the BOMARC. The crucial feature demonstrated here is the BOMARC Interlock Switch, which was the dual-key system designed to give each country a veto over use of nuclear-armed BOMARCs on Canadian territory. The procedures demonstrated below are clearly technical launch actions taken by the military, with little reference whatsoever to political authorization.

The interim BOMARC employment procedures, which were eventually codified for long-term use, were explained in January 1964 to Air Vice Marshal Hendricks, the Chief of the Air Staff. The Commander of RCAF ADC told him that the custody of the warheads would remain with the USAF until a nuclear release message from proper US authority was passed on by CINCCONAD. It was stressed that there would be consultation with the military committee only if time permitted. This authorization* would be passed by CINCCONAD to the US warhead release officer on duty at the Ottawa NORAD sector, the man holding the US BOMARC interlock key. Authorization for Canadian release of the weapons system would come to the Canadian release officer on duty at the Ottawa NORAD sector from CINCNORAD. It was stipulated that the release messages for the US and Canadian duty officers must be transmitted on different channels.[9]

Later regulations stipulated that the authorization from CINCNORAD at NORAD Headquarters in Colorado Springs would have to come from the Deputy Commander-in-Chief of NORAD, who was always a Canadian officer. "Action ... will not be taken until the Canadian authority to employ Canadian BOMARCs has been conveyed to CINCNORAD through the senior Canadian Officer present on the NORAD Battle Staff. Internal operational procedures within the NORAD COC have been revised to reflect this change."[10] This was the Canadian content in the BOMARC nuclear use chain of command.

DOCUMENT # 4
01 December 1968, Headquarters 41 NORAD Division, (North Bay) 41ND Regulations No. 65-5. from Colonel M.H. Vinzant, jr., USAF Commander, Nuclear Procedures, BOMARC SAFETY INTERLOCK PROCEDURES AND KEYS.

> 1. PURPOSE: To establish positive control of the BOMARC safety interlock switches on the Senior Director (SD) and Senior Weapons Director (SWD) consoles and to assure proper handling, transfer and the use of the interlock keys.
>
> 4. ACTIVATION OF INTERLOCK SWITCHES: Two BOMARC interlock switches are mounted on the SD console auxiliary panel and two corresponding BOMARC interlock switches are mounted on the SWD console auxiliary panel. The right-hand switch on each console auxiliary panel is operated by the USAF interlock key; the left-hand switch ... is

---

* The message would be sent via the NORAD voice alerting system and authenticated using the ACAS-90 Secret Two-Man authenticator system.

operated by the CF interlock key. The activation of either set of switches is sufficient to permit "USE BOMARC" switch action. The four switches are covered with plastic guards and safety sealed.

The switches shall not be activated unless the following sequence of events have taken place:

(1) The CF interlock key carrier has verified the authenticity of the NORAD Nuclear Employment Authority and verified this authority to the Battle Commander through the SD.

(2) The USAF interlock key carrier has verified the authenticity of the CONAD Release of Nuclear Weapons to NORAD and verified this release to the Battle Commander through the SD.

(3) The Battle Commander has given a specific order to employ live BOMARCs.

c. When ordered to employ live BOMARCs, the CF and USAF key carriers shall, independently:

(1) break the safety seals;

(2) remove the guards;

(3) insert and turn the keys in their respective switches on either the SD's or SWD's console auxiliary panel; and

(4) report to the Battle Commander that the interlock switches have been activated.

5. INTERLOCK AND AUXILIARY PANEL KEY CONTROL:

• • •

c. The keys will be carried on chains worn about the neck of the responsible officers. The keys are not to be taken out of the CC/DC building at any time.

d. The Senior CF and USAF Officers shall transfer their respective keys to the relieving CF and USAF Officers at the change of shift. AT NO TIME WILL THE CF KEYS BE IN THE POSSESSION OF A UNITED STATES NATIONAL NOR WILL THE USAF KEYS BE IN THE POSSESSION OF A CANADIAN NATIONAL. [emphasis in original document]

NUCLEAR WEAPONS RELEASE WITHOUT
CANADIAN GOVERNMENT APPROVAL

When nuclear weapons first arrived in Canada there was no standard procedure for Canada to give authorization for live use of the BOMARCs. As is clear from the above document on BOMARC Interlock Switch procedures, the Canadian battle staff officer on duty would receive his authorization for use from the Commander-in-Chief NORAD in Colorado Springs, USA. The Canadian officer therefore had no way of knowing whether the Canadian government had or had not already given a positive response to a US request for the use of nuclear weapons. This system would therefore allow for the release and firing of nuclear-armed BOMARC missiles without specific Canadian government authorization. Interim procedures were completely reliant on US military commanders. Six months after the arrival of BOMARC warheads, the Canadian high command issued orders stating that the Canadian political authorization for employment of Canadian BOMARCs would be conveyed to CINCNORAD through the senior Canadian officer present on the NORAD Battle Staff in Cheyenne Mountain, Colorado Springs.[11] This was a definite improvement in terms of Canadian control.

DOCUMENT # 5
06 January 1964, 1730Z from CANAIRHED to CANAIRDEF, written 01 Jan 64, secret, for A/V/M Hendricks from A/C Austin, 5 pages, refer to a message CPLN 1. file S0030-101,

> Custody of nuclear warheads will remain with the US until release is received from proper US authority. CINCNORAD will consult, to the limit which time will permit commensurate with the tactical situation, with COSC and JCS prior to employing nuclear weapons.
>
> C. US Release Procedures
>
> 1. Release from US custody will be by CINCCONAD only.
>
> 2. Release authorization will be communicated from CONAD HQ to the US warhead release officer on duty at the Ottawa Sector who will have exclusive access to the single US BOMARC Interlock key.

3. The US BOMARC Interlock Switch will not be activated until release authorization has been received from CINCCONAD and authenticated.

D. Canadian Release Procedures

1. Canadian release authorization will be by CINCNORAD only.

2. Release authorization will be communicated from NORAD HQ via Headquarters NNR and will be passed to the Canadian release officer on duty at the Ottawa Sector who will have exclusive access to the single Canadian BOMARC Interlock key.

3. The Canadian BOMARC Interlock Switch will not be activated until CINCNORAD's release authorization has been received and authenticated.

E. After US and Canadian releases have been received, RCAF CIM-10B's may be employed in support of the NORAD mission in accordance with approved rules of interception and engagement in NORADR 55-6. Approved NORAD authentication procedures will be used at each level to confirm orders associated with the employment of nuclear weapons.

Part Five. This Headquarters is preparing proposed permanent procedures governing the employment of nuclear weapons furnished Canadian NORAD forces.

Later, with some Canadian control procedures in place, it was still quite clearly the US command and control network which controlled the Canadian use of the BOMARC system. The BOMARC could only be used once the Commander-in-Chief of US Continental Air Defense (CONAD) had given authority for warhead release. This information was communicated on US lines to US units in Canada and to NORAD Headquarters in Cheyenne Mountain, Colorado Springs. At NORAD HQ the Canadian battle staff officer would add his input, assuming he had received authorization from Ottawa. The last line of the following document is most instructive as to the actual situation. The officer wrote: "Canadian authorization is assumed to have been given if the NORAD Employment Order is passed to Canadian NORAD elements."[12]

DOCUMENT # 6
21 October 1969, Annex A to V 3312-20(DNW), secret, Canadian
BUIC III/CIM10B (BOMARC) Operational History.

Continental Air Defence (CONAD) Command
represents US National release control over all nuclear
weapons used in NORAD including BOMARCs.
Nuclear weapons cannot be employed until this US
National release of the weapons has been given to
NORAD by CONAD. Continental Air Defence
Commanders down to and including Regions can
authorize the use of nuclear weapons in air defence
missions upon declaration of Air Defence Emergency
or a comparable state or readiness or when a
NORAD/Continental Air Defence Commander
declares an object hostile in accordance with the
applicable rules of engagement. CINC CONAD or
CONAD Region Commanders may further delegate
Nuclear employment authority to Division and BUIC
III NCC Commanders.

The governing regulation for authentication of
release weapons to Canadian Forces and subsequent
employment is NORAD/CONAD Reg 55-35.
CONAD through their voice alerting net advises the
BUIC III NCC USAF Custodial agent of the release
of nuclear weapons to Canadian Forces. The USAF
Custodial agent will authenticate the Release Order
using the USCAS-95 (SECRET-Two Man US-only
control). This authorizes the USAF custodian to turn
the USAF key in the BOMARC Safety Interlock
Switch assembly providing there is a state of Air
Defence Emergency. The NORAD Employment
Order authorizes NORAD forces to use nuclear
weapons. It is sent via the NORAD voice alerting
system and is authenticated using the ACAS-90
SECRET Two-Man Authenticator. The NORAD
Employment Order is normally given at DEFCON
One or Air Defence Emergency but must not
precede the CONAD release of weapons to Canadian
Forces. Canadian authorization is assumed to have

been given if the NORAD Employment Order is passed to Canadian NORAD elements. [author's emphasis]

CFB NORTH BAY

When Minister of National Defence George Pearkes stood in a stubbly field on that windy day, 16 May 1959, spread out a map and said "this will be the site," he probably did not imagine that it would take another four-and-a-half years to arm this new weapon.

The new 446 SAM Squadron attained its minimum operational capability in March 1962 and became fully operational, but without warheads, in August 1962. Once it passed the Initial Capability Inspection (ICI) held from 4 to 7 November 1963, the squadron was cleared to receive war reserve nuclear weapons.

As the missiles were in place for over a year prior to their arming, and they were useless without a nuclear warhead, Canada was in the curious position of having two full squadrons supporting 56 weapons 24 hours a day which had no live ammunition. Therefore, to give the personnel the feel of a live system, "in March 1963 warhead jumper cables were installed and both units reported status as though they were fully operational"[13] with W40 nuclear warheads.

Once operational, the wealth of military experience at North Bay, and the proximity to the Canadian NORAD HQ, made for the smooth running of the premier BOMARC squadron. This is not to say though that there were no accidents. On 04 September 1970 at 1915 GMT, 446 Squadron reported a Dull Sword on one of their missile/warhead combinations.* However, no information has ever been uncovered about this incident, and to this day it remains a secret.

INITIAL WARHEAD DELIVERY

Once it had been announced that the 16 August 1963 agreement had been signed, people naturally thought that warheads would soon be forthcoming. Minister of National Defence Paul Hellyer was asked in late November if there were any nuclear weapons on Canadian soil, and he replied "Not that I am aware of."[14] The vaguely amused Member went on to ask whether Hellyer would be aware of it if they were indeed stored on Canadian soil. Hellyer replied "I would hope so." However, there is evidence to suggest that as early as 1950 the

---

* Please see description of Dull Sword later in Chapter 2.

USAF was storing nuclear weapons in Canada without the MND being apprised of such.*

Two weeks later the Prime Minister was asked if there were US nuclear weapons at La Macaza, North Bay, or any other bases in Canada.[15] The fact that it is possible for there to have been SAC weapons at Goose Bay without the express knowledge of the prime minister is probably what lead Pearson not to answer, even though there were no such weapons at the five RCAF ADC stations. Again the Member pressed the PM for an answer, but Pearson replied that he still had not be advised "to that effect."[16]

Perhaps the most interesting statement given by the government concerning delivery was made by the Associate Minister of National Defence. He said that the delivery of nuclear weapons is subject to the authorization of the US president personally, and that "President Kennedy's untimely death has caused some delay."[17] Perhaps if it had not been for the assassination of Kennedy, the first BOMARC warheads would have arrived a month earlier.

On 30 December 1963, US President Lyndon B. Johnson signed a one page top secret memo for US Secretary of Defense Robert S. McNamara. This memo, still unavailable, authorized the shipment of US nuclear weapons to Canada for the arming of Canadian military systems.[18] Just over 24 hours later, the first warheads were in Canada.

The first warheads for the BOMARC arrived not in secret, as is usual for nuclear weapons shipments, but to a great fanfare of press coverage. Reporters from the *North Bay Nugget* were present as the convoy of warhead carriers moved down the highway from the airfield to the BOMARC launcher site north of town. Newspapers across the country carried the story, along with photographs, of the warheads arriving in Canada on New Years' Eve, 1963.

DOCUMENT # 7
08 November 1963, S0029-106-6(AMTS) secret, Memorandum, from AMTS A/V/M WW Bean, to CAS, re: 446 SAM Squadron North Bay Delivery of Warheads.

> Delivery to 446 SAM Squadron will be completed by four flights of one aircraft to North Bay. We will not receive a delivery schedule per se as the flights will

---

* The autumn 1950 SAC deployment to Goose Bay, NFLD, with 11 Mk 4 atomic bombs saw the MND cut out of the information chain in Ottawa.

be randomly scheduled. However, I will keep you advised of progress. For your information, we have established procedures so that we may stop delivery at any time during the process if such action should become necessary.

At approximately 10:00 PM, 31 December 1963, with only two hours left in the year, a USAF Military Air Transport Command C-124C Globemaster transport aircraft, serial number 0-20975, of the 19 LSS,[19] touched down at RCAF Station North Bay. The seven warheads were removed from the aircraft, and "convoyed to the BOMARC Site immediately on off-loading."[20] Three trucks marked "EXPLOSIVES" went from the airfield to the BOMARC site, and one stopped at the ordnance building for unloading. The remaining two trucks moved to the shelter area to deliver the warheads directly to the launchers. The next day MND Paul Hellyer would announce that the warheads delivered that night had been installed on the BOMARCs upon arrival.

Although the warheads had been expected, it is clear now that the Canadian government and military were caught slightly off guard by their arrival. A week after the initial shipment, not only was Paul Martin talking to Pearson about the "unexpected arrival of warheads."[21] but even the military was referring to the "recent sudden arrival of warheads."[22]

The other problem evident from the initial delivery was that the customs service intended to inspect each imported shipment, and insisted on normal customs procedures, such as clearly marked crates, and perhaps even import duties. In the end this was waived, but customs was still present at each delivery.

DOCUMENT # 8
28 November 1963, Memo to DL1 Division, External Affairs, re: Nuclear Warheads - Customs Requirements.

> The US authorities have apparently been informed that the Canadian Department of National Revenue is insisting upon the application to the entry of BOMARC warheads of the normal requirements of documentation, specifying value for all shipments of goods to Canada. They are also asking that crates containing the warheads be stencilled to show content

and value. Customs officers would be stationed at North Bay and La Macaza to effect clearance.

The Trade and Commerce Department eventually got their way, and External Affairs applied for permits for the import and export of US nuclear weapons on behalf of the United States. None have been found for the BOMARC, but the following document covered the nuclear weapons at Goose Bay only a few days after the BOMARC warhead arrived in Canada.

DOCUMENT # 9
Department of Trade and Commerce
In Reply refer to file No. 6731-2
            January 14, 1964
        Attention: Mr. J.R. McKinney,
        The Under-Secretary of State for External Affairs,
        Ottawa, Ontario
            Application #486695 has been received from the Deputy Minister of National Defence, Department of National Defence, Ottawa, dated January 13, 1964 for permission to export to USA the following: Nuclear air-to-air defensive weapons brought into Canada under the Canada-US Agreement of 28 and 30 September 1963 and any amendments thereto, and exported in accordance with the provision of that Agreement. This equipment is valued at $__ and is consigned to United States of America.
            I should be grateful if you would let me know whether an Export Permit may be issued to cover the above shipment.
                (signed for the)
                Deputy Minister of Trade and Commerce

The second of what came to be four initial shipments arrived at the airfield on 05 January 1964, and from the RCAF Station, a three-truck convoy proceeded north on #11 Highway.

The third shipment of warheads provoked the greatest concern. Like the first two deliveries, the USAF Globemaster arrived under cover of darkness on 08 January at 3:00 AM, and immediately off-loaded seven or eight W40 warheads. The problem then began when a freak geological occurrence caused an earthquake in the North Bay area only two hours later. Residents feared that a BOMARC warhead had exploded, and that the shaking of the ground was a sign of the nuclear detonation. Many calls to the police and to Station North Bay revealed to residents that the apocalypse was not beginning.

With the arrival of the fourth shipment of warheads three days later on 11 January 1963, 446 SAM Squadron was fully and completely armed.

In the early years, the 62nd Troop Carrier Wing, Detachment 1, 19th Logistics Support Squadron, was responsible for moving nuclear warheads into Canada.[23] Located at Kelly Air Force Base in San Antonio, Texas, the primary mission of the 19th Logistics Support Squadron was to "provide world-wide airlift in direct support of special weapons, and provide airlift for additional cargo as directed" by Detachment 1 of the 62nd TCW.[24] In the early years of the commitment, Canada would need at least 56 warheads for the BOMARC system, and at least 56 warheads for the Genie rocket. With the passage of time, replacements would be necessary, and warheads would be rotated between the central supply areas, the operational base, and the maintenance facilities. All of these moves were the responsibility of the 19th LSS.

DOCUMENT # 10
4 November 1963, from CANAIRHED, to ADCHQ Colorado Springs. Priority

> The Director of Air Force Movements (DAFM) at AFHQ has been appointed to make arrangements for the delivery for nuclear weapons on behalf of the RCAF. Detailed procedures have been made with Det 1 62 TCW Kelly AFB for this purpose. However the RCAF advises that the initial delivery actions for nuclear warheads for 446 Sdn RCAF North Bay not commence without specific approval of this HQ. It is expected that RCAF approval for initial delivery will be granted by classified message from this office immediately following the completion of ICI at North Bay. Thereafter routine arrangements as established by DAFM will be followed.

Official military film taken at North Bay on 31 December 1963 shows a C-124C Globemaster medium-heavy transport aircraft, serial number 0-20975, disgorging nuclear warheads unloaded via the internal lift system. This aircraft was assigned to the 19 LSS at this time. The Globemaster could unload smaller cargo directly from the hold using a lift system built into the centre of the body just aft of the wings. Using this, they lowered the large barrels containing a single W40 nuclear warhead each for the BOMARCs from the aircraft.

It became standard practice that the USAF aircraft moving nuclear weapons or components would inform the destination RCAF base's control tower of its cargo using the code signal "HAZARDOUS CARGO COCOA".[25] This would allow the tower to alert the fire fighters, ground handlers and special weapons personnel.

This comparatively simple procedure was repeated every few months at the six Canadian nuclear weapons sites for years. But with the closure of the BOMARC sites and Val d'Or in the early 1970s, and the denuclearization of CFB Chatham, there were only two sites to service. By the mid-1980s, with only the W25/Genie left in service at Comox and Bagotville, it is likely that the job of transporting nuclear weapons had fallen to the 6th Military Airlift Squadron. This was the US military's only prime nuclear airlift force serving foreign locations. The 6th flew the long-range C-141 aircraft out of Scott Air Force Base, and had 20 specially trained crews for this exclusive mission.[26]

UNIT NUCLEAR DELIVERIES AND REMOVALS

Squadron Base	Warhead Delivery	Warhead Removal
446 North Bay	31 Dec 63–11 Jan 64	04–17 Apr 72
447 La Macaza	01–15 Jan 64	06 Apr–15 May 72

UNIT NUCLEAR OPERATIONAL DATES

Squadron Base	Operational Dates
446 North Bay	c.13 Jan 64–31 Mar 72
447 La Macaza	17 Jan 64–31 Mar 72

446 SAM SQUADRON

With the motto "Vigilance Swiftness Strength," 446 Surface-to-Air Missile Squadron was formed on 28 December 1961 at Station North Bay. However, unlike their counterpart at La Macaza, 446 was only a tenant at North Bay, and the base provided all essential services and support for the unit. The squadron was not actually born in Canada, but came into being while various personnel were undergoing BOMARC training at the USAF training centre at Eglin AFB in Florida, US during October 1961. Those who remained in Florida fired 446 Squadron's first test BOMARC on 15 December 1961, at the Santa Rosa Island Test Facility.[27] The test flight intercepted a QB-47 drone bomber at an altitude of 12.3 km, 580 km out over the Gulf of Mexico. With the training under the guidance of the 4751st Air Defense Squadron (Missile) USAF/ADC, completed at Hurlburt Field, Florida, the Canadians proceeded home.

Once back at North Bay, work proceeded apace with the delivery of the BOMARC missiles by truck and aircraft from the Boeing factory in the state of Washington beginning on 19 October 1962.[28] Due to government and military fears that the Canadian population might not take too kindly to the new weapons, and that some people might actually try to stop them or at least protest, the missiles were delivered under a cloud of secrecy. Reports from Washington D.C. suggested that the RCAF "ordered that the route and time of shipments be kept secret because it feared that some Canadians opposed to BOMARCs might attempt to stir up demonstrations at communities along the truck's route."[29] The RCAF feared what was termed "possible pacifist demonstrations."

Along with their initial missile delivery, 446 had a busy autumn. That September some personnel again ventured down to Florida and launched a BOMARC which intercepted an F-104 drone at 7.7 km, 330 km down range. With the completion of the ICI in early November 1963,[30] 446 Squadron was ready to receive nuclear warheads: they would begin to arrive at 10:00 PM on 31 December 1963.[31]

Once armed, the squadron prepared for the first Operational Readiness Inspection on 25 February 1964. The four-day inspection took the squadron and Station North Bay through a gruelling series of tests and checks, resulting in a rating of "satisfactory."[32] Now the squadron was officially and finally cleared to carry out its primary role in NORAD.

In addition to their regular alert duties, various squadron personnel would venture down to Florida each year to fire the single test BOMARC allotted to each unit.

Often in the middle of a harsh winter, and much to the delight of the crews, a hand-picked team would move a BOMARC and its equipment to Florida for a couple of weeks. In 1965 and 1966 the 446 team successfully intercepted a USAF Ryan "Firebee" drone out over the Gulf of Mexico.[33] Each year until 1970 the tests were successful and the drones intercepted and destroyed. But to the shame of 446 SAM Squadron, the launch on 09 March 1971 did not result in an intercept. The squadron historian wrote "missile launched — intercept not achieved (nobody's perfect)."[34] There is no indication in the open documentation as to the reason for the failure.

425 MUNITIONS MAINTENANCE SQUADRON

The 425th Munitions Maintenance Squadron was the one unit responsible for all US nuclear weapons used by Canadian forces in Canada during the 1963–1984 deployment period. This USAF squadron took care of the BOMARC W40 warhead, and at the same time — but on four different sites — cared for the W25 Genie warhead. The squadron was divided into six detachments; two at the BOMARC sites, and four at the VooDoo/Genie bases. This particular unit was initially part of the USAF Air Defense Command (USAF/ADC).

USAF Munitions Maintenance Squadrons were established at each Canadian BOMARC and Genie site to accomplish the following missions:

1. Exercise and maintain custody of the warheads 24 hours per day prior to the release of warheads by proper US authorities.
2. Operate the US cryptographic system necessary for nuclear release and general nuclear weapons duties.
3. Receive, store, maintain, and monitor the handling of nuclear warheads.
4. Assure compliance with USAF BOMARC (GENIE) Safety Rules.
5. Provide personnel support to the Canadian Commander to accomplish maintenance.[35]

The 425th was based at Stewart AFB in New York state until December 1969 when it moved to Richards & Gebauer AFB near Kansas City, Missouri (Belton, Missouri).[36] Two years later, the unit made another permanent change of station when it moved to Peterson AFB in Colorado Springs, Colorado.[37]

At its height in 1969, the 425 MMS had 40 officers and 268 men assigned to the various detachments and the headquarters.[38] By mid-1972, the squadron was down to 33 officers and 215 men, having been withdrawn from the closed BOMARC sites.[39] On 01 January 1974 the

425 Munitions Maintenance Squadron (MMS) underwent a designation change and became the 425th Munitions Support Squadron (MSS), still having all the same duties as before. At the end of the 1970s, with only two operational detachments, the headquarters had only 4 officers and 12 enlisted men, while each detachment was authorized to have 6 officers and 42 enlisted personnel.[40]

The 425 MMS assumed new duties in early 1973 when they were assigned the difficult task of conducting command-wide inspections. On 06 February 1973 they were directed to undertake the Weapons Systems/Munitions Maintenance Staff Assistance Team (WMSAT) visits to various Air Defense Command and Air National Guard units.[41] This duty took both officers and NCOs to Fighter Interceptor Squadrons, Fighter Interceptor Wings, and Fighter Interceptor Groups in the US, and the All Weather Fighter units in Canada.[42]

Current secrecy provisions within the United States, and especially the US Department of Energy, have resulted in incomplete information being made public. Therefore, it has not always been possible to follow in strict chronological order such details as the identities of Commanding Officers.

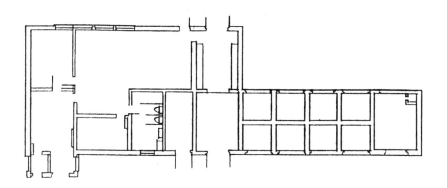

DIAGRAM #1
CFS La Macaza, Detachment #2 – 425 MMS Squadron USAF,
SAS building interior. Nine storage cells on the right side, and the maintenance and office facility on the left.

DETACHMENT 1

Based at CFB North Bay, Detachment 1 supported the 446 BOMARC Squadron beginning in 1963. This detachment had a rough start, as the person assigned to form the unit was unable to do so in 1962, and therefore returned on 15 September 1963 to try again. This time Captain Pickett succeeded, and within months the detachment would have nuclear weapons in its possession. The initial failure is directly attributable to the lack of progress made by the Diefenbaker Government towards signing the acquisition documents which would allow the nuclear warheads to come into Canada.

The detachment became inactive in the spring of 1972, but was not formally deactivated until 31 July 1972 under USAF Special Order G-165 of 18 July 1972.

CFS LA MACAZA

CFS La Macaza, Quebec and 447 SAM Squadron are really inseparable once 447 settled in at the site. The 447 was the only unit, and the site was built to house only 447. The 447 Squadron Commanding Officer was also the Station Commander, and the history of CFS La Macaza is also the history of 447 SAM Squadron, and vice versa. Like its sister unit 446, 447 was not formed in Canada. The unit was formed at Hurlburt Field in Florida during August and September 1962, then moved as a group to Station La Macaza in October.

The government had budgeted $7 991 850.00 for all construction at La Macaza, with $1.8 million for launcher/shelters, even though this was supposed to be a USAF responsibility. They also set aside $17 500 for a six-bay nuclear warhead storage facility.[43] The local MP, Gerard Girouard, commenting on the money spent in his riding, said that "even the workers of La Macaza, who helped my election, gave me the definite responsibility of opposing all acquisition of nuclear weapons."[44] The Quebec MPs would not be very nuclear-friendly.

Construction of the site began in 1960, with the first missile shelters ready for accepting weapons in July 1962. Launchers 1 through 14 were completed 15 January 1962, and launchers 15 through 28 were completed one month later. The Ordnance Building was completed and handed over on the same day. However, due to damage done by the contractors, the hydraulic system used to open the roof of the shelters leaked, and this posed a safety problem for the missiles.

CFS La Macaza, aside from those personnel directly concerned with the operation and maintenance of the BOMARCs, had a staff consisting of 4 medical attendants, 8 personnel staff, 31 security police, 26 communications technicians, 13 supply clerks, 41 construction engineers, and 9 fire fighters. That the engineers had some spare time was clearly demonstrated when in 1964 they built a station curling club, and in 1968 built an entire beach. They also hooked up a giant antenna and wired the entire site for cable at a time when cable TV was still in its infancy.

Records for Station La Macaza do not mention the initial arrival of warheads. However, it is clear that La Macaza and North Bay were armed at about the same time, and it is even possible that the USAF transporter which landed at North Bay then proceeded to La Macaza with another part of a larger shipment. It can be surmised, therefore, that the first W40 warheads arrived at La Macaza on 01 January 1964, near or soon after 1:00 AM. As with the first delivery, there is no public record of the second or third shipments. However, the fourth and final warhead shipment arrived at La Macaza on 15 January 1963, four days after the final shipment to North Bay.[45]

Once the BOMARCs had departed and 447 SAM Squadron deactivated, La Macaza was abandoned for about five years from 1972 until 1977 when the federal government moved the site from military control to Corrections Canada, and CFS La Macaza became a prison: the La Macaza Institution. Behind this prison, the shelters of the long-forgotten BOMARCs sit quietly decaying.

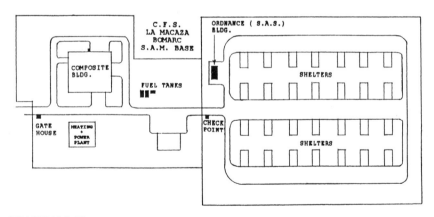

DIAGRAM #2
CFS La Macaza, 447 Squadron, BOMARC, site map. Shows only the 28 shelters/launchers, the SAS, and the supporting facilities. The station housing has been removed for clarity.

447 SAM SQUADRON

The 447 Surface-to-Air Missile Squadron was formed under Air Defence Command at CFS La Macaza on 15 September 1962. Under their motto, "Monjak Ecowi" or "Always Ready," an advance party had arrived at this outpost in the Laurentian mountains in January to begin the preparations for a full squadron deployment. All of this advance preparation was necessary as La Macaza was to exist only to support the BOMARC, and the squadron commander would also be the station commander, controlling everything. During the Cuban Missile Crisis, on 15 October, the Boeing Company representative handed over the completed BOMARC launcher site to the squadron commander, and the station underwent its first Initial Capability Inspection (ICI) from 13 to 15 November 1962. However, as no warheads were forthcoming, the work of the 240 military personnel and 97 civilians came to naught. With all of the missiles in place, but with no warheads, there was an air of unreality about the BOMARC sites. To combat this, RCAF ADC installed Warhead Jumper Cables in March 1963. This allowed the system to operate as though real war reserve warheads were on the missiles.[46]

The squadron would have its final ICI from 8 to 13 December 1963, and the installation of warheads would quickly follow. This is not to say, however, that the ICI went well. Many serious safety problems were highlighted. But this would not be their last difficult inspection.

DOCUMENT # 11
13 December 1963, USAF Air Defense Command Inspector General, Lt. Col. H.R. Junker, USAF Team Chief, secret, S1100-105-3, 3312-20, Statement of Facts, Initial Capability Inspection 447 SAM Squadron Held 8–13 Dec 63.

DISCREPANCIES.

1. USAF maintenance room did not have anti-panic handlebars on doors, and did not have an exhaust fan for proper ventilation.

2.a. Security radios were not available to sentries within the launcher area.

2.b. Unscreened personnel could have or control access to sensitive areas.

3. A significant amount of tools and equipment were not yet on site. 85% of tools and equipment for EOD capability, and 40% of tools for loading function had not arrived from USA.

4.a. Protective guards on drive belts on various machines were not installed.

4.b. A make up water meter had not been installed.

4.c. The fence was not properly grounded.

4.d. Instructions for the use of the hoists in the maintenance building had not been published.

4.e. The Station lacked 24 hour fire picquet coverage.

4.f. Damage to the exterior of the missile shelters had not been corrected and could cause damage to movable roofs during opening and closing.

4.g. RCAF lacked standardized grounding test procedures for BOMARC base systems.

5.a. No unit area safety surveys had been conducted.

5.b. The missile safety officer had not attended a formal safety training course, and his primary duty as Squadron Launch Area officer was in conflict with his safety functions.

5.c. An additional officer is to be assigned to help implement the Interim Nuclear Safety Rules.

Despite the many deficiencies reported during the ICI, the final recommendation of the inspection team was that warheads could be delivered soon, provided that the deficient areas were remedied. Therefore, delivery of the warheads proceeded apace with Station North Bay. Curiously, although they had many items to fix, and although they did not receive their final warhead shipment until after North Bay, CFS La Macaza was the first Canadian BOMARC site to become fully operational on 17 January 1964.[47]

Once operational, the heavy load of constant inspections descended upon them. The first to arrive was the ORI/CI (Operational Readiness Inspection/Capability Inspection) team on 02 March 1964, which stayed for four days. After four days the team concluded that 447 Squadron was only "Marginally Satisfactory"[48] as a nuclear-armed unit, and that significant improvement was needed.[49] Canada was not ready for the vast responsibilities of the nuclear weapons age. In fact, high level military officials considered the situation at La Macaza nearly disastrous, and worried that the nuclear warheads would be withdrawn. The Air Officer Commanding RCAF ADC told the Chief of the Air Staff that the "results of the ORI/CI at

La Macaza were almost disastrous and if at USAF unit would have caused removal of warheads."[50] Later inspections would reveal that CFS La Macaza had greatly improved.[51]

DOCUMENT # 12
25 March 1964, 1830z, to CANAIRHED from CANAIRDEF, priority restricted.

> It has become increasingly apparent that we must reshape our thinking and understanding in respect of the possession as opposed to the operation of nuclear weapons and the inspection as opposed to the operational evaluation of the weapons. As a beginning it is my firm opinion that the safety and security of the nuclear weapons is paramount and must take precedence over operational effectiveness. This view is supported by the fact that the retention of nuclear weapons would be denied only by a breach of the safety or security regulations laid down by the USA and agreed to by the Canadian government. In keeping our safety and security levels above minimum set by the USA we not only ensure retention of the weapon but reduce the possibility of a nuclear accident or incident to a minimum.

DULL SWORD, BROKEN ARROW

Despite the required change in thinking CFS La Macaza was not without its nuclear weapons accidents. Various "Dull Swords" or minor accidents involving live war reserve nuclear weapons were reported over the years. The first occurred just days after the fourth warhead delivery, when in the early morning of 18 January 1964 a Leading AirCraftman who shall remain nameless fell asleep while driving in front of BOMARC launcher/shelter #3 and thereby allowed his vehicle to hit the USAF Detachment Mobile Inspection Unit (MIU) van.[52] As there was a warhead in the shelter, and as the MIU van was in use monitoring the BOMARC system, this was considered a significant occurrence.

Another problem, this one not caused by lack of sleep but by system failure, was much more significant. A Dull Sword was declared and reported when it was discovered that the BOMARC launch control circuits were inadvertently switching control centres without action being taken by the human controllers.[53] Because this was a potentially disastrous event, it generated a great deal of paperwork and bilateral discussion.

Even more serious than a relatively simple Dull Sword was a Broken Arrow. The US military defines Broken Arrows as accidents or incidents which have the possibility of producing an unauthorized nuclear detonation, or which involve the theft of a war reserve weapon, the dispersal of nuclear material, or a fire in or around the war reserve weapon. One of these happened during the summer of 1967 when, during routine maintenance, RCAF personnel discovered a potential fire in the warhead section of the BOMARC in #28 launcher-shelter. With the fire fighters, security, and US custodians in attendance, the maintenance personnel opened the nosecone and found that several electronic components had been burned. The warhead was removed, the electronics replaced, and the missile re-armed. No cause was determined.

DOCUMENT # 13
10 July 1967, 2135z, secret, immediate, to CANFORCEHED from 447 SAM Sqn.

> During an MIU minor run, MIU van personnel noticed smoke coming from the electronics bay of the nose cone of missile number 1030 in shelter number 28. Alarm turned in to fire hall. A potential Broken Arrow was declared at 1945z and the Station NAR plan implemented. Power shut off on shelters 22, 24, 26, 28. Initial control point set up opposite shelter 18. On investigation by fire fighters no smoke was seen however upon opening of nose cone smoke and fumes observed, no fire detection. Maintenance personnel investigated, found electronics parts had burned. Down load then proceeded with on shelter 28 potential Broken Arrow downgraded to maintenance problem at 2030z.

With four sets of seven launcher/shelters, containing 28 armed BOMARCs, there was a great deal of work to be done keeping as many of the missiles as possible operational. Records for 447 SAM

Squadron show that there was always an average of 27 missiles ready to be fired in any month.*

The duties of the station and the squadron came to an end as the warheads were removed by their USAF custodians in the spring of 1972.

DETACHMENT 2
Based at CFB La Macaza, Detachment 2 supported the 447 (BOMARC) SAM Squadron beginning in 1963. Like Detachment 1 at North Bay, the La Macaza unit remained at full strength until disbanded with 447 Squadron.

DOCUMENT # 14
19 August 1965, Report of the USAF ADC Inspector General,
> The Detachment's Quality Control Program was unsatisfactory. Supervision and management of the Quality Control functions did not assure the accomplishment of minimum inspection requirements; planning and scheduling the Quality Control workload was inadequate; and inspections were not sufficiently thorough.

The detachment became inactive in the spring of 1972, but was not formally disbanded until 31 July 1972 under USAF Special Order G-165 of 18 July 1972.

PROTESTS AT LA MACAZA AND RCMP SURVEILLANCE
As one of the first two nuclear weapons sites in Canada, and due to its proximity to both Montreal and Ottawa, Station La Macaza was a natural target for those opposed to Canada's nuclear commitment. Through its operational life, the site would be a magnet for protestors opposed to Canadian nuclear armament and to the number of nuclear weapons sites inside Quebec.

Throughout the first summer, the protesters staged demonstrations and sit-ins at the main and side gates of the BOMARC site. On 24 June 1964, approximately 90 peace marchers

---

* Each month in 1970, 1971 and early 1972 CFS La Macaza reported an average of just over 27 missiles operationally ready at any one time.

sat down and blocked the main gate. On 06 August 1964, a peace demonstration and vigil at the main gate, called "Operation Hiroshima Day," was carried out by ban-the-bomb groups from across the country and from the United States. Later, "Operation Labour Day" was a week-long ban-the-bomb demo held during the first week of September.

But nuclear weapons were important to the Canadian government, and both the civilian and military authorities feared and distrusted those who disagreed with their nuclear policies and the nuclear deployments. The Royal Canadian Mounted Police (RCMP) were therefore called out to both provide security at the various nuclear bases, and to spy on the people and groups involved in peaceful and constitutionally-guaranteed protest: a right which Canadian soldiers had gone to war to protect three times in the previous fifty years. Freedom is indivisible, but this concept was lost on the government and its security forces.

While the RCMP were rarely involved in simple base security, they were the office of primary interest when it came to monitoring citizens' constitutionally-guaranteed legal dissent. The files of the RCMP security branch were transferred to the Canadian Security Intelligence Service (CSIS) when the new agency took over from the RCMP in the early 1980s, and after a few years, these old files were transferred to the National Archives, but kept under the control of CSIS. The files, which cover much of the RCMP effort to spy on Canadians who did not agree with government policy, can be requested from the Archives under a formal Access to Information process. However, the files will be reviewed by CSIS, and the agency is in the habit of making sweeping cuts. In the space of six months the author was able to get only 500 pages of documentation on RCMP surveillance of the protests at La Macaza. Finding aids tell us that there are massive RCMP files on protests, protesters, and anti-nuclear organizing across the country held by the National Archives.

The released files deal with the activities of the RCMP at La Macaza and other Canadian locations, and should be taken as representative of the state of RCMP interest at other nuclear sites such as North Bay, Comox, Chatham, and Bagotville. The standard practice seems to have been to take as many photographs as possible and then try to identify the persons protesting.[54] One officer even set up what he referred to as a "discreet observation post" near the

Supreme Court in order to take down licence plate numbers and possibly photograph people gathering to drive to La Macaza for a demonstration.[55] The RCMP was also involved in collecting anti-nuclear literature from both open and covert sources, and this information made its way into the files. Some documents belonging to a person or group opposed to the North Bay BOMARC nuclear weapons were copied by the RCMP North Bay Commander, Inspector H.F. Law, using a "Robot camera ... Kodak Tri X Film, time 1/25 second, distance 2'2" and setting F.16."[56] Whether Inspector Law was in the offices of the anti-nuclear group legally is questionable.

Files show that the RCMP gathered information on the "unwashed, uncut and uncouth"[57] peace demonstrators, and disseminated it to various RCMP detachments across the country. For instance, if a car was observed at a demonstration, the licence plate number was recorded, searched, and the information forwarded to the RCMP detachment nearest the owners home.[58] The purpose of forwarding the information was so that the local detachment could ensure "that a close watch will be maintained for any indication of such an occurrence," i.e., the development of anti-nuclear organizers, activists, and organizations.[59] Although there was no indication that people were doing anything that could be considered less-than-legal under even the broadest interpretation of Canadian laws, the government had those who disagreed with the nuclear policy closely monitored by the national internal security forces.

The paranoia was extensive, and resulted in many and varied breaches of personal privacy and security. For instance, "F" Division RCMP officers in Saskatoon, in following-up a La Macaza protest report, gained access to the central records office of the University of Saskatchewan at Saskatoon. They then built up their own file on a man whose name is erased from the reports, but who was identified as being active in the student Christian movement from 1959 to 1964. The RCMP officer had infiltrated the campus and knew the person by sight, having attended some of the same meetings.[60] This religious studies student in Saskatchewan was considered a threat to the security of the Liberal Government's continued deployment of nuclear weapons.

The depth of the paranoia is clear from the manner in which they treated even common information. A message from the RCMP officer at La Macaza to "A" division Ottawa dealing with an ongoing demonstration was classified as SECRET and sent through a secure line after being enciphered.[61] One has to wonder from whom this information was secret, as the protesters knew they were protesting, and they also knew the RCMP was watching and making reports.

SEMI-AUTOMATIC GROUND ENVIRONMENT

The SAGE system was the half-manual, half-computer air defence control system devised to bring North American air defence into the computer age and assist with the problems created by supersonic jets and missiles. The only SAGE centre located outside of the United States was built into a custom-made cavern in Reservoir Hill near North Bay, Ontario, making it the only hardened air defence control site other than NORAD HQ in Colorado Springs. The centre became fully operational when turned over to the Commander of Northern NORAD Region (NNR), AVM Harvey, on 26 September 1963.

The SAGE in North Bay was responsible for the NNR and the Ottawa NORAD Sector, which included the North Bay and La Macaza BOMARC sites. At the heart of the system are the giant FSQ-7 computers, originally weighing 275 imperial tons. The job of the computer system was to compute air interception courses and provide timely information to the battle commanders as to the best possible physical means for manned or unmanned interception of hostile targets. The computers were also programmed to select and target the BOMARC missiles, and prepare them for firing. As the name implies, the system is "Semi-Automatic" due to the retention of human operators to double check the system. As there was only one SAGE in Canada, and only a few in the United States, they were considered prime targets for a Soviet decapitation strike (i.e. a strike in which the eyes, ears, and brain of the government and military command are destroyed). Therefore NORAD, through the Canadian and US military commands, decided that there would have to be an extensive back-up system in place in both Canada and the United States. Thus BUIC was born.

BUIC: THE BACK-UP INTERCEPTOR CONTROL

There were two manned Back-Up Interceptor Control (BUIC III) sites built in Canada, and both were designated as NORAD Control Centres to back up the Northern NORAD Region/41 NORAD Division SAGE site at North Bay operating the BOMARCs in both the flight and intercept phases. The computerized sites in Quebec and New Brunswick were able to assume the operational responsibilities of the divisional headquarters or SAGE centres should SAGE be rendered inoperative.[62] Both sites could operate simultaneously, with one acting as the Division ALCOP and the other as a subordinate control centre. Each site had the capability to launch and control BOMARCs from both Canadian sites.[63] Like the SAGE sites, each BUIC III had a BOMARC Safety Interlock Switch assembly: the dual key switch covered with a plastic seal was the only safetied and sealed switch in the BUIC III System. The two national keys were kept by the RCAF Release Officer and the USAF Release Officer.[64]

BUIC III commanders were not allowed to fire nuclear weapons unless the target had been properly declared hostile in accordance with NORAD/CONAD regulation R55-6, after the CINCCONAD or CONAD Region Commander and CINCNORAD had granted authorization to employ nuclear weapons. Under autonomous operations caused by loss of communication, BUIC III commanders could have employed the nuclear-armed BOMARCs directly in their jurisdiction.[65]

CFS SENNETERRE

A small Canadian Forces Station between Nottaway and Senneterre, Quebec, CFS Senneterre was the site for one of the two BUIC III sites built by Canada and the USAF for the command and control of the BOMARCs. Originally part of the early-warning Pinetree Line, it was converted in the late 1960s. BUIC III site C8 at Senneterre, Quebec became operational on 01 December 1968, but it could not be used for primary BOMARC control as there were no USAF nuclear-qualified personnel stationed at the facility. Although all the equipment needed for the launching of BOMARCs was in the facility, the US launch keys were kept locked in the authenticator bulk safely in Canadian custody.[66] This was a clear violation of the nuclear safety rules for the Canada-US BOMARC system, but did not result in any disciplinary action. This is probably because the USAF was ashamed at not having their people on site in a timely fashion. In fact, it seems that the USAF had forgotten the site, and on 07 January 1969 a message was sent to remind the Director of Nuclear Safety at USAF Kirtland AFB that certain steps had to be taken with great haste at this point.[67]

CFS ST. MARGARETS

Originally part of the early-warning Pinetree Line, CFS St. Margarets was converted into the second BUIC III site in Canada in the late 1960s. BUIC III site C5 at St. Margarets, New Brunswick, became Operational 01 January 1969. However, due to poor planning on the part of the USAF, they experienced the same problems as CFS Senneterre: there were no USAF personnel on station.[68] The BUIC III system was useless as long as there were no USAF personnel on site who were qualified to carry out the custodial duties necessary under the dual-key arrangement.

PHASE-OUT AND DISBANDMENT AND CLOSE-OUT

On 24 August 1971, Minister of National Defence Donald S. MacDonald announced that Canada intended to disband both BOMARC squadrons and send the missiles and warheads back to the United States no later than 01 September 1972. Within one year this had been accomplished, and both squadrons were formally phased out as of 01 September 1972.[69]

The recent 1971 White Paper on Defence had brought the BOMARC issue to a close with the announced decision to end that commitment. The Canadian government, through External Affairs, had signed the CADIN (Continental Air Defence Integration North) Agreement renewal on 27 September 1971, at that time committing itself to ridding Canada of the BOMARC. Once the basic agreement had been signed, negotiations began towards the formulation of a government-to-government note on the phase-out. All items were worked out by February 1972, and the two squadrons ceased operations on 31 March.

In the United States, there was the hope on the part of USAF Air Defense Command that the ex-Canadian BOMARCs could be salvaged for re-use. ADC proposed that the 56 BOMARCs being repatriated from Canada be moved into the 48 shelters closed at the 35th ADMS at Niagara Falls, New York. The Pentagon decided that not only would ADC be prohibited from doing any such thing, but that they would also have to deactivate the remainder of their own BOMARC force within two years.[70]

The government and military moved with some speed to close the sites, and it was planned that the Canadian BOMARCs would stand-down from alert at midnight on 31 March 1972.[71] Although External

Affairs initiated talks with the US State Department on the impending closure, no records have been found of the government-to-government note dealing with this matter.[72] Each BOMARC site was told the date operations would end, and then told to commence with shipping the warheads with all speed.[73] Once the BOMARCs had ceased to be operational, unmating of the warheads, crating, and shipping would begin.

As the 1960s gave way to the 1970s, and the bomber threat from the USSR became even more remote with the greater emphasis being placed on ICBMs in the modernizing Soviet arsenal, the days were numbered for the BOMARCs. On 24 August 1971 Commanding Officer Major Randall told his 171 staff at North Bay that "it is the government's decision to retire the BOMARC missile system sited in Canada. While the date is not entirely firm, it is expected that operations will be phased out and the unit closed on or about 1 September 1972."[74]

The US military, due to decisions made during the McNamara era, was denuding itself of the BOMARC. With the final government-to-government negotiations easily completed, the Canadian BOMARC warheads were removed, packed, and shipped out in the spring of 1972. At the end of May, with all the weapons gone, the remaining 446 Squadron personnel began to destroy manuals and operational documents no longer necessary.[75]

With much less fanfare and press coverage than their arrival over eight years before, the warheads from the 56 BOMARC surface-to-air missiles were removed and shipped back to the United States in the spring of 1972. The large size of the warhead containers and the small size of the Special Ammunitions Storage (SAS) bunkers meant that once the warheads were removed from the BOMARCs, they could not all be stored in the SAS bunkers. Therefore, during the final phase-out, authority had been granted for the storage of two containerized warheads in a single BOMARC shelter.[76] Over a period of about five weeks, from 06 April 1972 until 15 May 1972, the warheads were flown out of both North Bay and La Macaza by a USAF nuclear weapon transport squadron[77] from Scott Air Force Base.

DOCUMENT # 15

S1920-3 (CO) Annex A, 25 Nov 71. Schedule of Activities for
Closure. 446 SAM Squadron, CFB North Bay.

Activity	Duration	Start	Finish
War Head Removal [sic]	10 days	4 Apr 72	17 Apr
Last Warhead Shipment			12 May 72

To ensure the safety of the system, and to ensure that as the system was being decommissioned no one could take the opportunity presented by the confusion to launch a BOMARC, certain precautions were taken. The critical components were removed and separated: the two launch keys were locked up separately; the target seeker data cards were locked up; the Status/Data circuits were destroyed; and the SAGE and BUIC sites safetied all BOMARC-related systems in the same fashion.[78]

The warheads were then trucked[79]* to the airfield and flown out by special weapons transporter aircraft based at Scott AFB to storage sites in the United States;** and the missiles, with the exception of a few kept as museum pieces and gate guards,*** would not be redeployed in the US, so the USAF chose to place them in storage or otherwise dispose of them.[80]

---

* At this time authorization was given to transport as many as six W40 warheads in a single truck.

** The common storage area for USAF nuclear warheads and bombs was the ultra-secure facility in the Sandia Mountains at Kirtland AFB, New Mexico.

*** One BOMARC was kept at CFB North Bay and one was given to the National Aeronautical Collection in Ottawa.

CHAPTER 3

STARFIGHTER: THE WEAPONS

Not until 1990, 25 years after the Starfighters began carrying their nuclear payloads, and more than 18 years after they were removed from Canadian service, did people know the true magnitude of the explosive force contained in these weapons. Paul Hellyer, the Minister of National Defence at that crucial time, wrote in 1990 that:

> The explosive power of the atomic bombs assigned to the RCAF's No. 1 Air Division was (a) ... closely guarded secret the military was reluctant to reveal to anyone — especially a politician. I was told the weapons could be adjusted to give them more than one level of explosive power, but no details were provided. It was only when I demanded, point blank, to see the figures, that I was told the bombs were capable of yields ranging from a few kilotons to something in excess of two megatons. I could now understand the air force's desire to avoid the kind of public relations "explosion" that would have been inevitable had this information become public.[1]

However, he had not always been so forthcoming. In his secret testimony to the Special Committee on Defence, the Minister said that "The yield of the bomb assigned would depend on the particular target but in most of these cases would be relatively low-yield — a very small fraction of the figures which have been used in the House and in the press."[2] This statement was made prior to Canada even signing the umbrella agreement which allowed for the RCAF and Army to acquire nuclear warheads. It is possible that at this time he had only been given the slimmest, and perhaps false, information by his air marshals. Members in the House took advantage of Hellyer claiming that Canada would only have a relatively low yield weapon in Europe. Hellyer confirmed on 28 June 1963 that he understood that a 20 kt bomb was a "relatively low yield" weapon.[3] This certainly does not line up with the information we now know to be true about the nature of the weapons equipping the Starfighters in 1964.

Information taken from military and civilian testimony in the United States, as well as data on nuclear tests now public, clearly demonstrates that the weapons used by the RCAF in Europe had various and high nuclear yields, although there is no indication that any weapon used by the RCAF exceeded 1.45 Mt in yield. The smallest was the 5–20 kt yield of the Mk 57 bomb, with the two largest being the 1000 kt (1 Mt) yield of the Mk 43, and the 1450 kt (1.45 Mt) yield of the Mk 28 thermonuclear bomb. However, as the Mk 28 series was a variable yield design based on changeable nuclear pits, it is extremely probable that only the nuclear pits for the lower yield versions were stockpiled at Canadian bases.

To the consternation of the government, Gordon Churchill, MP revealed in the House of Commons that he understood that there were several sizes (yields) of nuclear weapons for the Starfighter.[4] He was right, but the government would never comment on the variable yield aspect of the Canadian nuclear arsenal.

That the air marshals knew of the massive explosive power can be of no question. Their close relationship with the USAF and their preparations for RCAF deployment of the weapons would have put them in a position of knowledge. Three weeks later the Chief of the Air Staff told the same committee that "the weapons employed in these operations would be of the smallest possible yield commensurate with the task; rather than being in the megaton class, as has recently been suggested, they tend to be at the lower end of the scale."[5] Clearly, he was being very evasive, especially when you consider that the RCAF high command would eventually tell the Minister of National Defence that the weapons in question could exceed 1 Mt.

During the visit of the Special Committee on Defence to Germany in November 1963, the Air Officer Commanding 1 Air Division told members that the CF-104 was "a small airplane which obviously cannot carry a tremendous size bomb. I would say that it is a small bomb in the nuclear field, whether it is bigger or larger, I don't think I can actually answer that properly. But, I would put it this way: I think we would have to use more than one CF-104 to do the same damage."[6] It is unclear from the transcript of the testimony what he refers to when he makes the open-ended comparison of the level of damage. It is also unclear why more than one CF-104 with a megaton class weapon will be needed to destroy any target in central or eastern Europe, especially keeping in mind that this one small airplane would carry more explosive power than an entire thousand-bomber raid did during World War Two. This demonstrates the lengths to which the Canadian military high command was willing to go to protect its new class of weapons from what they saw as interfering and possibly hostile civilian politicians. Given their extensive espionage network, the Soviets probably already had a fairly good idea of the yields of various US nuclear weapons.

The other very important point is that although the aircraft was designated as an "F"-104, meaning fighter, and was called "Starfighter," that was not its mission while in Canadian hands. The reality was that the CF-104 Starfighter was to be tasked with the mission of a nuclear bomber. In fact, operating without a gun and carrying nothing but a thermonuclear weapon made the aircraft basically a low-level tactical-operational bomber. This was a big departure from the previous Canadian role in NATO which was high-altitude air defence with the Canadair CF-86 Sabre and the Canadair CF-100 Canuck.

Although a few of the Starfighters were fully armed with one of the three types of nuclear weapons at all times, they were always forbidden from flight during Quick Reaction Alert (QRA).* US and NATO rules stated that the aircraft, once armed with nuclear weapons, could not be launched, or even leave the alert facility: in fact, there was even an aversion to towing an armed aircraft. An armed aircraft was a grounded aircraft until the orders to attack a target were received.[7]

The Canadair CF-104 Starfighter carried four different nuclear weapons during its service life in the Royal Canadian Air Force and then the Canadian Armed Forces:

---

* QRA: Nuclear-armed aircraft with pilots standing by, ready for launch in minutes.

USAF Designation	RCAF Designation
B28EX	Weapon #1
B28RE	Weapon #1
B43	Weapon #2
B57	Weapon #3

It was RCAF practice to call them "Weapon #1," "Weapon #2," and "Weapon #3." "Weapons #1" referred to both the B28EX and the B28RE[8] without distinction. The exact reason for this is unclear, but perhaps this was for security, or because one of the B28 types was deployed to the RCAF after the original code-name system had been devised.

When not using the "Weapon #" system, the RCAF referred to all nuclear weapons as Mark-x bombs, i.e. Mk 28, Mk 42, and Mk 57, and as B-x bombs. It became standard practice in the US after 1967 to call gravity bombs by a B-xx name, i.e. B28, B43, and B57. The "Mk" reference in the US refers to and is synonymous with the Warhead "W" designation. In the case of the weapons carried by the CF-104 aircraft, all would have been called by either their Mark number or their B number depending on the date and the originating office of the documentation.

FIRST DELIVERY OF THE MARK 28

The Mk 28 was the first bomb to arrive for the use of Starfighter squadrons, and unlike the later systems, it sat in the SAS on Canadian bases for one to four weeks before being loaded onto operational aircraft. Deliveries by USAF MATS C-124 cargo aircraft occurred between 15 May 1964 and 08 June 1964, with aircraft standing QRA on 12 and 13 June 1964. From its official first alert on 01 July 1964, this bomb would remain in Canadian service until the Starfighter nuclear commitment was ended in 1972.

B28EX[9]

One of the B28 bombs carried by the CF-104 Starfighter was the B28EX "External," an externally carried, free fall, radar fuzed for airburst/ground burst, sealed-pit nuclear weapon. The weapon was "invented" on 05 February 1954 in the earliest days of thermonuclear weapons design, yet is remarkably small. It had a Category B PAL[10] (Permissive Action Link) which is a ground operable 4 digit coded switch and lock which prevents enabling the warhead without possession of the proper codes. Early versions allowed a user unlimited tries at entering the correct code, but later PALs would lock the user out after a certain number of incorrect codes had been entered. The PAL combinations would be kept in a USAF safe in the USAF custodial section, and could only be removed for use once confirmed authorization for the use of nuclear weapons had been received from NATO command.

The W28 warhead series had five different yields, with only four known: Y1=1.1 Mt (with either the Type 83 pit or the Type 93 pit), Y2=350 kt, Y3=70 kt, and Y5=1.45 Mt.[11] The Canadian units deployed only the lower yields of the Mk 28 design: probably only the 70 kt and 350 kt devices. The yield was only variable in the sense that a different yield required the installation at the maintenance facility of a different nuclear pit. However, it is possible that more than one yield was possible from a single pit, thereby allowing for a dial-a-yield system to be used. Testimony indicates that the yield would be selected by the ground crew from outside of the weapon casing once loaded under the aircraft in the QRA. The B28EX weighed 919–925 kg, and was 4.32 m long with a maximum body diameter of 0.51 m. The B28 contained plutonium and Lithium-6 deuteride and tritium; with either PBX-9404 or cyclotol as a 20 kg primary high explosive with a 40-point detonation system. The fuzing option had to be selected on the ground prior to flight for air or ground burst.

Due to the lack of a parachute system, only air or contact burst fuzing was used. It was delivered in an "over-the-shoulder" manner, or at low or medium angles by lofting. There was no "lay-down" bombing option with the B28EX as this variant had no parachute. The B28EX had the F28 nose cone (Mod 1, 4, 6, 8, or 9), and the EXSC tail cone with four (4) tail fins, one of which folded for greater clearance when loaded under the low-slung Starfighter. The lack of a parachute restricted delivery to medium and high altitudes. The B28 Mod 0 served in the USAF from 1958 to 1961; Mod 1 served from 1958 to 1976; Mod 2 served from 1962 to 1980; Mod 3 served from 1963 to 1969; and Mod 4 from 1964 to 1991. The RCAF/CAF could have used any of these versions, as the external shape remained unchanged. The RCAF 1 Air Division Starfighter strike/attack squadrons became operational with the Mk 28 weapon in June 1964."[12] The US Department of Energy built close to 4500 of the

Mk 28 series weapons between January 1958 and May 1966, (with a production break between March and August 1958), making it one of the most widely produced warheads in the US arsenal. Practice shapes or dummies for the bomb included the BDU-10/E as a drop shape, the MD-6 as a loading practice shape, the Mk 104 as a ballistic shape; and the BDU-26/E as a non-PAL shape.

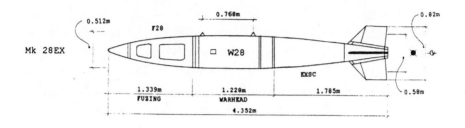

DIAGRAM #1
B28EX Thermonuclear free-fall gravity bomb.

B28RE[13]

The other B28 bomb carried by the CF-104 was the B28RE "Retarded External," an externally carried, free fall or parachute retarded, radar fuzing for airburst/ground burst, sealed-pit thermonuclear weapon. This is virtually identical to the B28EX, except that the B28EX had a parachute system. Development began in August 1955 and production ceased in May 1966. Like the B28EX, it also had a Category B Permissive Action Link (PAL), which prevented arming of the weapon without access to the proper combination.[14] Early versions had unlimited tries, but later PALs would lock the user out after a certain number of incorrect codes had been entered.

The W28 warhead series had five different yields, with only four known: Y1=1.1 Mt, Y2=350 kt, Y3=70 kt, and Y5=1.45 Mt.[15] The Canadian units deployed only the lower yields of the Mk 28 design. The yield was only variable in the sense that a different yield required the installation at the maintenance facility of a different nuclear pit. However, it is possible that more than one yield was possible from a single pit, thereby allowing for a dial-a-yield system to be used. The yield would be selected by the ground crew from outside of the weapon casing once loaded under the aircraft in the QRA. The B28RE weighed 984 kg, and was 4.21 m long with a maximum body diameter of 0.51 m. The B28 contained plutonium and Lithium-6 deuteride and tritium, with either PBX-9404 or cyclotol as a 20 kg primary high explosive with a 40-point detonation system. The fuzing option had to be selected on the ground prior to flight for air or ground burst.

The bomb was delivered in an "over-the-shoulder" manner, or at low or medium angles by lofting. The B28RE had the F28 nose cone (Mod 1, 4, 6, 8, or 9), and the RESC tail cone with three tail fins and a parachute receptacle. A 1.3 m pilot chute pulled out an 8.5 m ribbon parachute. The minimum altitude of delivery was 90–180 m. Using the parachute retarded version of the Mk 28 would allow Canadian Starfighter pilots a greater margin of escape from the lethal blast. The drogue system would give the weapon a flight time of between 25 and 35 seconds.

Dropping of the Mk 28 practice weapons was done "using a variety of deliveries, including laydowns, levels, and toss deliveries. Low Angle Drogue Deliveries (LADD) were practised with a 900 kg cement dummy weapon with the same aerodynamic shape and characteristics as the real thing."[16] The Mod 0 served in the USAF from 1959 to 1961; Mod 1 served from 1960 to 1976; Mod 2 served from 1962 to 1980; Mod 3 served from 1963 to 1969; and Mod 4 served from 1964 until the last was retired in September 1991. Practice shapes for the weapon included the BDU-2/B as a practice drop miniature; the BDU-4B as a practice profile shape; the BDU-29/E as a PAL simulator; and the BDU-14/E and BDU 15/E practice loading shapes. The Canadian War Museum has a BDU-14/E (Modified), built under RCAF contract by Hanson Brothers of Whittier, California in its storage facility in Ottawa.

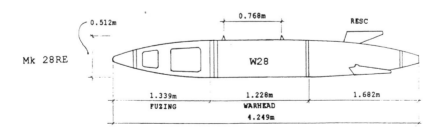

DIAGRAM #2
B28RE Thermonuclear retarded gravity bomb.

One of the few photographs of a CF-104 with a nuclear weapon shows aircraft #12864 of 1 Air Division, 3 Wing, Zweibrucken, with four pilots, and a B28RE nuclear bomb on trailer #25. The photo clearly shows the bomb nose cap, tail shape, access hatches, computer port, and hard points.[17] The lack of armed guards tells us that the weapon is a practice shape, but the access ports and movable nose demonstrate that it is fully functioning as a training device.

Once the B28 bomb had reached the Quick Reaction Alert shelter from the Special Ammunition Storage/Safe And Secure storage area on base, there was an average loading time of 30 minutes from start to final check-out.

Like all man-made objects, the B28RE would have accidents. The Mk 28 thermonuclear bomb was involved in more high profile accidents than any other nuclear weapon in the US arsenal. Notable USAF accidents include the dropping of four Mk 28RI bombs over Palomares, Spain, and the destruction of another load of the bombs over Thule, Greenland. Both incidents took place in the late 1960s. These accidents revealed that, after a crash, most of the safety features had failed. At both sites the high explosives had detonated, scattering plutonium over a wide area. Given the intricate loading procedures needed to place the large weapon under the small Starfighter, there was more than enough room for an accident if, during a routine loading of a war reserve weapon, faulty handling damaged a casing component.

DOCUMENT # 1
31 October 196?, [date obliterated] from 3 Wing Zweibrucken to CANFORCEHED, Secret Priority message,

> DULL SWORD, 30 1933Z Oct QRA 85A, 1 Mark 28 RE Serial Number 618630 JI Plug broken, CF-104, 3 Wing RCAF, Down Loading. During step 1-227 the bomb rotated slightly and a distinct snap was heard. On lowering the bomb the JI plug was found broken, 20 Apr Recertified 9 Oct, Cloudy, Hangar lighting, RCAF Weapons Loading Officer suspected that uneven pressure of rollers was prime factor. MJ1 Hoist standard.

In a continuing effort to prevent any accidents, the USAF had developed minutely detailed safety procedures. Just one small sample of such instructions shows that the RCAF had to be in strict compliance with all USAF safety regulations, or risk losing access to nuclear weapons.

DOCUMENT # 2
14 May 1964, secret, S1100-104-5(DNW), 3313-22, copy #23, RCAF Nuclear Weapons Instructions, NWI 64-202. CF104 Weapon System Safety Rules (T-1517 AMAC).

1. The following Safety Rules apply to all phases of CF-104/Mk28RE and Mk28EX Weapon Systems involving War Reserve Weapons during peacetime. These safety rules are mandatory.

2.b. Two Man Concept: During any operation affording access to a Mk 28 Bomb, or weapon-loaded aircraft, a minimum of two authorized persons, will be present. Only US personnel will be authorized such access for weapon maintenance operations directly associated with Mk 28 Bomb(s).

2.d.(1) Mk 28 Bombs will be stored in US approved, locked and secure facilities.

(2) The Mk 28 J-2 ARM/SAFE Plug will be maintained in the SAFE position except where specific maintenance procedures, require otherwise.

2.e.(1) The Mk 28 J-2 ARM/SAFE Plug will be maintained in the SAFE position during all ground transportation, loading and unloading operations. This does not preclude placement of the Mk 28 J-2 ARM/SAFE Plug in its ARM position during postloading operations for Quick Reaction Alert.

2.f.(7) One USAF Weapon Custodian may have custody of two Mk 28 Bombs provided they are not separated by more than 100 feet.

2.f.(8) Configuration for Quick Reaction Alert (QRA) will be as follows:

(a) 1. Interlock Lever — OS (OFF-SAFE), safetied and sealed.

(a) 2. Option Selector Switch — OFF, except that it may be placed in its safe position when monitoring the safe condition of the weapon.

(b) Special Weapon Drop Lock Switch — SAFE — cover down, safetied and sealed.

(c) Special Weapon Selector Switch — SAFE.

(d) Weapon J-2 ARM/SAFE Plug — may be in the ARM position.

FIRST DELIVERY OF THE MARK 43

The Mk 43 thermonuclear weapon was the last addition to the Canadian nuclear arsenal in Europe. Arriving at 4 Wing during the second half of September 1968,[18] it would become operational immediately. The Wing had already passed the inspection required for the operation of a new weapon,[19] and alerts commenced with each new shipment. 4 Wing had a full complement of weapons and was fully operational with the Mk 43 by 01 October 1968.[20]

B43[21]

The B43 Mod 1[22] bomb carried under the CF-104 Starfighter was the externally-carried, free fall or parachute retarded, radar fuzed for airburst/ground burst thermonuclear weapon. The weapon was accepted for production in March 1960 as a Strategic Air Command (SAC) weapon, but was transferred to Tactical Air Command (TAC) that November. It was equipped with a Category B PAL (Permissive Action Link).[23] This PAL required that a four digit code be correctly entered into the bomb arming circuits on the ground prior to flight.

The W43 warhead had a single, massive, non-variable yield: 1 Megaton. The long-nose B43-1 weighed 961 kg, and was 4.16 m long with a maximum body diameter of 0.46 m. The Mod 0 nose had the impaling spike for laydown strike, but the Canadian weapon sported the Mod 1 nose with the radar fuzing system for airbursts. The B43 contained plutonium and lithium-6 deuteride and tritium for fusion. The fuzing option had to be selected on the ground prior to flight for air, contact, or ground burst.

The bomb was delivered in an "over-the-shoulder" manner, or at low or medium angles by lofting. In order to be used in the retarded mode, the body contained a parachute receptacle in the tail. The minimum altitude of delivery was 90–180 m. The US Air Force had originally conceived of the bomb as being designed to destroy "high value urban-industrial targets and moderately hard military targets." The tail fins had frangible, break-away sections which would simply fall off if the fins struck the runway while the Starfighter was on take-off or landing.

Production of some 1000 units began at the Pantex Plant in Texas in April 1961 and lasted until October 1965. The B43 Mod 0 was deployed to the USAF between 1961 and 1972 and then converted to a Mod 4; Mod 1 between 1962 and 1991; Mod 2 between 1965 and 1991; Mod 4 between 1973 and 1976; and Mod 5 between 1965 and 1991. The final bomb, a Mod 2, was retired on 01 May 1991.

Practice shapes for the weapon included the BDU-8A/B retarded shape; the BDU-18A/B free fall shape; the BDU-6/E non-PAL loading shape; and the BDU-35/E PAL loading shape.

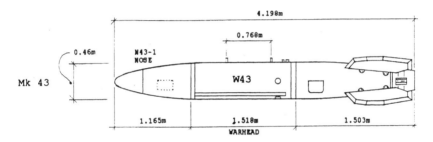

DIAGRAM #3
B43 Mod 1 Thermonuclear retarded gravity bomb.

As it was unacceptable to both the USAF and the RCAF to have the pilots do their flight training with live war-reserve nuclear bombs, the RCAF had to acquire practice shapes. The BDU-8/B practice bomb was one of the training shapes for the B43 nuclear weapon which was purchased by Canada, and RCAF pilots got their nuclear qualification on the BDU-8/B. In the first year of the deployment of real war reserve nuclear bomb to the RCAF in Europe, the RCAF spent $571 000.00 on a number of BDU-8/B training ballistic shapes.[24] They would then continue to spend an average of half-a-million dollars per year to buy more ballistic shapes for the Starfighter pilots to drop at the bombing ranges around Europe, but primarily at Decimomannu, Italy.

Curiously there is no record in the main estimates of training shapes being purchased for either the B28 or B57, but as the pilots did drop them, and they are referred to in RCAF/CAF documentation, there is no doubt that millions more were spent on various other training and ballistic shapes.

The B43 was the shortest-lived nuclear weapon in RCAF European service, seeing alert duty with the Starfighter squadrons only at the end of the 1960s. In mid-September 1968[25] the Mk 43 Mod 1 weapon was brought to the SAS at RCAF 4 Wing at Baden-Soellingen and made operational on 08 October.[26] It would see service with no other Canadian units. The only other curious aspect of the deployment was that the Pre-Atomic Capability Inspection had to be carried out with a dummy training warhead because the USAFE had not yet delivered the war reserve bombs to the USAF custodial unit at the Baden SAS[27] as the USAF custodial unit was still uncertified.

Original plans for the Mk 43 called for the weapon to be emplaced at 3 Wing. However, since 3 Wing was to be disbanded on 01 July 1969, it was decided that 4 Wing should be trained on the new weapon. Training for 4 Wing started in March 1968. Members of USAF 17th Air Force from Ramstein Air Base conducted training and certified the 4 Wing load crew team. At this time CF Air Division HQ queried USAFE HQ if the Mod 0 or the Mod 1 (long nose) weapons would be used at 4 Wing. The USAF confirmed that Mod 1 was the weapon destined for 4 Wing.[28] This showed that at times even the highest staff at RCAF Air Division HQ were unaware of the exact nature of the beast with which they had to deal.

By early 1969 the military was already talking about the USAF-planned withdrawal of the Mk 43. Not to be left naked in the nuclear world, the RCAF and USAF discussed replacing the Mk 43 with additional Mk 28 thermonuclear weapons at 4 Wing.[29] The final outcome of these discussions remains hidden, as we do not know if additional B28 or B57 nuclear weapons were deployed.

FIRST DELIVERY OF THE MARK 57

As the RCAF had already gone through the process of acquiring a nuclear weapon type once in Europe, the acquisition of the Mk 57 was both smooth and relatively fast. Both 3 and 4 Wings were certified on the new weapon on 01 April 1966,[30] received their Mk 57s in the latter half of March,[31] and stood operational QRA with the new weapon as of May.[32]

DOCUMENT # 3

28 February 1966, 0928z, V3312-22, to CANFORCEHED from USAFE, Secret.

Subject: Mk 57 Weapon.

USAFE has requested shipment of weapons from CONUS to Zweibrucken for week of 14 March 1966 and week of 21 March 1966 for Soellingen. These dates are contingent upon airlift availability and are therefore subject to slippages.

B57[33]

The B57 bomb carried by the CF-104 Starfighter was the externally carried, free fall or parachute retarded, radar fuzed for airburst/ground burst, sealed-pit nuclear fission weapon. It too had a PAL (Permissive Action Link),[34] which had to be operated on the ground by USAF custodial personnel prior to flight.

The W57 warhead was a "Nominal yield" weapon, like the Hiroshima bomb, of less than 20 kt. This is often referred to as a 5–10 kt bomb, but is more likely actually in the 15–20 kt range. This low-yield weapon was the smallest free-fall atomic bomb in the US arsenal. It was originally developed for the US Navy and US Marine Corps in response to their request for a small (size and yield) tactical atomic bomb.* The B57 weighed 231 kg, and was 3.02 m long with a maximum body diameter of 0.37 m. Given the low yield, the B57 was probably a fission bomb containing a plutonium core, and contained none of the secondary stages necessary for thermonuclear fusion. The fuzing option was probably selected on the ground prior to flight for air or ground burst.

The bomb was delivered in an "over-the-shoulder" manner,** or at low or medium angles by lofting. The minimum altitude of delivery is 90–180 m. CF-104s, on their final run down the bomb release line, would be travelling at 540 km/s towards the target. If the target was sighted visually, the accuracy of bombing with the Mk 57 could be as good as 35–65 m. However, deep inside East Germany, in unfamiliar territory and in bad weather and while bombing by radar, the accuracy could degrade to as much as 1000 m. Accuracy for all four

---

* Please see Chapter 7 for a discussion of Maritime Air Command nuclear requirements.

** See Chapter 3.

bomb types was heavily dependent on meteorological conditions and the ability of the Canadian military's meteorological staff to predict them throughout central Europe. As it was a US Navy weapon, it was also designed with depth pressure sensors to have an anti-submarine capability, but this was never used by the RCAF/CAF.

Production of some 3100 units began at the Pantex Plant in Texas in January 1963 and ended there in May 1967. The final weapon was retired in June 1993. Seven different Mods were produced in the 1960s, with the USAF and USN getting Mods 0, 1, 2 and 5 in 1963, and Mods 3, 4, and 6 in 1966. Mods 5 and 6 were designed for carriage by the massive B-52 strategic bomber. The RCAF/CAF could have used any of the first five versions, as their external characteristics were virtually identical.

Practice shapes for the weapon included the BDU-11A/E for loading, and the BDU-12A/B as a drop shape. However, there is no record of Canada purchasing such items.

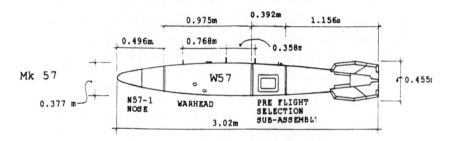

DIAGRAM #4
B57 Nuclear retarded gravity bomb.

Before the RCAF could hang the bomb under a single Starfighter, the USAF detachments had to be trained and certified. Certification came in February 1966, pre-positioning inspections followed in March, and munitions standardization inspections came in April.[35] Previously, in November and December 1965, a program to provide initial training of loading crews on the Mk 57 weapon system was arranged with USAFE 7232nd Munitions Maintenance Group. The training was carried out at 3 and 4 Wings between 22 November and 10 December 1965.[36]

On 01 April 1966, the CF-104 and CF-104D dual seat trainer were certified to carry the new Mk 57 weapon, and in May 1966, all squadrons received their initial Tactical Evaluation on the CF-104/Mk

57 weapons system.[37] This made the CF-104D dual seat trainer the only training aircraft in Canadian service certified as a nuclear weapons delivery vehicle. However, the aircraft never stood QRA, and served only in a reserve capacity.

DOCUMENT # 4
28 February 1966, 0928z, V3312-22, secret, to CANFORCEHED from USAFE, Subject: Mk 57 Weapon.

> 7232 MMG will complete 3rd and 4th Wing certification requirements at Soellingen during week of 14 March 1966 and at Zweibrucken during week of 21 March 1966. US Detachment at Zweibrucken has been certified by USAF MSD. US Detachment at Soellingen will be certified during week of 14 March 1966. You are reminded that US Custodial Detachment cannot support strike units operational alert with new weapon until USAFE Inspector General has inspected US unit. This inspection must take place after receipt of weapons.

Use of the Mk 57 was widespread, and the relatively small bomb was available to all of the six strike/attack squadrons at various times.

RCAF Squadrons Certified on the Mark 57, in May 1966[38]

3 Wing — Zweibrucken	4 Wing — Baden Soellingen
427 Sqdn–16 CF-104s	421 Sqdn–16 CF-104s
430 Sqdn–16 CF-104s	422 Sqdn–16 CF-104s
434 Sqdn–16 CF-104s	444 Sqdn–16 CF-104s

At first, the relatively small B57 bomb was thought to be too large for Canadair CF-104 aircraft, as the four-finned "plus" (+) configuration allowed the lower tail fin to nearly touch the ground. the RCAF solved this problem by *removing* the lower fin. In May 1965 taxi tests at 3 and 4 Wing showed that there was sufficient ground clearance for the carriage of the Mk 57 weapon in full four-finned plus configuration.[39] Given that the Mk 57 was the smallest nuclear bomb carried on the Starfighter, it is curious that there is no documentation showing this problem with the earlier deployments of the bigger Mk 28 and Mk 43 weapon shapes.

Ground tests, with CF-104s carrying test shapes around the aerodrome, down the runway, across the taxiways, and through the QRA shelters, confirmed that there was a clearance concern, but that it was minor. The final report noted the following clearances for the CF-104/Mk 57 weapon system:[40]

a) normal:	2.50 inch fin clearance (63.5 mm)
b) in QRA:	1.85 inch fin clearance (47 mm)
c) taxi bounce:	0.75 inch fin clearance (19 mm)

There is no available record showing that the US Air Force used a four-fin plus-configured weapon shape, as all references to the USAF B57 show a four fin X tail configuration. The maximum span of the tail fins in the X form is 0.64m. These same fins rotated 45 degrees into a plus form would give a shape which rested dangerously close to the ground. It is unknown why the RCAF did not get the X-form tail shape for its Mk 57 weapons.

The USAF did consider this enough of a problem to place restrictions on the delivery of the four-fin plus configuration weapon. However, after further testing in New Mexico, the restriction was lifted for the free-fall delivery of the Mk 57.[41]

Although it may have been said in jest, the suggestion that the clearance problem be solved by removing the lower fin was taken seriously. Some responded that the fins were all there for a reason, and that the ballistic performance of the bomb might well be affected by alterations, but testing showed otherwise.

DOCUMENT # 5
23 October 1964, O 3312-22, secret, minute sheet, from DArmEng to DNW, re: Project Ukulele.

> This Directorate … released one BDU-19B free fall shape and three BDU-12B retarded shapes with the lower fin removed. The BDU-19B drop confirmed that the weapon remained ballistic for at least 50 feet (15 m) after release. The BDU-12B drops confirmed that there was no degradation in the flight path or parachute deployment of the retarded shapes and miss distances of 75 feet (23 m) and 100 feet (31 m) were

recorded. The fin interference problem can be resolved by removal of the lower fin.

Being the smallest of the nuclear weapons deployed on the Starfighters, the Mk 57 was chosen as the weapon to be carried by the CF-104D Mark 2 dual-seat training aircraft.[42] The CF-104D would never stand alert, but was certified to give each squadron additional delivery vehicles in time of war.[43] In early 1966 the dual-seaters were found satisfactory for the emergency carriage of war reserve weapons, and the crews were trained on the new aircraft type. These 16 aircraft, serial numbers 12653 through 12668, are unique in Canadian military service as being the only dedicated trainers to be certified as nuclear carriers.

The biggest problem the RCAF faced with the Mk 57 was that the CF-104 was unsuitable to carry the new weapon. The bomb rack, originally designed for the Mk 28, was considered a danger to the new weapon by the USAF. Testing in New Mexico at the US Air Force Weapons Laboratory had revealed that the existing bomb rack would cause "damage to the weapon pull-out cables when the weapon was loaded on the aircraft."[44] The RCAF, in Project Ukulele, set about redesigning the rack, as well as adding larger sway brace disks, and reworking the ejector piston assemblies. They also had to move the weapons away switch located in the rack during the April through December 1965 programme.[45] By August 1966, the deficiencies had been overcome, and the hold order issued by the USAF against the RCAF carriage of the Mk 57 was lifted.[46]

PAL RELEASE
Once political authority had been granted by the Canadian and United States governments, there was still the question of the actual physical release of the weapons. On the PAL (Permissive Action Link) equipped weapons used on the CF-104 Starfighters, the USAF custodians would have to open the USAF safe in the Canadian QRA, get the combinations, and enter them into the weapon to allow for final arming of the warhead. Both procedures were accomplished upon receipt of the appropriate coded message from the NATO SACEUR. The same safety procedures applied to the army Honest John system in Europe.*

---

* See Chapter 5.

In practice, this meant that "all nuclear weapons remain in United States custody until released by an authenticated SACUER/USCINCEUR R-Hour or S-Hour message." At that point

> notification of authority to release weapons may be received through US channels or through NATO channels, and such notification must be certified by US and RCAF agencies. Authentication of the USCINCEUR code word, and acquisition of the PAL code, are accomplished by the US Alert Duty Officer (ADO) and the US Custodial Agent manning the QRA safe. Authentication of the SACEUR code word is accomplished by the RCAF Operations Duty Officer and passed to the QRA Alert Pilots.[47]

Final arming of the bomb would not take place until the aircraft was airborne and on its way to the target. The pilot would use the bomb option selector switch to supply aircraft power to the weapon, and then choose either the GND (ground) or AIR settings to operate the bomb safety switches for either ground burst or air burst respectively. The pilot would also have to enter the PAL codes received just before flight from the US and Canadian duty officer. Once entered in the PAL code device in the cockpit, the bomb enable selector switch could be positioned from OFF to EN (enable) to initiate electronic comparison of the PAL code entered by the pilot with the PAL code held inside the arming device in the weapon. If the numbers matched, the bomb would then proceed to arm itself for air or ground burst as previously chosen. If the numbers did not match, then the enable status light would remain on continuously after the initial 30 seconds. If correctly entered, the light would be on for 30 seconds, and come on again if pressed for confirmation.

THE CANADAIR CF-104 STARFIGHTER

The Canadian government and Canadair had purchased the right to manufacture their new bomber for European deployment from the US maker, Lockheed. The Canadair version of the Starfighter, the CL-90, used a single General Electric J-79 turbojet engine to power the relatively light (12.156 tonnes all-up) aircraft to a maximum speed of Mach 2. When conserving fuel, the pilot could take the CF-104 out to a combat radius of close to 1300 km. This small aircraft was only 17.75 m long and 4.12 m high, and had a tiny wingspan of merely 6.68 m with tip-tanks. While in nuclear strike service, the aircraft were finished in bare metal with gloss white wings.

Costs for the Starfighter were $1 950 000.00 per aircraft, or $463 762 000.00 for 200 single-seat fighters and 38 dual-seat trainers. On 14 August 1959 the government announced that the Starfighter would be built by Canadair of Montreal (airframe), and Orenda of Toronto (J-79 engine). Whether the aircraft itself was a danger when armed with a nuclear weapon is debatable. The seemingly high accident rate when flown close to the ground is undeniable, yet the aircraft performed well in Canadian hands. The biggest problem was that the aircraft had never been designed to carry nuclear weapons, having been originally conceived as a high-speed, high-altitude bomber interceptor. Flying at low-levels to evade detection by radar took its toll on both aircraft and pilots. However, the Starfighter was an excellent bomber.

THE BOMB TRAILER
One of the other dangers to safety discovered by Canadian and US safety inspectors was the trailer they used to transport the bombs from the SAS to the QRA. The MHU-12/M bomb trailer had constant tow-bar problems, and many breakages. This was considered a Nuclear Safety Hazard, and much paperwork was generated about the problem. In the end, the trailer continued to serve at all Wings.

TARGETING OF THE NUCLEAR WEAPONS
Minister of National Defence Paul Hellyer stated in committee that the CF-104 aircraft in 1 Air Division were to be used to bomb "tactical" targets, such as "military bases including dockyards and airfields; radar installations and military command and control centres; depots and dumps containing fuel or other supplies directly supporting enemy combat forces; key road, rail or waterway facilities used for supporting the combat area, etc."[48]

The Chief of the Air Staff then told the same Committee that the CF-104s would be used for "the destruction of targets of immediate and direct significance to the conduct of military operations against Allied Command Europe. For example, airfields and the aircraft thereon would be subject to immediate attack as part of the process of quickly gaining air superiority. Major bridges would be destroyed to delay the advance of enemy troops, as would ammunition, fuel and other depots."[49] Planned targets included corps and division level storage depots for armour groupings of the Group of Soviet Forces in Germany (GSFG), and the command and control sites for these forces. Why Canada needed to use thermonuclear weapons with yields exceeding one megaton to destroy bridges and airfields was never explained to the Committee members who were also never told the explosive yield of the bombs. In fairness to the military, it has to be noted that at a briefing for members of Parliament visiting Europe, Air Vice Marshal Bradshaw and his staff told the visitors that "the fellow who wins, wins — we think — and the fellow who loses, loses; sometimes it is a debate as to who wins."[50] At least they had recognized that war with nuclear weapons was not likely to produce a clear victor, but did produce a lot of losers.

The one problem with the targeting was that it was a gross duplication of the nuclear efforts of the United States. In fact, US Secretary of Defense Robert McNamara had told Paul Hellyer that "all the targets assigned to the RCAF were also targeted by the US Strategic Air Command. Some targets were covered as many as three, four, or five times by different missiles or bombers."[51] The exact targets were supplied to the Wings by SACEUR, but it was up to the individual units, and even to the individual pilots, to do all of the detailed mission planning. They would prepare a complete attack route and bombing profile based on NATO-supplied intelligence about the surrounding threat and target type. Once all of this was done the pilot would present the entire attack profile to a target evaluation board for review and (hopefully) acceptance. Once accepted in principle, the plan had to be transmitted to Omaha, Nebraska, so that it could be included in the planning of the Single Integrated Operational Plan (SIOP). This would allow the US nuclear commanders to de-conflict the Canadian missions from all other missions, as no pilot wanted to be flying directly into a thermonuclear fireball from someone else's attack. This also meant that the Canadian strikes were timed to the second, with pilots expected to drop their weapon within a 30-second window. In reality it was often deemed possible to not only meet this window, but to fulfill it to within 10 seconds. Although Canada supplied 20% of the day and night nuclear strike force in the 4th Allied Tactical Air Force of NATO, its nuclear role had more to do with Alliance (NATO) cohesion than with the nuts and bolts of attempting to fight a nuclear war.

DOCUMENT # 6

22 October 1959. S981-101-87(COR). Memorandum to VCAS from COR A/C WW Bean, "Operational Characteristics Strike/Reconnaissance Aircraft — OCH 1/1-87." Secret.

> The role of the aircraft is as follows:
>
> **Part I — Strike** (a) The effective delivery by day or night of nuclear stores from low or medium levels, not above 20,000 feet (6000 m), under visual or limited blind bombing conditions against pre-selected targets.
>
> (b) The effective delivery by day or night of nuclear stores or a variety of air-to-ground weapons from low altitude under visual conditions against tactical targets of every description including armoured vehicles, troop concentrations, lines of communication, airfields, and targets of opportunity.

BOMBING

Once the decision had been reached by people far removed from the RCAF and Canadian government as to what targets were to be struck, the RCAF Starfighter pilots and their CF-104's in Europe had four general types of nuclear bombing tactics in the strike role.[52]

1. **Dive Mode.** The pilot uses the Gunsight as an aiming reference, and Radar Range to measure the distance between him and the target.

2. **Level Identification Pass.** The pilot must be able to see the terrain below him, and then uses some prominent feature on the ground a known distance from the target as an Identification Point. As the aircraft flies over the identification point the pilot presses the Freeze Button (computer button) located on the control stick, this tells the Computer to make the final calculations for bomb release. The pilot then continues on the same flight path and the bomb is dropped automatically.

3. **Blind Target Identification Point.** This is similar to the Level Identification Pass except that instead of the pilot seeing the Identification Point, the Radar "sees" it for him.

4. **Over The Shoulder.** This mode is used when it is necessary for the aircraft to get beyond the lethal range of the unretarded bomb. The

pilot must be able to see the target itself. As the Aircraft flies over the target the pilot presses the Freeze Button and pulls up in a steep climb, the computer drops the bomb at the proper instant in time, the pilot rolls out at the top and is on his way home before the bomb hits the target.

Most often, the bombing was done with only the radar able to "see" the target. This meant that the mission planning had to be extremely exact.

In these bombing modes, the nuclear gravity bomb was released automatically, after the pilot pressed the Freeze Button. The computer depended on the pilot to press the Freeze Button at the proper time and thereafter to fly the aircraft within certain limitations for accurate bombing. After the bomb was gone the WEAPONS AWAY light in the cockpit flashed for 30 seconds.

All of this electronic wizardry was accomplished using the CF-104 Armament Systems Equipment consisting of the ASG 501 Fire Control System, and the APG 502 Radar System. The ASG 501 was divided into two sub-units, the Bomb Toss Computer, and the Sight Optical Display and Computer.

Another, though unofficial, method was known as TLAR, or "That Looks About Right" bombing. Practice bombing was often done by first sighting the target, then pulling the aircraft up in a climb and lofting the bomb. This was not an overly accurate system, but it was kept in mind that, with a high-kiloton or one megaton bomb, close counts.

The pilots themselves best described the bombing mission when some unidentified crew from 3 Wing wrote "we are capable of delivering medium and low yield nuclear weapons to targets in Eastern Europe. The mission for this delivery is flown low level (50'–500' AGL) at speeds varying from 450 Kts to 0.85 Mach. The methods of delivery are: level, estimated manual release, low-angle drogue deliveries or laydown — most of these are possible on radar also, with variations."[53]

SECURITY

Keeping the various and numerous nuclear weapons safe from the public and possible paramilitary groups was the job of security personnel. Most of these were provided by the RCAF, with the exception of those USAF personnel serving in the SAS maintenance compound. Each Special Ammunition Site required 53 RCAF guards, and each QRA complex required another 46 guards. On top of this had to be added the 60 firefighters needed for each airfield having a nuclear weapons responsibility.[54]

By 01 June 1964 the bulk of essential USAF and CF security personnel had been processed through phase I and II of Security Squadron Training, and were ready to guard nuclear weapons.

Standard security procedures for nuclear bases required a 24-hour manning of a security guard post adjacent to each nuclear-armed aircraft, in addition to access gate guards and roving patrols. Roving patrols were often accomplished in the company of guard dogs. Unfortunately for the dogs, the RCAF had placed the kennels at 4 Wing too close to the aircraft run-up pads, and the dogs were suffering from the *high noise levels*.[55] The kennels were relocated in 1966. The dogs stationed at 4 Wing in 1965 were Prinz, Duke, Bodo, Asko, Ilk, Hasso, Bero, Rolf, Jeep, Cito, Olaf, Rex, Birko, Dole, Roon (smallest at 28 kg), and Alf (largest at 40 kg).

DOCUMENT # 7
4 Wing Monthly Historical Records, 1964. Technical Summary, 1 Jan 64–31 Dec 64.

> With the acquisition of the nuclear weapons during the summer months, security became of prime importance. The south dispersal area was zoned off for storage of these weapons and to facilitate fast weapon loading, adjacent to this area, combat ready [CF-]104 aircraft were parked. The weapon storage and aircraft parking areas became known as QRA (Quick Reaction Alert). American servicemen were the custodians of the nuclear weapons and the storage area was security enforced by the construction of a high double fence between which sentry dogs patrolled at night. American and Canadian guards also patrol the area day and night.

WEAPON INSPECTIONS

The US Air Force was nothing if not absolutely fanatical about the safe treatment of nuclear weapons. Safety came ahead of operational capability, and a unit could lose their nuclear certification by failing any one of many annual and semi-annual safety and operational inspections.[56]

During their work-up period, when the squadron was training on dummy weapons and teaching pilots and load crews their tasks, a Pre-Atomic Capability Inspection would be held. This determined the status of the preparations, and would help set the date for Initial Capability Inspection (ICI) and the introduction of nuclear weapons. If possible, a real war reserve nuclear weapon would be used, but this was only possible if the custodial unit was certified, and if there were already war reserve weapons in the SAS for another unit.

The ICI was required to verify that the RCAF strike wing and US custodial detachment were capable of receiving initial delivery of nuclear weapons. This was accomplished before the initial introduction of weapons for storage. The ICI consisted of inquiry into the following areas:

a. Safety requirements
b. Facilities and equipment
c. Physical security
d. Road access
e. Support agreements
f. Availability of personnel

A "satisfactory" rating in the ICI meant that nuclear weapons would soon move into the SAS. From then on, there would be a constant series of Semi-Annual Inspection, or SAI. These divided into six different inspection regimes:[57]

1. Joint Safety Inspection.
2. Joint Security Inspection.
3. Loading Standardization Surveys of RCAF/CF Load Crews, (conducted by USAFE 7232 MMG/26TRW).
4. Capability Inspection of US detachments.
5. Standardization Visits to US detachments.
6. Capability Inspection of RCAF/CF strike Wings.

Other than the standard scheduled inspections, there were two other types: the Spot Check, and the Reinspection. The Spot Check could include any aspect of a nuclear weapon unit's activities at the discretion of the inspecting agency. This was usually done by the USAF Inspector General's office. Reinspections would only be required to evaluate the capability of a unit which had received an inspection rating of unsatisfactory.

Lastly, and purely on the operational side, were the RCAF/CF-sponsored Tactical Evaluations. The responsibility of the Air Officer Commanding RCAF 1 Air Division, the "Tac Eval" was conducted to ascertain and evaluate the state of training, readiness, combat capability, logistic support, and the ability of the RCAF strike wing to execute its mission to drop nuclear weapons in Eastern Europe.

These inspections could take from a few hours to an entire week. The ICI was generally about four days long, while reinspections limited to a single item could be over in an hour.

BOMB LOADING

Little exists in the open literature on the load crews, other than that their performance was constantly subject to training, tests, inspections, and certifications. However, as part of an exercise to develop visual aids for training servicemen, 1 Air Division commissioned a short film demonstrating the proper bomb loading technique.[58] The film was never completed, and commentary never added. For years the eight-minute film sat in the military film storage facility in Ottawa, untouched.

What the film shows is a load crew consisting of four men, including a crew chief. They are loading CF-104 serial #89 with a BDU-14/E, the training shape for the three-finned B28RE nuclear weapon. Each man wears identical white cover-alls, and has a sign stencilled on their backs reading:

SPECIAL WEAPON
LOAD CREW

Each of them also wears a dark baseball-style hat with a light-coloured (northern) hemisphere containing a dark letter "S".

After the crew chief checks to see that everyone's hands are clean, work proceeds. One crew member pulls the nose cone slightly away from the B28 bomb, and then rotates it and looks inside. Satisfied that some device was correctly set, he then shouts to the rest of the crew.

While one crew member monitors the cockpit to ensure that all switches are safetied, the bomb is then lifted from its trailer with a very low-slung bomb-loader forklift truck, and positioned under the CF-104 from the forward starboard side. After being lifted into position.by the loader, the crew attaches the bomb to the centreline bomb rack, tightens the sway braces, attaches the umbilical cables and pull-out cables, and sets the safety plug on the bomb to ARM. Presumably this operation took less than 15 minutes in skilled hands.

DOCUMENT # 8
1 Air Division Historical Narrative, 1964. Appendix B.
V-Munitions and Weapons. Secret.

> April–May 1964, After an RCAF self-training programme for RCAF loading crews a second stage training was given by the USAFE 7232 Munitions Maintenance Group to the RCAF loading crews at 3 and 4 Wings. Six load crews were certified at each of 3 and 4 Wing in time for the initial capability inspection and Tactical Evaluation. At the same time initial nuclear delivery certification checks were carried out on the 3 and 4 Wing aircraft.

CHAPTER 4

STARFIGHTER: THE SQUADRONS

RCAF (and later Canadian Armed Forces) CF-104 Starfighter tactical aircraft standing nuclear Quick Reaction Alert (QRA) operated under a chain of command flowing from:

- *NATO Headquarters (NATO HQ)*
- *Allied Command Europe (SHAPE)*
- *Allied Air Force Central Europe (AFCENT)*
- *4th Allied Tactical Air Force (4 ATAF)*
- *1 Air Division (1 Air Div)*
- *RCAF/CAF 1 Wing, 3 Wing, 4 Wing*
- *RCAF/CAF Strike/Attack Squadrons*

The release of nuclear weapons to the pilots standing alert in the QRA hangar came about through two channels. Firstly, once the US president had authorized the use of nuclear weapons, this was conveyed through the Worldwide Military Command and Control System (WWMCCS, pronounced Wih'mex) to the various appropriate Commander in Chiefs (CINC) and to the appropriate field commanders. For the purposes of the Canadian Air Division this information would be transmitted to the Supreme Allied Commander Europe (SACEUR), who was also dual-hatted as the US forces Commander in Chief Europe (CINCEUR). As CINCEUR he would then authorize the release of nuclear weapons by the USAFE custodial detachments holding them at Canadian bases. As SACEUR he would, through a completely different channel of communication, authorize their use by various NATO forces. Once both the US custodians and the Canadian QRA duty officer had received the release order, they would both open a two-combination safe kept in the QRA containing the PAL codes. These codes would then be handed to the pilot already in the Starfighter cockpit. Once aloft and on the way to the target, the pilot would enter the four- or six-digit code into the PAL device located in the cockpit and connected directly to the weapon slung beneath the aircraft.

1 AIR DIVISION, RCAF

The Canadian 1 Air Division HQ had been based in France until the increasingly nationalistic moves by the government of Charles de Gaulle forced its removal on 31 March 1967. After a Cabinet decision of 14 July 1966, it was then based at Lahr, Federal Republic of Germany. The initial problem with Lahr was that with the French then occupying the site, there was not enough room for the Canadians.[1] In early 1967 the French were withdrawing their forces to French territory, and Lahr was opened up to become the new headquarters of 1 Air Division and a strike base.

Under the command of 1 Air Division in early 1964, eight squadrons were reactivated as strike/attack or strike/reconnaissance units.[2]

Strike/Reconnaissance or Strike/Attack, Base,	Date Activated
441 St/R Marville, France	20 Jan 64
439 St/R Marville, France	02 Mar 64
427 St/A Zweibrucken, West Germany	01 Feb 64
430 St/A Zweibrucken, West Germany	26 Feb 64
434 St/A Zweibrucken, West Germany	01 Feb 64
421 St/A Baden-Soellingen, West Germany	26 Feb 64
422 St/A Baden-Soellingen, West Germany	01 Feb 64
444 St/A Baden-Soellingen, West Germany	01 Feb 64

The reactivated squadrons had their first Tactical Evaluations for strike duties on 8–11 June 1964 at 3 and 4 Wings, and on 1 July 1964 all six strike/attack squadrons assumed an alert commitment.[3] It is crucial to note that six of the eight squadrons were nuclear-armed, and therefore essentially immobilized. The United States had widely distributed nuclear weapons among the NATO allies, and the constant inspections, heavy security, and burdensome nuclear procedures prevented any of the forces assigned nuclear duties from being flexible and usable in any conventional sense. The RCAF did not even train their Starfighter crews in conventional weapons use until at least 1970. By 1970, the Canadian military, prompted by the Trudeau Government, was pushing for a conventional role for the CAF in Europe. Of course, once Canada got back into the conventional area, all of the other air forces desired the same thing. This led to an increasing conventionalization of NATO air forces and their ability to take action, much to the dismay of the United States. For the US government, a grounded European air force was a safe air force which could not disturb the delicate balance of military relations with the Soviet Union.

Under SACEUR's plans, 1 Air Division was tasked with providing three to four aircraft from each of the RCAF squadrons in Europe to be on Quick Reaction Alert at all times and this involved the aircraft actually being armed with nuclear weapons.[4] Because of limited numbers of both aircraft and personnel, the military found it difficult to meet the minimum requirements, and SACEUR lowered the number of alert aircraft required to two per squadron.

DOCUMENT # 1
11 September 1963, S0029-106-1 TD 32418(CAS), 3314-22, to Chairman, Chiefs of Staff, Ottawa, from Chief of the Air Staff, Air Marshal C.R. Dunlap, re, Special Weapon Storage Facilities.

> The SACEUR Nuclear Strike Plan, in part, requires that strike squadrons with an aircraft establishment of 15 or less must maintain two aircraft on Quick Reaction Alert, whereas strike squadrons with an aircraft establishment of 16 or more must maintain four aircraft on Quick Reaction Alert. SACEUR has indicated that he is prepared to accept only two aircraft on QRA until it is possible to increase this number in accordance with the Nuclear Strike Plan.

As time went by, and the squadrons became more proficient at doing more with less, 1 Air Division was able to field greater numbers on alert. By 1967 the Quick Reaction Alert (QRA) states of readiness for the Wings were as listed below:[5]

QUICK REACTION ALERT TIMES

Peacetime QRA	4 aircraft/Wing in 15 minutes
Augmented QRA	12 aircraft/Wing in 6 hours
Sustained QRA	18 aircraft/Wing in 12 hours (30–45 days)
Full Generation	25 aircraft/Wing in 12 hours
	(70% of Unit Establishment aircraft)

Although the readiness was improving, the numbers of aircraft was shrinking. On 01 April 1967 Canadian aircraft in SACEUR's operationally ready forces were reduced from 126 to 108 aircraft. This left 1 Air Division with four squadrons of 18 aircraft each for a total force of 72 aircraft committed to the strike role: a reduction of 24 aircraft. While the numbers might seem small, they actually represented a significant force of 20% of 4 ATAFs all-weather strike capability.[6]

The draw-down of forces had been planned for years, and the Starfighter force in Europe was the first to experience the trimming of the Canadian nuclear commitment. Explaining his 1964 defence White Paper to Cabinet, Paul Hellyer said that it "was deliberately somewhat indefinite on this score because of the impossibility of foreseeing what the future might require. The Air Division would be run down through attrition and would also be given a dual role with a conventional capability. There was a clear indication that forces now employing nuclear weapons, with the possible exception of the Honest John, would be phased out over the years ahead."[7] Clearly everything was up for re-negotiation within NATO and NORAD, and 1 Air Division would be the first to be cut.

EXERCISES[8]

Nothing could tell us more about the actual tasks of the strike/attack squadrons than the exercises they carried out on a weekly, monthly, semi-annual, or annual basis. The list below shows that all aspects of the Wing and squadron operation were subject to constant practice, drill, and exercise.

"Fast Strike" This exercise was designed as a command post drill to practice implementation of the Nuclear Strike Plan, and to provide training in staff procedures.

"Front Centre IV" This procedural exercise provided training for staff personnel in the operations of a War Headquarters, and in

procedures associated with implementation of Emergency Defence Plans.

"Fallex" This annual NATO-wide autumn exercise was a large scale command post exercise, jointly scheduled and conducted by SACEUR and SACLANT. It was designed to exercise command and control by SACEUR and his lower formations, and to practice procedures for meeting and dealing with aggression less than general war, and leading to implementation of all tasks associated with all-out nuclear war.

"Max Effort" 4 ATAF sponsored this exercise testing Wing capability to survive and continue operation effectively under conditions realistically simulating a reasonably successful enemy attack.

"Sardinia Salvo" RCAF/CAF strike/attack squadrons utilize the Capo Della Frasca range in Sardinia for live non-nuclear bombing practice, and to carry out nuclear weapon delivery qualifications.

"Soft Sand" This live flying exercise combined Combat Profiles Missions with practice weapons deliveries, and was carried out on a continuing basis at Vhliehors range in the Netherlands.

"Simplex" This exercise provided training for operations personnel at the Wing level in the execution of duties associated with the implementation of the strike plan and subsequent strike operations. It was played twice weekly.

"Round Robin" This exercise entailed a turnaround by CF-104 aircraft at other bases to test cross-servicing within 4 ATAF.

DULL SWORDS

Dull Swords are defined by the US military as all non-significant accidents involving nuclear weapons. Non-significant, they referred to anything less than the unauthorized detonation or possible detonation of a nuclear weapon, or its theft or destruction. These more serious accidents are called Broken Arrows and Bent Spears, and there is no record of the RCAF/CAF reporting this class of accident. However, a Dull Sword still meant that there was a danger surrounding some aspect of the handling of the nuclear weapon which had to be remedied immediately.

As 1 Air Division HQ was not in physical contact with nuclear weapons, reports on accidents found in divisional files have been very vague. However, records indicate that in 1965 1 Air Division squadrons had 9 Dull Swords, while in 1966 this number dropped to 6 Dull Swords.[9] Canadian units tended to have fewer accidents involving nuclear weapons than similar USAF units. This is due for the most part to a greater professionalism of the smaller RCAF, and to the fact that there were actually two levels of safety for RCAF units, as opposed to a single one for the USAF units. In addition, the RCAF was not responsible for all aspects of the nuclear weapon, and therefore had less room for contributing to an accident.

Despite the Dull Swords, RCAF strike units were amongst the highest rated in 4 ATAF. In fact, 1 Air Division was the only air division in 4 ATAF to attain a rating of "ONE" (highest) in Tactical Evaluations.[10]

1 CANADIAN AIR GROUP

The 1 Air Division was replaced with the 1 Canadian Air Group in August 1970, but the organization remained similar to its predecessor and continued to perform the same tasks. There was, by this time, less than 18 months left in the Starfighter nuclear weapons commitment. A change in organizational name and structure did nothing to affect the nuclear operations of the two Starfighter squadrons standing QRA.

DECIMOMANNU TRAINING RANGE

The RCAF and CAF pilots found little room to fly in Europe as compared with Canada. Small ranges were available in various NATO countries, but Canada and other NATO allies maintained the Italian range on Sardinia, Italy, for training and bombing practice. In 1968, the only year for which records are available, the operation at Decimomannu, Sardinia, brought a total of 203 pilots to SHAPE standards for the delivery of nuclear weapons. That year they also dropped a total of 14180 bombs and ballistic drop shapes in training and as part of the nuclear weapons qualification process.[11] This explains the cost of at least half-a-million dollars per year for the ballistic shapes for the hardly-used B43 weapon alone.

USAFE 7232 MUNITIONS MAINTENANCE GROUP

Vitally important to the Canadian nuclear weapons effort in Europe was a small US Air Force unit called the 7232 MMG. Comprised of detachments of the USAF (Europe), the 7232 Munitions

Maintenance Group (MMG) was tasked with providing the custody and maintenance services for all of the nuclear weapons used by the RCAF/CAF in Europe between 1964 and 1967.

Due to the fact that all records of the 7232 Munitions Maintenance Group and its successor, the 26 Tactical Reconnaissance Wing, have been classified as containing US Restricted Data or Formerly Restricted Data, otherwise known as nuclear weapons secrets, they cannot be declassified by the US Air Force alone: they must be declassified by the US Department of Energy, the agency responsible for developing and producing nuclear weaponry. As this has not yet been possible, little is publicly known about the two units which supported the Canadian Starfighter squadrons based in West Germany.

What is known is that the 7232 MMG, and its subordinate units, the 306 Munitions Maintenance Squadron, and detachments 1900 and 2100, were responsible for the custody, care, and field maintenance of the three basic types of thermonuclear weapons used by the RCAF in Europe: the Mk 28, the Mk 43 and the Mk 57 gravity bombs.

Although the USAFE was anxious to have the Canadian contribution, and had even earmarked the 7232's detachments for support, there was a problem. Because Canada had delayed finalizing the government-to-government agreement for so long, the USAFE was put in the position of having to consider reassigning the custodial units to other NATO nations. In the end, Canada acted fast enough to keep the services of the 7232.

DOCUMENT # 2
18 December 1963, 1546z, to CANAIRHED from CANAIRDIV, priority, secret. Also noted as to CAD from AOC.

> Strong possibility exists that custodial detachments requisitioned by USAF for Three and Four Wings will be reassigned to other NATO nations if Technical Agreement is not signed by 05 Jan 64. These personnel are presently en route to Europe. Assignment to our bases was programmed to commence 01 Jan 64 however EUCOM will not authorize such assignment unless Technical Agreement has been signed. If custodial personnel are not assigned to us by 05 Jan 64

then they will be reassigned to other non RCAF commitments and a minimum period of 90 days will be required before another group can be assigned to us. Strongly recommend that Tech Agreement be signed by 05 Jan 64.

The prime purpose of the USAF units assigned to Canadian bases was one of custody. Each weapon had a US custodian whenever it was not locked in its SAS, and each nuclear-armed RCAF Starfighter was under constant custodial control. The manner of the custody was rather curious in that during the early years, the 7232 had equipped its detachments with small mobile huts which the custodians would wheel into the path of the Starfighter in the QRA. However, later NATO policy changes recognized that the security fence was enough of a barrier to aircraft operations, and this meant that US soldiers would no longer be sitting in small boxes in front of nuclear-armed Canadian aircraft 24 hours per day.[12]

Between July 1967 and January 1968 the 7232 MMG was reorganized at Ramstein Air Base and several units were deactivated or redesignated under a different command.[13] This signified that the 7232 had evolved into the 26 Tactical Reconnaissance Wing (26 TRW).

306 MUNITIONS MAINTENANCE SQUADRON

The 306 MMS of the 7232 MMG of the USAFE, although just one squadron, was vitally important to the RCAF, as it was the squadron through which the detachments present at the Canadian bases operated. There is little mention of them in Canadian records, as these records tend to refer only the 7232 MMG or the detachments associated with each Wing. The 306th was not only responsible for nuclear weapons used by Canadian squadrons, but for those used by USAF units in northern Germany and Belgium.[14]

26 TACTICAL RECONNAISSANCE WING

With the reorganization of the US Air Force in Europe, the 26 Tactical Reconnaissance Wing took over the duties of the 7232 MMG between July 1967 and January 1968. Based at Ramstein Air Base, Federal Republic of Germany, the 26 TRW continued to perform the same taskings as the former 7232 MMG, and provided support for the 326 MMS and detachments 3 and 4. This change did not affect the Canadian deployments or duties at all, and were merely changes to the US military structure and deployments taking place at the height of the US war against the South Vietnamese.[15]

326 MUNITIONS MAINTENANCE SQUADRON
The 326 was formed from the 306 in late 1967, and was a subordinate unit of the 26 TRW. Falling under the 326 control were detachments 3 and 4 which directly supported RCAF/CAF bases, Wings and squadrons in Germany. This was the only munitions maintenance Squadron of the 26 TRW. Like the 306, it oversaw the two detachments which serviced the three nuclear weapon types deployed on the Canadian Starfighter strike/attack aircraft.

1 AIR DIVISION WINGS
The RCAF maintained four Wings in Europe, but disbanded 2 Wing in the early 1960s. The bulk of the nuclear weapons commitment was borne by 3 and 4 Wings, with 1 Wing taking over from 3 Wing in 1969. Only strike/attack (S/A) squadrons had nuclear weapons duties.

WINGS, SQUADRONS, and OPERATIONAL DATES
#1 Wing HQ Lahr
(nuclear role transferred from #3 Wing, 1969)
430 S/A (24 Feb 1969–01 May 1970) (from #3 Wing)
441 S/A (01 May 1970–01 Jul 1970) (439 and 441 S/R Squadrons combined to form 441 S/A Squadrons, 01 May 1970)

#3 Wing HQ Zweibrucken
(Wing deactivated 1969: duties transferred to #1 Wing)
427 S/A (1964–moved to #4 Wing Jun 1969)
430 S/A (1964–moved to #1 Wing 24 Feb 1969)
434 S/A (1964–disbanded 01 Mar 1967)

#4 Wing HQ Baden-Soellingen (final nuclear RCAF Wing)
421 S/A (1964–01 Jan 1972)
422 S/A (1964–disbanded 01 Jul 1970)
427 S/A (1969–disbanded 30 Jun 1970)
441 S/A (01 Jul 1970–01 Jan 1972) (from #1 Wing)
444 S/A (1964–disbanded 01 Apr 1967)

The CF-104 Starfighter was the only Canadian nuclear weapons system to use more than one type of warhead. But while the RCAF/CAF utilized three different warheads, the nuclear weapons were not all in Canadian service at the various Wings at the same time or in all years

NUCLEAR WEAPONS ARRIVAL AND OPERATIONAL DATES

The Mk 28 arrived at RCAF sites 15 May–08 June 1964.

DELIVERIES	STANDING QRA
3 Wing, 15 May–08 June 1964.	13 June 64.
4 Wing, 15 May–08 June 1964.	12 June 64.

The Mk 57 arrived at RCAF sites 14–28 March 1966.

DELIVERIES	STANDING QRA
3 Wing, 14–21 March 1966.	immediately.
4 Wing, 21–28 March 1966.	immediately.

The Mk 43 arrived on site 12–30 September 1968.

DELIVERIES	STANDING QRA
4 Wing, 12–30 September 1968.	immediately.

1 WING RCAF/CAF

Under the motto "Armed for Peace", 1 Wing at Lahr, Federal Republic of Germany, had nuclear weapons for almost exactly one year: mid-June 1969 until mid-June 1970. The nuclear weapons arrived after the Initial Capability Inspection of 3–5 June 1969 had been passed, and before the Nuclear Safety Inspection on 23–26 June 1969.[16] Documents indicate that the weapons were delivered by the USAF Military Airlift Command between 6 and 19 June 1969.[17]

DOCUMENT # 3

06 June 1969, Minute Sheet to VCDS from DNW.

> 1 Wing is ready to receive weapons. They will be moved into storage within the next two weeks. Assuming all goes well at that time, 1 Wing is in business in the strike role.

Following the deliveries and the initial work-up of the squadron and base, the first Tactical Evaluation team arrived. Although initially sceptical that a new base could be up to speed with nuclear weapons in such a short time, the Tactical Evaluation "drew highly complimentary remarks from the USAFE and 4 ATAF Teams who had had grave doubts the schedule could even be met."[18]

The nuclear commitment at 1 Wing had been transferred from 3 Wing, which was being closed. The problem was that delays at 3 Wing were delaying the transfer of USAF custodial Detachment 4 to 1 Wing, and these delays could have thrown the inspection schedule off. Under command pressure, the delays were cleared and Detachment 4 moved on to Lahr.[19]

In 1969 when the wing assumed its small nuclear duties, there were two reconnaissance squadrons stationed at the base, and one strike/attack squadron, 430 Strike/Attack Squadron. 430 would be replaced by 441, only to have 441 moved to 4 Wing after only two months of nuclear service.

When the Wing ended its nuclear commitment, the Mk 28 and Mk 57[20] bombs were flown out as "hot cargo" within 48 hours of the deactivation on 01 July 1970.

DOCUMENT # 4
03 March 1970, V3313-22(DNW), Visit Report to HQ USAFE Weisbaden 3 Feb 70, 4 Wing Baden 4 Feb 70, and 1 Air Div Lahr 5 and 6 Feb 70. Secret.

Visit set up to determine schedule for removal of nuclear weapons from 1 Wing and other matters.

USAFE advises the weapons at 1 Wing should be removed within 48 hours of deactivation and that no CF support other than that normally provided during Hot Cargo deliveries would be required.

1 WING NUCLEAR SQUADRONS

430 Strike/Attack	1969–1970
441 Strike/Attack	1970–1970

430 STRIKE/ATTACK SQUADRON

Sporting their mascot "Sydney the Silver Falcon," Falcon Squadron was re-formed at 2 Wing 30 September 1963, but moved to 3 Wing Zweibrucken on 24 February 1964. This provided 3 Wing with its third strike/attack squadron.

Originally based at 3 Wing, 430 Squadron became operational in June 1964 with the Mk 28 nuclear weapon. The next addition to the Canadian nuclear arsenal saw the unit affix the new Mk 57 bomb underneath their aircraft in May 1966.[21]

The squadron would not stay still, and on 24 February 1969, "Sydney" moved to 1 Wing at Lahr. Although in place as a strike squadron, the lack of completed SAS and QRA facilities at Lahr until April postponed armed QRA status for 430. At Lahr 430 would form the only nuclear strike squadron on that base in 1969, using both the Mk 28 and Mk 57 nuclear weapons. The squadron was disbanded on 01 May 1970 and later re-formed as a tactical helicopter squadron.[22]

439 STRIKE/RECONNAISSANCE SQUADRON

Operating under the motto "Stalk and Kill," 439 Squadron holds a curious place in Canadian nuclear history. The squadron was one of two squadrons to be converted from a reconnaissance role to a nuclear role late in the commitment. 439 had been activated on 20 January 1964 in Marville, France, for strike/reconnaissance duties. In April 1967 they relocated to Lahr, and there served their last month as a reconnaissance squadron in April 1970. They were then combined with 441 Squadron to make up the sole Canadian strike/attack squadron at Lahr on 01 May 1970. On 01 July 1970 they moved to 4 Wing at Baden-Soellingen as the nuclear commitment at 1 Wing was ended.

441 STRIKE/ATTACK SQUADRON

The Silver Fox squadron combined with 439 Squadron to become the last CF-104 squadron in Europe in 1984. It was also the last CF-104 squadron to become a strike/attack unit. It received the new designation as a strike/attack unit on 01 May 1970. With changes to the Canadian nuclear commitment to NATO happening on 01 July 1970, all 441 pilots attended the Conventional Weapons (conversion) Course at CFB Cold Lake, Alberta.

USAFE DETACHMENT 4

The USAFE unit supporting the short-lived nuclear 1 Wing at Lahr was probably Detachment 4 of the 26th TRW which was no longer needed at 3 Wing.

The first BOMARC W40 warhead container is loaded on to a truck at RCAF Station North Bay for transport to the SAS. DND negative PMR 94 487.

The truck carrying the first W40 nuclear warheads and an armed escort enters the guarded North Bay BOMARC site at about 2330 hrs, 31 December 1963.

DND negative PL-143809.

BOMARC training missile, RCAF/CAF #446, 446 SAM Sqdn, CFB North Bay. National Aeronautical Collection, **Ottawa.** Photo by author.

Aerial photograph of the Station La Macaza BOMARC site showing 28 missile shelters, 2 erect BOMARCs in shelters #11 (top centre), and #18 (left), security perimeter and gate, ordnance building/SAS, and composite building.

DND negative PCN 4496.

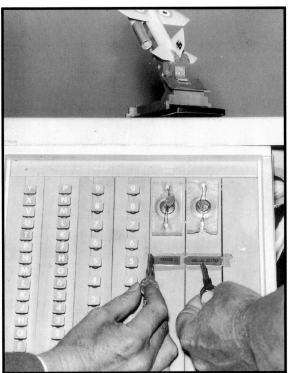

Part of the BOMARC control panel showing the two-key concept (Dual Key) with both Canadian and US keys, and sealed key-holes covered with special sealing wax and wires. Station North Bay, May 1965. DND negative PCN 5528.

Honest John training warhead is mated by crane to an Honest John rocket of the 1 SSM Battery at 1 RCHA Gun Camp, Munsterlager, Germany, 24–25 April 1969.

Photo by Spellmeier. DND negative IB69-16.

Launcher crew of 2 SSM Training Battery at Shilo readies an Honest John for a practice firing. c. 1965. DND photo courtesy of CFB Shilo Museum and author.

Officers and crew inspect the decapitated Honest John and launcher after the failed launch at Soltau Range on 12 April 1966. DND photo courtesy of CFB Shilo Museum.

The author with an Honest John training round on an erect launcher at CFB Shilo. Photo by P. Zeiss.

CF-104 of 417 Squadron at CFB Cold Lake showing weapons and ground
support equipment of RCAF in the 1960s. On the trailer are the training versions
of the Mk 28EX (left), and the Mk 43 (right) thermonuclear weapons, and on the
MJ-1 bomblifter truck is the Mk 28EX with folded fins for greater ground and
aircraft clearance. DND negative PL 140-767.

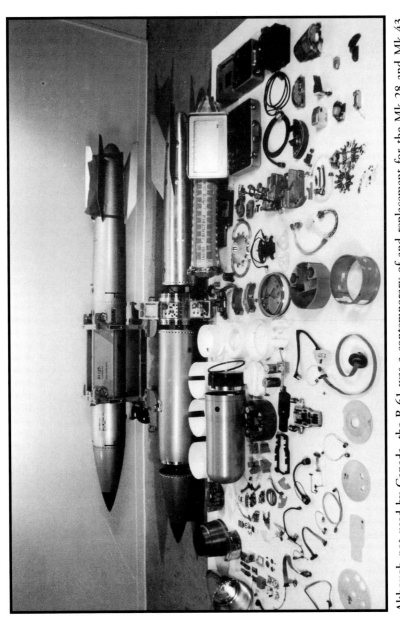

Although not used by Canada, the B-61 was a contemporary of and replacement for the Mk 28 and Mk 43 bombs. This shows some of the more than 6000 parts in this 3.6-metre-long thermonuclear gravity bomb.

Pantex negative # 0992-045-1.

Four live B-57 war reserve nuclear weapons in transport.

Permissive Action Link (PAL) lock and ARM/SAFE switch on Mk 28RE bomb.

Photo by author. Weapon courtesy of Canadian War Museum, Vimy House.

Two live war reserve Mk 57 nuclear gravity bombs go to their final resting place: the disassembly chambers at Pantex in Texas, March 1993. Pantex negative # 0393-008-3.

Four man crew load a Mk 28RE on the centre pylon of CF-104 #12838 at 4 Wing, Baden-Soellingen, inside a double-fenced compound using an MJ-1 bomblifter truck. DND negative PCN 69-109.

CF-104 #12864 of 3 Wing at Zweibrucken and four pilots stand with a training Mk 28RE nuclear bomb on trailer #25. The bomb nose cone, tail shape, access hatches, computer port, and hard points are clearly visible.

Photo by Thomas. DND negative CF66-576-7.

CF-104 #12864 of 3 Wing with a Special Weapons Load Crew member and a training Mk 28RE thermonuclear weapon. The nose cone is being removed for preliminary fuzing. DND negative CFC-66-54-8.

CF-101B VooDoo 101008 sits idle in Winnipeg ten years after the nuclear Genies had been removed from its base at CFB Chatham. A baggage pod has replaced the **weapons.** Photo by author.

VooDoo CAF 101009 of 425 Squadron from Bagotville firing one Genie rocket and carrying a second under the bomb-bay. 1972. DND negative BNC72-2844.

Genie rocket being positioned under CF-101B VooDoo CAF-038 by ground crew. 1977. DND negative BNC77-2841, Wallet #463, Neg. frame #23A.

Genie rocket being uploaded rotary bomb-bay door of a CF-101B at the "William Tell 1976" air weapons competition at Tyndall AFB, Florida, on 7 December 1976. DND negative NBC76-1940 Wallet #457, Neg. frame #18A.

RCAF Maritime Air Command Neptune #24123 from Station Comox, equipped with jet pods and tip tanks, 29 April 1960. The Mk 101, and later the Mk 57, could be carried inside the bomb bay. DND negative PCN-1825.

RCAF Maritime Air Command Argus #20725 from 404 Squadron, Station Greenwood, drops two practice conventional depth charges over the Atlantic, 31 January 1959. Either the Mk 101 or the Mk 57 could be carried inside the bomb bays. DND photo by Lindsey. DND negative PCN-736.

RCN CS2F-2 Tracker landing on HMCS Bonaventure, 02 January 1964. A single Mk 101 or Mk 57 could be carried inside the bomb bay.

DND photo by Haynes. DND negative EKS-1487.

RCN CHH-2 Sea King on HMCS Assiniboine, DDE-234, 04 August 1964. A single Mk 101 or Mk 57 could be carried on the outboard starboard store.

DND photo by Porter. DND negative DNS-33905

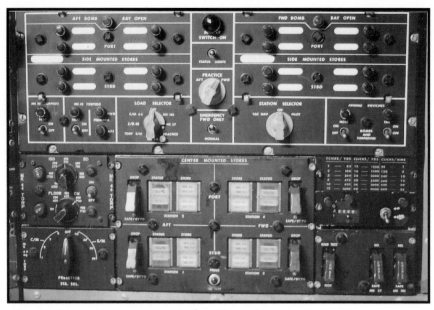

Argus nuclear weapons Armament Control panels. Photo by author.

Argus Stores Release control panel. Photo by author.

Once in place at Lahr, Detachment 4 underwent an Initial Capability Inspection along with 1 Wing, and on 5 June 1969 was certified as "satisfactory." A further Joint Nuclear Safety Inspection later that month also showed that the quick move had not degraded the detachment's ability to support the RCAF.[23]

Much effort was put into moving an entire nuclear weapons establishment from the disbanded 3 Wing to 1 Wing by Dominion Day (Canada Day) 1 July 1969. The SAS was closed and the nuclear role had passed to Lahr. At Lahr, Detachment 4 had supported nuclear weapons #1 and #3, the Mk 28 and Mk 57.

BASE CONSOLIDATION

The European strike nuclear commitment was the first to be drawn down by the Pearson Government. As part of the dramatic restructuring and down-sizing of the military which went along with unification, 3 Wing at Zweibrucken would be closed and all operations would be consolidated at 4 Wing Baden-Soellingen and 1 Wing Lahr. This change would end the nuclear duties at Zweibrucken and transfer them, albeit on a slightly smaller scale (1/3), to 1 Wing at Lahr.

The original plan had been to both consolidate the QRA strike duties at two bases and to reduce the number of aircraft deployed in that role. However, the Soviet invasion of Czechoslovakia in August 1968 had forced a reconsideration of the timing. While the reductions would still take place, they would be moved along into at least the 1970–1971 period.

Base consolidation moved ahead with the completion of the SAS and QRA facilities at Lahr on 01 April 1969: the start of the fiscal year in Canada. A month later CFB Lahr would undergo its Initial Capability Inspection for nuclear duties, and a month after that experience its first Capability Inspection. By Dominion Day, 01 July 1969, the Air Division had assumed a two base posture with a nuclear commitment at each.

3 WING RCAF/CAF

Under the motto "Freedom's Vanguard," 3 Wing was formed at Zweibrucken, Federal Republic of Germany, on 02 February 1953. It was closed by a Cabinet decision on 01 July 1969.

Even before the weapons arrived, 3 Wing would have a significant place in the history of Canadian nuclear weapons. On 31 January

1964 the Wing hosted A/C/M/ Huddleston, AAFCE Commander, and USAF General Gabriel Disosway, Commander 4 ATAF. During this visit the officers signed the RCAF/USAF Service-to-Service Technical Arrangement for the provision of nuclear weapons to the RCAF in Europe.[24]

With the successful Initial Capability Inspection, the way was cleared for the operational deployment of nuclear weapons at 3 Wing on 14 April 1964. The fact that both 3 and 4 Wing passed their ICIs was not immediately clear from the message traffic. In fact, the US message dealing with the inspections[25] failed to mention that both Wings were rated as "satisfactory" and therefore ready to operate nuclear devices. RCAF officers feared that various USAF officers would think that the Canadian units had failed the inspections,[26] and would therefore not be willing to provide appropriate nuclear weapons support.

With nuclear weapons in place, 3 Wing stood for its first Tactical Evaluation on 08 June 1964, passed, and was ready to take up its readiness posture and stand QRA commencing 13 June 1964. The following week Minister of National Defence Paul Hellyer visited the Wing.*

DOCUMENT # 5
1964, 1 Air Division Historical Narrative, Appendix F, Operations Section.

> Tactical Evaluations:
> 8–11 June 1964, the final TacEvals were conducted by 4ATAF at 3 and 4 Wings, and on 01 July all six Strike Squadrons assumed an alert commitment.

Before cost-cutting had become an issue, the military had planned to extend the types of nuclear weapons deployed in Europe, and it was originally planned that 3 Wing would be the first to get the Mk 43 thermonuclear gravity bomb. However, with the impending base closure, this duty was transferred to 4 Wing.[27]

The custodians provided by the USAF were organized into Detachment 2100 of the 306th Munitions Maintenance Squadron of the 7232 Munitions Maintenance Group, Ramstein Air Base. In 1967 the unit was reorganized as USAF Detachment 4 of the 26th Tactical Reconnaissance Wing.

---

* MND Hellyer visited 3 Wing on 14 June 1964.

3 WING NUCLEAR SQUADRONS
427 Strike/Attack Squadron   01 Feb 64–1969
430 Strike/Attack Squadron   26 Feb 64–1969
434 Strike/Attack Squadron   01 Feb 64–1967

427 STRIKE/ATTACK SQUADRON
The "Lion" squadron at 3 Wing Zweibrucken was re-formed on 16
December 1962. It was the first RCAF squadron to be equipped with
the CF-104 in Europe, getting the aircraft on 10 January 1963.
Despite the practice, the Tactical Evaluation gave them the lowest pass
mark allowed (a rating of "three") on 08 June 1964. Their second Tac
Eval in November 1964 gave them an improved score of "two." The
squadron assumed nuclear duties with the Mk 28 in the QRA area on
15 June 1964. In May 1966 the Mk 57 weapon would be added to
their capabilities and commitments.

Their duties were best described by a couple of unnamed pilots in
the unofficial squadron diary:

> The Squadron is broken down into two flights: A and
> B. We had at this time (March–April 1966) an
> establishment of 21 pilots and our own ground crew
> located at one end of our building. The Squadron also
> had its own aircraft, and our ground crew handled
> minor unservicabilities. Each flight provided a pilot
> daily to hold "Q". QRA thus saw the same pilot
> appear approximately once a week. "Q" is served for a
> 24 hr period: the pilot relegated to a closed compound
> with nuclear weapon loaded aircraft.[28]

During June 1969 the squadron moved from 3 Wing to 4 Wing
at Baden-Soellingen. The Lion was then closed out on 30 June 1970.

430 STRIKE/ATTACK SQUADRON
The information on 430 Squadron is in the 1 Wing Strike/Attack
squadrons section previous to this.

434 STRIKE/ATTACK SQUADRON
The time in nuclear service for the Bluenose squadron at 3 Wing
Zweibrucken was short, covering 15 June 1964 until the unit was

deactivated on 01 March 1967.[29] 434 thereby became one of the first Canadian nuclear units to be decommissioned as Canada slowly started to shed it nuclear commitments within NATO. However short their operational life, the squadron did manage to become operational with two different nuclear weapons. Initially all units used the common Mk 28, but in May 1966 the squadron became certified to use the relatively new Mk 57.[30]

USAFE DETACHMENT 2100 or DETACHMENT 4
The USAFE unit serving 3 Wing was originally Detachment 2100 of the 7232 MMG, but changed its affiliation in late 1967. By November it was Detachment 4 of the 26th Tactical Reconnaissance Wing. Detachment 2100 was responsible for the custody and maintenance of the various nuclear gravity bombs used by the three strike/attack squadrons at 3 Wing.

This unit officially closed at 3 Wing on 01 July 1969, and moved to 1 Wing Lahr to support the new nuclear strike commitment at that base.

4 WING RCAF/CAF
Flying under the motto "On Guard," 4 Wing was formed at Baden-Soellingen, Federal Republic of Germany, on 01 July 1953.

With the passing of the Tactical Evaluation carried out by 4 ATAF on 11 June 1964, the Wing took up its operational strike role on 12 June 1964, with each squadron placing two pilots on QRA at all times. Each 4 Wing pilot did QRA duty every 6–7 days.[31] Within days of the Wing being cleared for operations with thermonuclear weapons, Paul Hellyer paid a visit and spoke to all service personnel on his new National Defence White Paper. There was no mention of the nuclear weapons.

At Baden-Soellingen, the south dispersal area was zoned off for the storage of nuclear weapons. The Wing decided that to facilitate fast weapons loading, the combat-ready CF-104 aircraft of the three squadrons would be parked nearby when preparing for QRA duties. This became the Quick Reaction Alert area, and both Canadian and US Air Force guards patrolled between the high double fences day and night.[32]

The Wing was first stocked with the Mk 28 thermonuclear bomb, and later with the smaller Mk 57 bomb.[33] What is notable is that 4

Wing was the only unit to operate the Mk 43 thermonuclear weapon, which had originally been planned for a deployment to 3 Wing.[34] A Pre-Atomic Capability Inspection of the Mk 43 Mod 1 weapon, 4 Wing, and Detachment 3 of the 26th Tactical Reconnaissance Wing, was done 9–11 September 1968, and all involved were cleared for the reception of the new weapon.[35] The inspectors noted, however, that there was no Mk 43 weapon on the base, and a Type III training weapon had to be used for the proficiency demonstrations.[36] This was considered odd as the base and units had already been cleared for holding nuclear weapons.

The deployment of the Mk 43 was not a long one, and by early 1970 the weapon had already been removed from the SAS site at Baden-Soellingen.[37] The Mk 28 types and the Mk 57 would remain in use until 01 January 1972.

4 Wing managed to become the longest serving nuclear unit in Canadian service in Europe despite some impressive obstacles. There was a great deal of pressure placed by the officials of the nearby town of Baden for the relocation of the air base. On 18 January 1968, the Baden Minister of Finance stated that he was requesting the German Ministry of Defence to give up Baden-Soellingen air base and thereby remove the Canadians. It was said that the townspeople would settle for having the runway shifted to cut down on noise, but were unwilling to part with even one square metre of land for such construction.

Periodic maintenance was always a problem, and by 1968 it was obvious that the runway at Baden had to be resurfaced. This meant that the strike/attack squadrons (422 and 421) would be moved to 3 Wing to serve their QRA. Beginning on 24 February 1969 and lasting for 100 days, the operational squadrons and all of their associated equipment were moved to Zweibrucken. This shuffling of squadrons also meant that the nuclear weapons were moved, and that there would be a problem with maintaining the stockpile. It seems that the USAFE would not be able to restock the Mk 28 at Baden until after another Capability Inspection once the squadrons had returned to their base, thus leaving the Wing essentially unarmed for a short period of time.[38]

The last surviving nuclear Wing in the CAF in Europe was stood down from that nuclear commitment on 31 December 1971.[39] As of 01 January 1972, 4 Wing and the entire Canadian Air Group were tasked with conventional weapons delivery.

4 WING NUCLEAR SQUADRONS

421 Strike/Attack	14 Feb 64–1972
422 Strike/Attack	01 Feb 64–1972
421 Strike/Attack	01 Jul 70–1972
444 Strike/Attack	01 Feb 64–1967

421 STRIKE/ATTACK SQUADRON

"Red Indian" Squadron was originally reformed at 2 Wing on 21 December 1963, and then switched over to the command of 4 Wing on 14 February 1964.

Tasked to perform day and night strikes with nuclear weapons against pre-selected targets and/or targets of opportunity of enemy forces positioned within SACEUR's theatre of operations, 421 held its first QRA with the Mk 28 on 01 October 1964,[40] making it the last strike squadron to come on-line at 4 Wing. This late start was due to a lack of establishment pilots and the fact that the staff was still in the training phase.[41] In those first years of operation, the attack role, which meant the use of conventional weapons, "was all but ignored."[42] In May 1966 a new weapon was added to the arsenal of Mk 28s carried by the unit when they became certified to deliver the Mk 57.[43]

Although always a 4 Wing squadron, 421 did serve some QRA time at 3 Wing. It moved there on 24 February 1969 for 100 days to allow the runway at Baden to be resurfaced.

After standing its last nuclear QRA on 31 December 1971, the squadron assumed a conventional role on 01 January 1972. Although it did not acquire nuclear weapons as early in 1964 as some other strike/attack squadrons, 421 was the last Starfighter unit in the RCAF/CAF to be equipped with nuclear gravity bombs. This made it the longest-lived nuclear weapons squadron in 1 Air Division, RCAF/CAF.

422 STRIKE/ATTACK SQUADRON

Tomahawk Squadron at 4 Wing Baden-Soellingen was activated 15 July 1963 with the first CF-104 delivered to 4 Wing,[44] and the first squadron aircraft was flown on 19 July. 422 and 444 Squadrons would be the first operational nuclear units to begin QRA duties at 4 Wing on 15 June 1964. The unit would start its QRA carrying the Mk 28 bomb, and in May 1966 would add the new Mk 57 to the inventory of weapons certified for use on the CF-104.[45]

Although always a 4 Wing squadron, 422 and its sister squadron 421, did serve some QRA time at 3 Wing. They moved there on 24 February 1969 for 100 days to allow the runway at Baden to be resurfaced, returning in June.

The squadron would be disbanded on Canada Day, 1970, after flying 33 800 hours and losing four aircraft and two pilots to crashes.

444 STRIKE/ATTACK SQUADRON

With its mascot Cecil the Snake and the motto "Strike Swift Strike Sure," Cobra Squadron moved into 4 Wing Baden-Soellingen on 21 May 1963. On 31 January 1964, 444 Reconnaissance Squadron became 444 Strike/Attack Squadron. It was fully operational with the Mk 28 bomb after the Tactical Evaluation on 11 June 1964, during which they flew over 100 missions.[46] Then in May 1966 it became operational with the new Mk 57 nuclear weapon. This would last for less than one year. In 1966 the squadron was commanded by Gerard Theriault, who would later become the Chief of Defence Staff at the time the last nuclear weapons were removed from bases in Canada.

With the news from Ottawa that "effective 1 April 1967, 444 Strike/Attack Squadron, Baden-Soellingen, Germany will be reduced to nil strength and made dormant"[47] the unit prepared for the end. Cecil flew his last flight on 31 March 1967, and the squadron was disbanded 01 April 1967.[48]

USAF DETACHMENT 1900 or DETACHMENT 3

This USAFE unit serving RCAF 4 Wing was originally Detachment 1900 of the 7232 MMG, but changed its affiliation in late 1967 to become Detachment 3 of the 26th Tactical Reconnaissance Wing. Their task was to provide the custodial oversight and the maintenance of the three types of nuclear weapons assigned and deployed to 4 Wing for the three (later two) strike/attack squadrons.

At its inception, Detachment 1900 under the command of Major RP Cady and his team, served RCAF 421, 422, and 444 Squadrons. In 1972 the detachment, by this time called #3, would be disbanded as the nuclear commitment at 4 Wing was ended.

THE FINAL WEAPONS

The last nuclear weapons used by the RCAF in Europe were stored at the 4 Wing Baden SAS. The strike/attack squadrons stood their final

QRA on New Year's Eve, 1971. After their final use in the QRA on 31 December 1971, the next 12 days were used for the removal of the weapons. By 12 January 1972 the SAS at Baden was empty, and 4 Wing became the last Starfighter unit to stand alert with nuclear weapons. The previous year, 1971, had seen the last remaining nuclear weapons removed from 1 Wing, which had only acquired them in 1969.

DOCUMENT # 6
18 November 1971, V3313-22 DNW, Restricted Memorandum, re: DNW Field Activities — 1 CAG Final Visit.

> It is felt that the experience gained from the previous phase out of the strike role from 3 and 1 Wings would serve to accomplish nuclear weapons removal and phase out at Baden in a safe and efficient manner.

DOCUMENT # 7
17 January 1972, 1910Z, from VCDS/CANFORCEHED to Commander 1 CAG/CANAIRGRP Lahr.

> Final phase-out of special weapons on 12 January (1972 at 4 Wing Baden) marked the end of an era which started in 1964. Thank you for the great credit which you have brought to the Canadian Armed Forces in Europe.

CHAPTER 5

HONEST JOHN: THE WEAPON AND THE BATTERIES

The Honest John battlefield rocket was the only nuclear weapon system deployed by Canada outside of the Royal Canadian Air Force. The Canadian Army bought a total of six mobile launchers, and deployed four to their only nuclear unit, the 1 Surface-to-Surface Missile Battery of the Royal Canadian Artillery (1 SSM Bty, RCA) stationed in the Federal Republic of Germany between 1964 and 1970.

THE RATIONALE

The rationale for acquiring and using the Honest John battlefield nuclear weapon system was explained in secret to a Conservative member of Parliament: a member whose own party had acquired the Honest John in the first instance.

DOCUMENT # 1

21 June 63, HQTS 1625-7 TD 3165 (DMO&P 3) Top Secret answer to question by Member of Parliament Mr. G. Churchill (PC) on 30 May 63 prepared for the MND by DMO&P and approved by DGPO Brig HW Love.

  The Army requirement for nuclear weapons is based upon the NATO strategic concept to counter Soviet aggression in Europe. This concept is contained in NATO Document MC 14/2. Since no Canadian reservation was made, it is assumed to have the same effect and meaning as though it were approved by the Government of Canada. The Strategic concept of

NATO is that since the rapid overrunning of Europe could not be prevented unless NATO immediately employed nuclear weapons both strategically and tactically, NATO must be prepared to take the initiative in their use.

In order to achieve this task each element of the NATO force, including the Canadian Army brigade group, must be highly trained, flexible, and have integrated nuclear capability ready for immediate use should conventional weapons fail to contain the aggression. To meet these requirements, it is essential that the Canadian brigade group have nuclear weapons deployed and operationally ready to fight with full effectiveness on D-Day.

Conventional warheads are not economical to use, since this weapon is designed as a nuclear delivery system.

The Canadian Army would never receive a conventional warhead for the Honest John, although earlier versions deployed by other nations did come so equipped.

THE FINANCES

Prior to the purchase of the Honest John for Canadian troops, the military and the government had shown more interest in the US Army's Lacrosse nuclear weapon rocket. This interest had been so serious as to have the Cabinet approve the procurement of four launchers and 12 Lacrosse training rockets.[1] The early Honest John had also been considered, but the price for a complete, inert, demonstration round was considered exorbitant.[2] In the late 1950s, however, rocket science was progressing at a phenomenal rate, and the Lacrosse was soon surpassed by another system, the Honest John.

In May 1959 a decision was made to consider the purchase of the Honest John rocket by Canada.[3] By the autumn of 1959 the Army had decided that the Honest John was superior to the earlier-proposed Lacrosse, and it was assumed by the military that "a nuclear capability is required" for the Canadian Army.[4] Supreme HQ Allied Powers Europe (SHAPE) had recommended that Canada buy 230 rockets, but this was cut to 115, as even the Canadian Army felt that this was "a fantastic amount of explosives to provide in support of a brigade."

In early 1959 the Minister of National Defence argued to John Diefenbaker that the Lacrosse project should be terminated, and that a cost-benefit analysis supported procurement of the Honest John. The Minister pointed out that the Lacrosse would cost $22 401 457.00, and that the Honest John would only cost $5 387 940.00 — approximately one-quarter of the Lacrosse's cost.[5] The matter would soon be discussed at the Cabinet Defence Committee.

The Chief of the General Staff wrote to the Minister of National Defence the following spring, telling him: "Approval is being sought for the procurement of six launchers together with associated equipment and 115 operational and 36 training rockets (three years training supply) at a total cost of $4 612 514.00. Four launchers will be employed in Europe to meet the NATO force goal for Canada; two launchers will remain in Canada for training and rotational purposes."[6]

Along with the brief note, the CGS sent along a draft memorandum to the Cabinet Defence Committee outlining the views of National Defence on the procurement of the Honest John. The memorandum noted that the 762 mm Honest John nuclear delivery rocket was being recommended to the forces of the United States, the United Kingdom, France, the Federal Republic of Germany, the Netherlands, and Belgium. A few days later the Chief of the General Staff once again wrote to the Minister, telling him that the expected costs had dropped for the 115 operational rockets the Canadian Army wished to buy. The figure had decreased from the original, to an undetermined amount, and finally to $2 237 342.00.[7]

The Cabinet Defence Committee approved the purchase of Honest John rockets, in place of the expected Lacrosse rockets, on 25 March 1960, for $2 799 573.00. "On 25 March 1960 the Cabinet Defence Committee authorized the Canadian Army to procure six 762 mm rocket launchers, 36 training rockets and associated equipment. Contract demands for the procurement of the equipment and rockets from the US are now being processed. Delivery has been requested by 1 Jun 61."[8] Whether the Minister told Cabinet that the initial cost only covered launchers and training rockets is unknown, but the reality was that the 115 operational Honest John rockets would cost another $2 237 342.00 over the next year.[9] The Minister's office at NDHQ wrote a speech the next day outlining the change in procurement, and on 30 March 1960, the Minister announced that the Canadian government, on the advice of the Army, had decided to purchase Honest John rockets instead of Lacrosse rockets.

Although the Army was pleased to be acquiring new battlefield weapons, there was a price to pay. In order to make room for this new function, the Army had to give up another function, and anti-aircraft defence was dropped from the Army's order of battle for over ten years. All resources were funnelled from the disbanded Royal Canadian School of Artillery (Anti-Aircraft) at Camp Picton, into the new 1 SSM Battery and 2 SSM Training Battery newly formed at Camp Picton. Most of the original personnel were drawn from the 1st Light Anti-Aircraft Regiment of the Royal Canadian Artillery, and from the RCEME Light Aid Detachment, both of which were disbanded on 30 September 1960.

By 1960, the US Army had fielded its first improved Honest John rockets, and the Canadians got a better idea of its refined capabilities. The Chief of the General Staff was told that the new Honest John and warhead would have a Mk 31 nuclear warhead with a 2–10–30 kt variable nuclear yield; a range of between 5000 m and 38500 m; and a delivery schedule bringing the bulk of the rockets to Canada before 01 October 1961.[10]

With the decision having been made to purchase the weapons, the Canadian Army moved to prepare a user unit. 1 and 2 SSM Batteries were authorized for formation on 05 July 1960.[11] 1 SSM would get four launchers, and the remaining two launchers would stay in Canada as part of 2 SSM Training Battery.

By July 1961 Canada had the four launchers it would deploy to Germany in December.[12] But the Canadian Army was still three years from being able to arm their new rocket. The *Canadian Army Journal*,[13] that the new Canadian rocket for the 1 SSM Battery carried either nuclear or conventional warheads, but this was not the case: in fact, it was a lie. The Army had no interest in having the public worked up over another nuclear deployment, and they endeavoured to keep their collective heads down. The original Honest John had been built as a dual-capable weapon, with provision made to carry nuclear, conventional, and chemical weapons: but this was not the weapon Canada intended to acquire. The Canadian Army wrote on 30 June 1961 that it had bought the Honest John "primarily as a nuclear delivery system," and to fulfil this role, "conventional warheads were not to be procured." The Honest John rockets would provide "nuclear general support" for the division, firing in a counter-battery or harassing fire manner. There would be no close-support role for the Honest John.

THE HONEST JOHN ROCKET

The MGR-1B (M50) Honest John[14] was a short-range, free flight, mobile, solid propellant, surface-to-surface, nuclear-capable ballistic rocket, which could fly from 5.0–38.0 km at 1.5 mach. At maximum range the rocket would be in flight for 112 seconds. To achieve some stability for the rocket and thereby increase the accuracy, the Honest John incorporated four spin rockets mounted just behind the warhead section, and four short tail fins skewed at a one-degree angle. Burning for 0.19 seconds, the spin rockets would rotate the rocket clockwise twice per second.

It was the weapon's relative lack of sophistication, plus the fact that it was a free-flight rocket and not a guided missile, which made it impervious to electronic counter-measures during flight: it would proceed towards its intended target despite electronic counter-measures, or jamming. This weapon type was usually aimed at tactical targets such as headquarters, command posts, masses of armour, and enemy battlefield nuclear weapons. It had an accuracy of about 0.3 km to 1.6 km after the rocket motor had burned for the standard 3.4 seconds.

Carried on an open truck, the rocket had to be warmed by electric blankets for 24–48 hours prior to firing to raise the fuel temperature to about 25°C for an even propellent burn. The Honest John was a "Shoot and Scoot" weapon system: after firing the rocket from the rear-mounted rail launcher on the truck, the vehicle quickly drove away (the "scoot" capability) to avoid being targeted by the enemy due to the flash and smoke of the launch.

HONEST JOHN ROCKET STATISTICS:

Range: maximum 39 000 m with XM27, XM47, XM48 warhead
         minimum 5000 m with XM27, XM47, XM48 warhead
Accuracy: 300 m–1600 m at 5000 m–30 000 m range
Length: 7.57 m
Diameter: 762 mm, warhead section
Fin Span: 1.37 m (original model)
Weight: 2140 kg at launch.
Stages: single stage, solid fuelled, rocket.

THE W31 MOD 0 NUCLEAR WARHEAD[15]

The Honest John rocket acquired for the Canadian Army carried the US built and owned W31 Mod 0 boosted nuclear warhead. The W31 used Oralloy (Oak Ridge Alloy) as fissile material and probably cyclotol as the primary high-explosive detonator. There was also a tritium booster in the physics package to increase the yield. Selectable fuzing allowed for ground bursts, and air bursts up to 1900 m. Production of the W31 at the Pantex nuclear warhead assembly plant in Amarillo, Texas saw about 1650 W31 warheads built between October 1959 and December 1961 for the Honest John rocket worldwide. When the last active US Army Honest John unit was deactivated in 1979, approximately 1000 W31 warheads were returned from Europe to the United States by the US Army in 1980. By 1983 it was estimated that there were only about 200 W31 warheads for Honest John rockets left in storage, and by 1987 all warheads had been dismantled.

The warhead was small by today's standards, and was often referred to as a 20 kt weapon, i.e. a Hiroshima or "Nominal" size bomb. The W31 Honest John warhead had three separate warhead sections, each having a different yield: the M27, the M47, and the M48. The Canadian Army definitely used the M27 warhead and the M72 training warhead. If the M27 is 2 kt, the M47 is 20 kt, and the M48 is 40 kt, then the Canadian M27 warhead section of the W31 had a yield of about 2 kt. The warhead had the M7 timer fuze with air or ground burst options, and height-of-burst settings. Additional safety features were incorporated into the W31 Mod 2 warheads in 1959, but these were not used in the Honest John system, instead seeing service in the air defence version used in the US Army. Security against unauthorized deliberate detonation was provided by the early Category A Permissive Action Link (PAL) consisting of a few-digit, unlimited try, mechanical combination lock device in the warhead section. The XM72 and XM27 warhead section had the safety/PAL Atomic Weapon Locking Device XM81 and/or XM82.

Retirement of the W31 Honest John warheads from the US inventory began in July 1967 while they were still serving with the Canadian Army, and continued until mid-1987. The W31 was also used in the Nike-Hercules air defence missile, and as the charge in the US Army's Atomic Demolition Munition.

W31 WARHEAD STATISTICS
Warhead: W31
Warhead Sections: M27, M47, M48.
Canadian Warhead Section: M27
Yields: 2 kt, 20 kt, 40 kt.
Fuzing: Ground and Air Burst (Height Selectable)
Fuze: M7 timer fuze
Weight of Full Warhead Section: 561 kg
Security: Category "A" PAL, multiple-try mechanical combination
PAL: Cat. A, XM81 and XM82
Production Run: approx. 1650 built
Production Dates: Oct. 1959–Dec. 1961.
Shipping container: 3.4 m x 1.12 m x 1.32 m

THE TRAINING WARHEAD

The Canadian Army had a different relationship with the nuclear weapon it was to utilize than did the RCAF. The RCAF required that the warhead be loaded on the missile, as in the BOMARC system, or that the bomb be loaded under the airplane, as was the case with the CF-104. However, the Canadian and US armies operated slightly differently. The Canadians would rarely see the actual war-reserve nuclear warheads meant to be launched atop their Honest John rockets.[16] Instead, the warheads were always kept under close custody by the US Army in the Special Ammunition Storage igloos near Hemer, and the Canadians used only training rounds.

The Canadian Army, therefore, had to acquire at least "One Warhead, Section, Training, Inert XM72 (nuclear)," NATO Number 1115-00-967-9958 w/container XM136E1, to allow the troops of the 1 SSM Battery simply to carry out their daily training and operational routine. Use of the M72 training section was governed by two basic manuals: the TM(C)9-N-1100-200-12 (c.1964), which dealt with the XM72E1, and the TM9N-1100-200-12. The US Army described the XM72 as "a training (not-to-be-fired) warhead section which is similar to the tactical XM27 warhead section in size, shape, weight, centre of gravity, and all external controls, connections and features. (A) user checkout panel is located on the left-hand side." The troops of 2 SSM Training Battery never received a training warhead.

By early 1965 the Army had acquired five training warheads of the M72 class: 1 x M72, and 4 x M72E1. The problem was that although Canada was to use only one warhead in battle, they had two different warhead training sections. It was requested that the M72 be upgraded to match the M72E1 training section for the sake of comparability. However, their problems were not to end here. The M27 warhead set aside for 1 SSM Bty had a locking device not found on even the upgraded M72E1 training section.[17] For this warhead an M72E2 training section was required, but not purchased, by Canada. One major problem was that training nuclear warheads were never provided to the training unit at Shilo, Manitoba.

THE SERVICE-TO-SERVICE TECHNICAL AGREEMENT

When the Pearson Government signed the Exchange of Notes on 16 August 1963 for the provision of nuclear warheads to support Canadian weapon systems, the Canadian Army knew that their day was soon at hand. The Army already had the rockets: what it needed now were the atomic warheads designed to be mated to the Honest John battlefield nuclear support rocket.

In early 1964 the Chief of the General Staff informed the Minister's aide that 1 SSM Bty had rockets but had yet to receive warheads of "either conventional or high explosive."[18] The Chairman of the Chiefs of Staff wrote that these warheads were to be provided to Canada under a "service-to-service technical agreement."[19] Once a draft arrangement had been concurred in by HQ US Army Europe, HQ British army of the Rhine, and the Canadian financial advisors in Europe prior to 17 February 1964, the final document was prepared. This last draft of 19 March 1964 was forwarded by the Chief of the General Staff to External Affairs for the final political touches. This would be the final political act before the Canadian Army was equipped with nuclear warheads.

The document to be signed by Canada actually required little negotiation, as it had been in existence for some years already. In fact, it was originally negotiated by the British for the support of their Honest John Regiment, also stationed at Hemer, Germany. Canada was simply appending its name to the arrangement, and would be the junior partner to the British Army. The British Army would be in charge of Explosive Ordnance Disposal and site security, and its commander would coordinate any actions in the event of a nuclear accident. (After devising a plan for security, the British commander commented that the plan was "assuming that the site still then needed securing"[20] after a nuclear detonation.)

With the final negotiations completed between the Canadian Army, the British Army, and the US Army, the technical arrangement was ready for signature. Brigadier Mike Dare, the Canadian Brigade Commander, wrote to the US Army chief in Europe and announced that all three governments were in agreement and that he, the brigadier, was authorized to sign for Canada. He went on to ask that the document be signed at the Canadian HQ in Germany during the week of 15 June 1964.[21]

The actual "Service-to-Service Supplementary Arrangement" was signed in Germany on 18 June 1964 by the Commander of the Canadian Army National Force, Europe; the Chief of Staff of the British Army of the Rhine; and the Commander in Chief of the United States Army, Europe. Due to the stunningly long name of the original UK-US agreement, the document was always referred to as the Heidelberg Agreement of 30 August 1961. (The document is found in the Appendix of this book.)

1 SURFACE-TO-SURFACE MISSILE BATTERY, RCA

The Canadian Army had only one nuclear armed unit, the 1st Surface-to-Surface Missile Battery of the Royal Canadian Artillery.

Army headquarters moved to make the new unit official on 05 July 1960, and the Army Chief of Staff wrote that "the formation of the undermentioned units of the Canadian Army (Regular) is authorized the date shown: 1st Surface-to-Surface Missile Battery Royal Regiment of Canadian Artillery, 15 Sept 1960."[22] By the end of its first year 1 SSM Bty had 13 Officers, 5 Warrant Officers, 47 NCOs and 146 men on strength.

The new shock troops of the 1 SSM Bty had been trained at the US Army's Honest John Cadre Course at Fort Sill, Oklahoma, from 15 April to 26 May 1961.

The unit then formed at Petawawa, and by the autumn of 1961 had demonstrated its ability to fire the Honest John rocket. On 27 October 61, 1 SSM Bty fired their first Honest John rocket, in the presence of the Minister of National Defence, at the Petawawa, Ontario, weapons range. By this time there were 14 Officers, 22 WO and NCOs, and 199 men on strength.

But the 1 SSM Bty was not to stay in Canada for long. Plans had already been made for shipping the entire unit to Hemer-Menden,

Germany.[23] An advance party went by RCAF flight from Trenton to Germany on 3 December. Within weeks of the successful rocket firing at Petawawa, the 1 SSM Bty of 228 officers and men set off from Canada on Greek Line ship QSS Arkadia. They left Canada on 8 December 1961 and arrived in Bremerhaven, Germany on 17 December, but did not leave the ship until 18 December. This would be one of the final rotations of Canadian units to Europe by ship. From there they made their way by land to their new home, Fort Prince of Wales, Deilinghofen, 4 km from Hemer, Germany, in the Westphalia region. In the autumn of 1968 they would move into new quarters at Fort Qu'Appelle, Iserlohn (Hemer), Germany, only a short distance from Fort Prince of Wales.

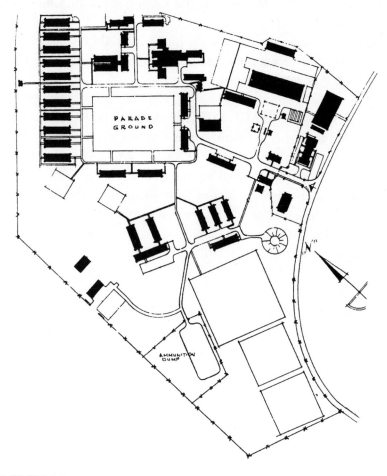

DIAGRAM # 1
The Canadian Army's Fort Prince of Wales, the first home in Germany of the 1 SSM Bty.

The Canadian Army troops would soon become familiar with the city of Iserlohn and its 52 000 people, which, at 10 km distance, was the closest city to Fort Prince of Wales. Their operational site was Hemer, and the Commanding Officer of the British Army 50th Missile Regiment, as the senior partner, was the Site Commander. Fort Prince of Wales was shared with the US Army 69th Missile Support Detachment. Together with the 69th Detachment, 1 SSM Bty had adopted an orphanage in the area and provided it with activities and picnics and various parties.*

The new battery moved its 16 first line rockets[24] and some 100 of the operational and testing Honest John rockets into the rocket storage bunkers near Hemer. The unit would test fire two Honest John rockets per launcher per year, and this quickly ate up the available rocket bodies. This was acceptable as long as the sixteen war-use units were not touched. The Canadians would only be provided with 16 nuclear warheads for the entire unit in times of war; and, as there was "no known wartime function"[25] for the SAS all warheads would have to be deployed at once. This meant that, in times of war, 1 SSM Bty would not be dashing back to Hemer for a warhead refill. The unit establishment of 115 operational rockets was further broken down into "16 1st Line" and "99 Reserve" Honest John rocket motors. From this fact we gain another clue that there would only be 16 nuclear warheads provided for 1 SSM Bty in times of war from the SAS site at Hemer.

The 1st Surface-to-Surface Missile unit was a battery upon formation, and this caused certain problems. In the 1st British Corps organization, for which 4 CIBG (Canadian Infantry Brigade Group Germany) was often considered an operational equivalent, a battery was responsible for two missile launchers, but 1 SSM had the launchers, ancillary equipment, and support organization equivalent to those of a regiment in other NATO nations. In addition, within the usual chain of command, a battery is normally subordinate to a regiment, and therefore 1 SSM was often considered to be under the command of an RCA Regiment, co-located at Deilinghofen. This was not true, as operationally 1 SSM was responsible directly to 4 CIBG. It was therefore recommended that 1 SSM Battery become 1 SSM Regiment.[26]

---

* The Kinderheim Marien Frieden in Neheim-Husten.

In Europe, the 1 SSM Bty operated under the command of the 4 CIBG, while its own HQ was near Deilinghofen, Germany. The commanding officer of the Royal Canadian Horse Artillery was the senior artillery officer for all of 4 CIBG, and as the Honest John was considered an artillery-class weapon, was technically responsible for 1 SSM Bty. The unit passed its first summer in West Germany with 64 live rockets and 8 training rounds.[27] But there was something missing, and it continued to be missing for another two years.

The unit worked with two other units at Hemer during its time in Germany: the British Army of the Rhine's 50 Missile Regiment; and the US Army Europe, US Army Special Ammunition Storage Command, 69 US Army Missile Warhead Support Detachment (69 US Msl Det). 1 SSM Bty received direct support from the British Army in the form of loaned training warheads, loaned training manuals, and the like until the Canadian stores were provided. The 69 US Msl Det was responsible for Honest John warheads assigned to 1 SSM Bty Honest John rockets.

AUTHORIZATION FOR RELEASE AND USE

Authorization for the use of nuclear weapons by 1 SSM Bty came through a few channels. First the release of nuclear weapons would be authorized by the US president in a first-strike situation. It may have been possible to get this authorization and transmit it within 20 minutes. However, if this stage of the war had passed, there was the possibility that release could be authorized by duly delegated high commanders on site. This meant that SACEUR/CINCEUR may well have had authority granted him by the president to use nuclear weapons at his own discretion. The authorization for the release of nuclear warheads to the non-US NATO units would be transmitted to the US Army 69th Detachment by radio. The 69th had a radio station inside the 1 SSM Bty barracks which directly connected them to the communications centre in the Pentagon. However, it is likely that their actual release orders would come from within Europe, from SACEUR.

Canadian authorization for the use of nuclear weapons would come to the commanding officer of 1 SSM Bty from the commander of 4 CIBG. The two men would be in close quarters in wartime, so this could have been accomplished verbally. The 1 SSM Bty commanding officer would then radio his dispersed units using a code on a one-time disposable pad. Divided into transmission bursts, and lasting a total of only 30 seconds, all targeting, timing, and burst information would be sent to the four launchers. However, the authority to initiate targets was held by the corps commander, a British officer. This authority was delegated to him by SACEUR after presidential R-hour release. The warheads were also controlled by the corps commander, but he did not have the authority to order their use unless it had been pre-delegated to him by the US.

The question of how the decision to use nuclear weapons deployed by non-US NATO forces was to be implemented is a very complex one and far beyond the scope of this operational history. However, it is clear that the NATO Military Committee would have to make the world's most difficult decision in the shortest period of time and under the most severe circumstances, and this does not lend one confidence. But, on a smaller, and more Canadian scale, if the prime minister had granted his permission, and if the US president and/or SACEUR had so directed, it would have been technically possible for Canada and Britain to engage in a nuclear war alongside the US in Europe without other NATO partners. The chances of this actually happening were close to nil.

With the signature of the technical arrangement, the way had been cleared for provision of warheads. The Initial Nuclear Safety Inspection of the unit was held between 28 and 30 September 1964, and upon attaining a satisfactory rating, the unit was certified as ready to receive nuclear warhead support from the US Army.

The SAS site at Neheim-Hueston was also supporting the British Army Honest John Regiment, and at least 48 warheads would already have been in place. After the Service-to-Service technical agreement was signed the US Army would have moved in at least 16 more warheads to support the added Canadian Honest John forces. Unfortunately, there is no open record of additional warheads arriving.[28] All that is known from Canadian open documentation is that 1 SSM Bty became nuclear certified after the unit passed the Initial Nuclear Safety Inspection of 28–30 September 1964. The only reference to the initial access to nuclear warheads is a historical report footnote. The unit had neglected to mention their new nuclear status in their 1964 annual historical report for Department of National Defence, and so managed to work it in as an additional note to the 1965 report.

DOCUMENT # 2

1965 Annual Historical Report, 1 SSM: 1451-1, 4 Feb 66.

> Note: as of Sep 64 this unit became the only
> nuclear capable unit in the Canadian Army.
> (signed) Major A.C. Moffat, CO.

The warheads arrived on site from Minden carried by large moving van-style trucks in the dead of night. Accompanied by a US Army's armoured car regiment, the moving vans disgorged their load of 16 warhead boxes into two SAS bunkers in a single night's work. When they departed, the exterior of the dark facility was guarded by about 30 rather nervous young Canadians, and only a tiny handful of US Army servicemen. Once fully stocked to handle all three units in the area, the SAS would hold some 48 W31 nuclear warheads.

This storage site was a twenty-minute drive from the 1 SSM Bty barracks, yet the unit was expected to have a platoon of 30 men on 30 minutes notice to deploy as an additional external perimeter security force. However, the security force was normally provided by both the British and Canadian armies, along with a token US custodial presence.

DOCUMENT # 3

Nuclear Safety Inspection of the 1 SSM Battery, Royal Canadian Artillery (Trip No 10C) (FY 65). 6 Nov 1964.
from Office of the Inspector General, US Army, Europe, thru CO 1 SSM and CO 4 CIBG, to CINC US Army Europe. written by Lt. Colonel William H. Clausen, Team Chief, US Army Inspector General.

> In accordance with the above references, an initial nuclear safety inspection (NSI) of the 1 SSM Battery, Royal Canadian Arty, Deilinghofen, Germany, was conducted during the period 28–30 September 1964. A technical proficiency inspection of the 69th US Army Missile Detachment, supporting the 1 SSM Battery was made during the same period.
>
> As a result of this inspection it was concluded that the battery was qualified to receive nuclear weapons support.

Although the Nuclear Safety Inspection found that 1 SSM Bty "was qualified to receive nuclear weapons support," there were still problems. The safety report noted that the unit had not been placed on the distribution list for the warhead operator and maintenance manual, and that the manual used during the inspection was on loan from the 69th US Army Detachment. The inspectors also found several nuclear safety deficiencies which suggested a lack of strict adherence to the exact procedures deemed necessary. They pointed to the lack of close inspection of the warhead shipping container, the improper placement of the tie-down straps on the warhead container, improper installation of the warhead mating bolts, and failure to inspect the warhead firing plug prior to the installation of the plug in the fire-safe receptacle. The inspectors also commented on incorrect procedures for removal of the warhead and the fact that the training warhead being used was on loan from the British.[29]

It turns out that the Army had purchased all the launchers and associated equipment, and over 100 live rockets, and had negotiated for the provision of nuclear warheads, but had not bothered to acquire a training warhead for the unit. Months after they became nuclear certified, the Director of Nuclear Weapons wrote that "No 1 SSM Battery can be congratulated for having progressed as far with their nuclear preparations as they have without the use of their own training round. The one XM72 nuclear training warhead available to the battery is on loan from the British." The Director went on to comment that from a nuclear safety point of view, 1 SSM Battery had to be provided with training nuclear warheads, and that he would bring the matter to the attention of the appropriate directors.[30]

It may not have been all that the troops on the ship imagined while crossing the Atlantic: nuclear weapons duty was tiresome and muddled in a sea of bureaucratic regulations. Within a year of acquiring warheads for the rocket, it became clear that the mobile Honest John system might not be so mobile. The US Army forbade the warheads to be more than 15-minutes night-travel time by foot from the central assembly location unless the wartime R-hour message had been received.[31] This meant that a loaded launcher could not be dispersed outside of a 15-minute walking-radius circle.[32] The commander of 1 SSM commented that the restrictions on dispersal "will have the effect of having all our nuclear weapons in a position of being destroyed by one enemy nuclear strike"[33] and pleaded with the commander of 4 CIBG to speak to the proper authorities in order to have the travel-time rules relaxed and to have the officer and Warrant Officer establishment of the 69th Detachment increased. The manning of the 69th was a perennial problem, as in the early days there was only one captain, one sergeant, and three enlisted men assigned.

The plan with a two-troop formation was that one troop would be deployed to cover the forward zone while the second was held back. This would provide a leap-frog set-up. However, two things combined to destroy this military plan: first, the US Army had the regulations preventing non-US nations from deploying nuclear weapons more than a 15-minute walk from a central location; and second, the Canadian government cut the Honest John launcher deployment in half.

1 SSM BTY TABLE OF ORGANIZATION, 4 LAUNCHERS, 19 MAY 1966

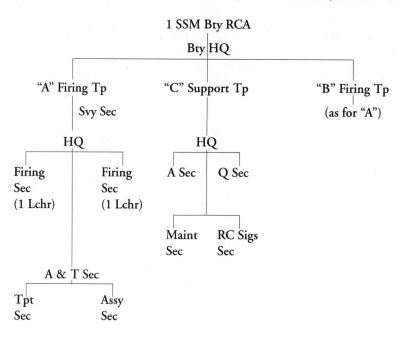

Another problem 1 SSM Battery had was that, although they were equipped with Honest John rockets, and serving NATO, they were not in a position to have repairs done within the NATO infrastructure. All of the NATO-European Honest John systems were supported by the NATO Maintenance Supply and Services Agency (NMSSA) or System (NMSSS), which was the purchasing and third-line repair activity for the European Honest John system. Canada was not a member of the NMSSA and was therefore not entitled to use the services of this agency for Honest John logistics and engineering support.[34] In 1961 it was estimated that Canadian participation in the NMSSS would cost $30 000.00 per year. Canada had not joined and therefore never paid. For the first little while, the Canadian Army got by with the benevolence of the US Army.[35] However, that would not last long, and soon the US Army was demanding cash for services. The Canadian Army refused, and soon 1 SSM was in danger of failing Nuclear Safety Inspections as some of their equipment was nearing the end of its certification period (which expired 01 March 1969). This had to be resolved or the Canadian Army risked grave embarrassment, and the possible withdrawal of warhead support.[36] The US Army was refusing to test, for free, the M62 cranes and all the warhead slings at their facilities at Munster, Westphalia. Without certification, the equipment could not be used in a nuclear role.

The 1 SSM Bty, as a non-US NATO unit with US nuclear weapons, was responsible for "providing transportation, equipment and personnel necessary for local evacuation of weapons positioned in support of their forces" and for "developing local evacuation plans, including routes, communications procedures, and security measures." This meant that if the area was about to be overrun by Soviet forces, authorization for weapons evacuation would come from the US custodial detachment commander who received his authorization from US CINC Europe. The detachment commander was also allowed to make this decision on his own in special cases.[37] Therefore, a US Army captain would be in a position to give evacuation orders to the Canadian brigadier regarding Canadian equipment and US warheads — a situation which did not seem to please the Canadian planners.[38]

If the weapons were to be evacuated, all of the warheads would have to be shipped from the SAS in no more than four increments. This included both the Canadian and British warheads. In 1965, the first full operation year, the 69th Detachment could only provide 16 personnel (10 trained and 6 untrained staff) to ride in the Canadian warhead load carrier vehicles as custodial agents.[39] Since each warhead required a custodial agent when outside of the SAS bunker, it is reasonable to conclude that the Canadian Army would go out into the field in an emergency (war) situation with 16 warheads, or four per launcher.

DOCUMENT # 4

03 November 1965, 1 SSM: S/6001-H2. from 1 SSM Bty CO to HQ, 4 CIBG. re: Employment of US Personnel.

> The 69th Missile Detachment can provide sixteen personnel to ride in the required load carriers. Legally then, if any of these personnel are absent on leave, course or sick, one warhead for every absent person cannot be moved.

If there was no time for evacuation, or if the request to evacuate was denied, the custodians would then destroy the weapons with Canadian and British assistance if necessary. Regulations[40] required that US nuclear weapons be destroyed if it became apparent that they were about to fall under enemy control. This destruction was to be accompanied by US equipment and US personnel, and could not be dependent on Canadian or British personnel or machines. However, the US detachment could request Canadian and/or British assistance for supporting tasks.

The Honest John, as with any man-made object, was not without its faults. Despite careful planning and maintenance, there was bound to be a failure sometime, and that time came on 12 April 1966. The unit had been participating in Exercise Mardi Gras near Hohne NATO Camp, from 01 through 15 April 66. It was to fire eight rockets. The Historical Report for 1966 notes that the "first rocket malfunctioned on the rail and never developed full thrust it then fell off rail and burnt on ground, *no injuries.*" Major Moffat, the Commanding Officer, was a bit more eloquent, and wrote that:

> On April 12, 1966 a weapon system malfunction occurred on the Soltau Ranges, during the Battery's annual firing position. At "X" hour the Sergeant pressed the firing button, and a series of minor ignitions occurred lasting for five to twenty seconds, at one to two minute intervals. The thrust of the rocket was emitted through both the nozzle and pedestal

sections (fore and aft). During this time the rocket tore itself loose from the Launcher rail and dropped to the left side of the launcher, at the same time blowing the warhead free from the rocket motor, (the warhead landing approximately ninety meters in front of the Launcher, making it a truly "short-range" rocket).[41]

Major Moffat also included a poem, which is one of the few literary artifacts of the Canadian nuclear era. There is a rumour that he may even have penned it himself.

Countdown Soltau
Honest John Firing
April 1966 [42]
Twas a stormy snowy evening
A goodly crowd was there,
To witness our launching
Of a rocket in the air.

Over in one corner
Stood a soul with fingers crossed,
This was his first launching
And he didn't know the cost!

There stood the guests of honour,
Some dependents travelled along
All tense in expectation,
Could anything go wrong?

Then hark! the order cometh,
The current went down the wire.
All eyes were fixed upon the rail
But the weapon didn't fire!

Shot One went o'er the wireless,
Surveyors peered through the hail.
We knew that this was useless,
The rocket fell off the rail.

Now why should this have happened?
Oh! you naughty little dart.
Did you fall in love with the launcher
And from it refuse to part?

Now certainly there's an answer,
The fault lies not with us.
But they simply wouldn't listen
They just climbed on their bus.

Oh! you terrible little rocket!
Upon the rail you smoulder.
The pain, the burden for ever more
Your L.P.O.* must shoulder.

But never worry, never fear
We've only seven of the things.
We'll simply call the Master Gunners,
Let them build us rubber slings.

(*L.P.O.: Launch Position Officer.)

Other exercises throughout the years were more successful. These included, but were not limited to, Exercise Checkmate with 2 Division from 10–20 October 1966, and the nuclear supply drill Exercise Gay Gordon on 11–15 September 1967. In Exercise Checkmate, 1 SSM Bty served as the nuclear regiment from "Mapleland."

With the reorganization of the Canadian military in 1967 and 1968, there was a shrinking of the army commitment in Europe. 1 SSM Bty was to be halved on 30 April 1968 by giving up two of its four Honest John launchers[43] — transferring excess rocket motors to the 1 British Corps operational reserve at Hemer — and having 23 men cross-posted to 1 RCHA. The problem with the force reduction was that the Canadian Army had chosen to do it unilaterally and without consultation with the British and US Armies, and this resulted in a situation where 1 SSM Bty was still responsible for the lift and evacuation of the rockets and nuclear warheads associated with a four-launcher posture even in their new two-launcher mode. The 4 CIBG commander pleaded with commander of the 1st British

Corps to see that "excess holdings are removed from the Canadian Igloo" at the Hemer SAS site.[44]

A year and a half after being halved, 1 SSM learned of its fate from Minister of National Defence Leo Cadieux. On 19 September 1969 he announced, among other things, that the "brigade in Germany will drop the Honest John nuclear role when it is reconfigured next year." This was part of the new defence posture to be pursued by Pierre Trudeau, who had succeeded Pearson as prime minister.

Just prior to its disbandment, the unit had its final Nuclear Surety Inspection on 11–15 May 1970 by the US Army. For the first time in the history of the unit, no observations were made and no deficiencies found, and 1 SSM Bty was given another satisfactory rating.[45] The inspection team leader, US Army Lt. Colonel D.G. Manring, found that "the units performance was, in his opinion outstanding, and one of the best he has ever conducted."[46] This would be their last great moment with their peers.

The men of 1 SSM Bty had their final workout during Exercise Gravy Train of 19–22 May 1970. Twelve officers and 173 men took part in the "Final Live Shot" of an unarmed nuclear rocket in the Canadian Army on 19 May. Little more than a week later the battery had its final parade on 01 June 1970. US Army Colonel R.S. Friday, commanding officer of the 570th Artillery Group, presented 1 SSM Bty RCA with the Outstanding Performance Award 1963–1970 on behalf of the officers and men of 514th Artillery Group. The unit was then disbanded on Canada Day, 01 July 1970.

Although aware of the coming disbandment, the unit remained ready and armed until the final day of its existence. There was no draw-down period. In fact, the US Army continued to supply perhaps twice as many warheads as necessary after the unit was halved in the spring of 1968. Unlike the other nuclear weapons systems the Canadians used, the support for the W40 warhead used on the Honest John would continue for the British Army unit at the Hemer site. Therefore, there were no Canadian arrangements made for the removal of the warheads as 1 SSM Bty prepared to close down on 01 July 1970. 1 SSM simply had their nuclear warhead support withdrawn by the US Army 69th Detachment on 30 June 1970. This also meant that all warheads would be available right up until the disbandment.

The Honest John nuclear commitment would turn out to be the

shortest-lived of all, yet this was not the original thinking. In the discussion of the defence White Paper of 24 March 1964, Minister of National Defence Paul Hellyer told Cabinet that his new White Paper would be somewhat vague on the point of nuclear armaments, but that "there was a clear indication that forces now employing nuclear weapons, with the possible exception of the Honest John, would be phased out over the years ahead."[47] Strangely enough, the government seemed to feel that the least advanced weapon they would deploy would last the longest.

69 US ARMY MISSILE WARHEAD SUPPORT DETACHMENT

The 69th US Army Missile Warhead Support Detachment, also known as the 69th USA Msl (Whd Spt) (HJ), was based at Hemer, Federal Republic of Germany, and supported the 1 Surface-to-Surface Missile Battery. Under the command of the 514th US Army Missile Group, it was responsible for all Honest John warheads assigned to Canada in Germany. The 69th also supported the British Army 50 Missile Regiment, which also used the Honest John, at the same site. The records for this unit are kept in a US Army and federal government storage facility in St. Louis, Missouri, and are currently unavailable to researchers.

The 69th was organized under the US Army Special Ammunition Storage Command (SASCOM) at Heidelberg, and fell under the operational control of the 514th US Army Artillery (Missile) Group commanded by Colonel Wilson at Munchengladback (sic).[48] In this capacity, the 69th operated safe and secure Canadian "Igloos" for storage of nuclear warheads at or near Hemer, Germany.

The biggest problem Canada had with the US Army was that staffing of the 69th never seemed to be a priority, and stability of personnel was never guaranteed. In fact, turnover was so great that the operational readiness of the 69th could well be called into question.

DOCUMENT # 5
02 March 1969, 1 SSM: 3030-1765/1, from 1 SSM Bty to
CANLANEUR, secret, re: "Offr Estb 69th USA Msl Det".

> 1. The officer establishment of 69th USA Msl Det to enable this unit to operate in accordance with Ref A is minimum of four officers. Since previous CO, Lt. Murphy was posted out on 19 Feb 69 after holding

appt for only three months Msl Det has been one officer short. New CO informed of posting out 24 March with new CO due to arrive 31 Mar 69. Det will be two officers short for seven days then one officer short.

2. Continual change of Det. COs makes the required close working association difficult and endangers credibility of operational readiness of Det. Further, a shortage of even one officer makes it impossible for supported units to fulfil their role because of applicable US stringent regulations on custody of nuclear warheads.

3. Request that US authorities be asked to fill officer estb of 69th Msl Det to allow unit period of stability. In this regard during tenure of command of CO 1 SSM thus far 69th Det have had five COs with a sixth to report on 31 March.

After the closure and departure of 1 SSM Bty in 1970, the 69th Missile Support Detachment commanded by US Army Captain Glossmeyer continued to serve at Hemer into the early 1980s, still providing custodial duties for the Royal Artillery of the British Army 50th Missile Regiment.

2 SURFACE-TO-SURFACE MISSILE TRAINING BATTERY

In theory, 2 SSM Training Battery was supposed to provide trained personnel for 1 SSM in Europe.[49] Yet in the beginning, 2 SSM did not have a training programme which included the nuclear requirements of the Honest John system. The commander of 1 SSM complained that he was having to train people on the spot, even after their time with 2 SSM, to the standards of a nuclear-capable unit.[50] Despite a rough start, during its short existence 2 SSM Trg Bty would train over 700 replacement staff for rotation to 1 SSM Bty in Hemer, Germany.

The unit was formed along with 1 SSM Bty at Camp Picton, Ontario, and then moved to Camp Shilo, Manitoba, in August 1962. By the end of its first year, 2 SSM Trg Bty had 7 Officers, 3 Warrant Officers, 46 NCOs, and 74 men on strength. Since the unit would never have nuclear weapons or be required to have them at any time, no custodial unit from the US Army was ever provided to this Shilo unit. Clearly it would have been preposterous to have a short-range battlefield rocket stationed in Canada armed with a nuclear warhead.

While their first firing of an Honest John (at Shilo for a distance of 22 km)[51] was a notable success for 2 SSM, there was also a notable failure. During a live-fire training exercise sometime in 1964, the crew of the truck-mounted launcher forgot to remove the tie-down straps from the Honest John rocket body. When the rocket engine was ignited and developed full thrust, the rocket pulled the unfortunate launcher vehicle down the range, resulting in extensive damage to the launcher and to the reputation of the crew.

After their live firing at Shilo on 13 February 1968, as witnessed by MND Leo Cadieux, 2 SSM Trg Bty was closed on 01 September 1968. This was the last Honest John rocket test-fired in Canada. One launcher vehicle remains intact at the Royal Canadian Artillery Museum outdoor artillery park at CFB Shilo to this day. Despite being battered by harsh winters and scorching summers, the launcher and accompanying Honest John rocket are still in fairly good shape.

CHAPTER 6

THE CF-101B VOODOO AND GENIE ROCKET

The 1960s saw a great upheaval in the air defence of Canada. With the growth of the intercontinental ballistic missile as the primary threat to North America, and the decrease in the theoretical threat posed by manned bombers, Canada's air defence seemed to lie in knowing when the missiles were approaching, rather than in shooting down the encroaching red hordes flying suicide bomber missions over the north pole.

In a wildly overblown response to the mythical "Bomber Gap" of the 1950s, Canada had opted to defend the country by building nearly 700 CF-100 Canuck all-weather fighter/interceptor aircraft meant to shoot down the Soviet bombers. As the 1950s ended the Canuck was considered outdated and ill-equipped, despite being all-weather capable and having two engines. As there was no Canadian interceptor in the design or manufacturing stages, a replacement aircraft would have to be acquired from the United States. The F-101B VooDoo was the logical choice for the time, but nuclear armament came as part and parcel with the VooDoo.[1] The 1960s brought the VooDoo interceptor aircraft and its nuclear weapons to the Canadian arsenal. But even before the VooDoo and the nuclear Genie were considered, the RCAF had its eyes on another weapon. In July 1958, six months after it was cancelled by the US Navy, the RCAF was requesting atomic warheads for the Sparrow air-to-air missile.[2] Of course, this requirement fell through, and the Genie became the weapon of choice.

DOCUMENT # 1

17 May 1961, State Department, MEMCON, US Ambassador
Merchant and Prime Minister Diefenbaker.

> The Ambassador said that the United States'
> considered military judgement was that to make the
> transfer of these fighters currently in the USAF
> inventory and currently equipped with nuclear-tipped
> rockets would result in a degradation rather than an
> improvement of our air defenses if they were armed
> with conventional rockets.

The Genie was a part of the Canadian plan for nuclear-armed air
defence fighters from the beginning. In December 1960 Diefenbaker's
Minister of National Defence, Douglas Harkness, outlined the present
position of the Canadian government in respect to nuclear
commitments. He told Cabinet that Canada had accepted a nuclear
commitment for the CF-104 strike aircraft in Europe, for the Honest
John rocket battery in Europe, and for the BOMARC air defence
missile.[3] There was no special mention of the VooDoo-Genie weapon
system. However, Harkness did tell Cabinet that there might possibly
be a need for nuclear weapons "for fighter aircraft in Canada"[4] used
by the RCAF. The reason for this coy presentation by the Minister is
unclear, as in December 1959 he told the CDC that Cabinet had
already agreed to have military staff negotiate for the acquisition "of
MB-1 nuclear air-to-air rockets for use of the RCAF in Canada."[5]

In the end, three CF-101B VooDoo squadrons were armed with
the Genie air-to-air atomic 1.5 kt anti-bomber rocket, and on 29
September 1965[6] the VooDoo squadrons would become the last
operational units in the Canadian military to be armed with nuclear
weapons. Two Genies could be carried internally on the rotary bomb
bay/missile bay door under the CF-101B VooDoo interceptor aircraft.
This was the final type of US nuclear weapon to be brought to
Canadian soil, and the final one to be returned to the United States in
the spring and summer of 1984.[*]

Although the VooDoo-Genie system was Canada's longest serving
nuclear weapon system, the Canadian government, and particularly

---

* An anonymous source at NDHQ told the author on 14 Nov 84 that the last nuclear
weapons left Canada in July 1984, and that there had been 54 warheads for the Genie
stored at Comox and Bagotville. There were 24 warheads at Comox, the last base, at the
end of June 1984.

the military, were loathe to mention it. Official secrecy was pervasive, and even as late as 1982 the pretense of secrecy was upheld. When a member of Parliament, soon to be in attendance at the UN Disarmament Conference, asked about the VooDoo and Genie nuclear weapon: "are they on Canadian soil, or are these planes simply equipped to handle nuclear weapons?" General Ramsey Withers from National Defence Headquarters replied "Mr. Chairman, our policy is that we neither confirm nor deny the presence of nuclear weapons." All the bemused MP could do was thank the General.[7]*

THE ROCKET
The Genie AIR-2A unguided short-range nuclear capable rocket[8] was designed for strategic interception of Soviet bombers coming over the Atlantic/Pacific/Arctic oceans.

Thousands of Genies were produced prior to 1962; however, by 1983 there were only about 200 of these old nuclear weapons remaining in the US arsenal. Although the Genie was developed for Strategic Air Command (under the name MB-1), responsibility had moved to Air Defense Command by the time Canada acquired the weapon. The Genie was designed for automatic firing by the fire control system on a lead collision type of attack. This McDonnell-Douglas missile is made up of the warhead, the fuze assembly, the motor (complete with tail assembly), and the nose assembly.

Length	2.92 m
Diameter (max)	0.441 m
Weight (total)	377.8 kg
Throw-weight	approx. 68 kg

A Genie with a live W25 war reserve test warhead was fired and detonated at the Nevada Test Site, Indian Springs, Nevada, on 19 June 1957. Test "John" of Operation "Plumbbob" saw a Genie fired from a USAF F89J aircraft to a mid-air target 4.3 km away. The rocket covered the distance in 4.5 seconds, and the W25 warhead produced a nuclear yield of approximately 2 kt when it exploded at an altitude of 4500 m.

Capable of being carried in the missile bay of the CF-101B were the live Genie, the training rocket called ATR-2N, the simulator called ATR-2A, or the conventional trainer called ATR-2L. The rocket was considered very inaccurate, as it had no guidance system or

---

* However, in 1979 Tory Minister of National Defence Allan McKinnon stated that there were nuclear weapons in Comox, thus causing quite a stir.

fixed stabilizers. Flight times varied from between 4 and 12 seconds at ranges of 2.5 to 9.5 km at Mach 3. The Genie was originally known as High Card, Ding Dong, and the official "MB-1" designation. The rocket was designed to be fired automatically and detonated by the fire control system in the VooDoo. Canada was the only Allied user of this nuclear weapon system aside from the United States. Through the 1961 Canada-US reciprocal procurement deal to bring the VooDoo into Canadian service, Canada was to acquire 330 of the MB-1 Genie rockets with nuclear warheads.[9] Canada would pay $12.23 million for the Genies, four flight simulators and a mobile training unit.[10] A full war load of the W25/Genie on RCAF/CAF CF-101B VooDoos was two rockets carried inside the aircraft.

DOCUMENT # 2

15 September 1959, Letter to the Minister of National Defence from the Chairman, Chiefs of Staff, re: Storage of Defensive Nuclear Weapons at Goose Bay and Harmon Air Force Base. Top Secret.

MB-1 Air Defence Atomic Missile

1. The MB-1 is a long-range unguided rocket armed with an atomic warhead containing four major components.

2. The MB-1 rocket has no air-to-ground, ground-to-air or ground-to-ground applications; it is purely an air-to-air defensive weapon.

3. The MB1 is designed for automatic firing by the fire control system on a lead collision type of attack. The weapon can be carried externally on wing pylons or internally in a belly bay. It can be adapted for either ejection or rail launch. It can be completely assembled and checked in 30 minutes.

4. Safety Features — The missile has the following safety features:

(a) In Storage — The individual components are physically separate in storage so that an accidental explosion cannot occur.

(b) Installed on the Aircraft —

(i) Prior to Take-Off — Safety pins are installed in the warhead and in the rocket motor so that inadvertent launching and/or accidental explosion cannot occur.

(ii) After Take-Off — Final arming of the missile does not occur until after it is launched from the aircraft. After launch the missile must first accelerate and then decelerate and then continue on course for a finite time before detonation can occur. It is this feature which permits the missile to be jettisoned safely in flight.

(c) The weapon will not be employed against targets less than 5000 feet above terrain.

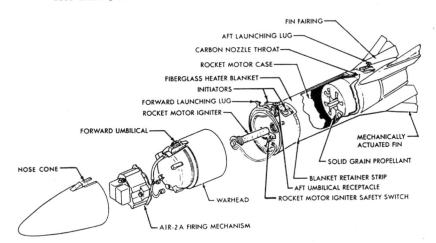

DIAGRAM #1
AIR-2A Genie Rocket, break-away view.

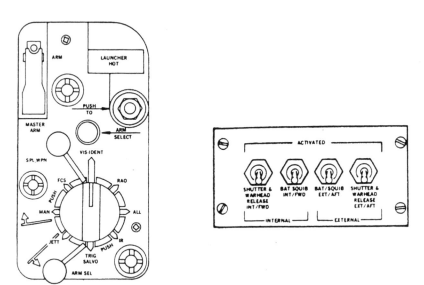

DIAGRAM #2
AIR-2A Genie armament control panel in VooDoo.

THE W25 NUCLEAR WARHEAD[11]

The Genie rocket carried the W25 nuclear warhead which had an explosive yield near 1.5 kt. Despite its small yield, the weapon was not to be employed against targets less than 1500 m above the ground. The warhead, or physics package, was designed by Los Alamos Laboratory, and the warhead was assembled between 1956 and 1962. W25 warheads had been designed and built exclusively as an air defence warhead for the Genie rocket. It was a combination plutonium-oralloy (Oak Ridge Alloy) fission weapon, probably containing Cyclotol (75% RDX) as the primary high explosive component.

Safeguarding features are still classified thirteen years after the W25's retirement, but we do know that the warhead was assembled too early to have included Permissive Action Link safety locks. Once the weapon was loaded into the aircraft and the safety pins were removed, it could be physically fired without further input. As one of the earliest of the new "sealed pit" or pressurized weapons, the W25 did not allow for automatic in-flight insertion of nuclear materials.

After 1958 the safety features included an early Environmental Sensing Device (ESD) for barometric pressure and an accelerometer. Only after readings consistent with high altitude flight had been registered by the ESD would it allow the arming of the warhead. A message to the Minister of National Defence confirmed that the W25 would also have to sense acceleration and then deceleration and continue on a flight path for a finite time before detonation was possible.[12] Declassified records now show that the two ESDs would have to record an acceleration of 28Gs, followed by a deceleration down to 15Gs. The warhead was transported in its H-490A shipping container, the bottom of which could be used as a transporter base without the top attached. The W25 could be assembled into the Genie rocket and checked for use in 30 minutes.

The W25 warhead, unlike all other weapons for the Canadian military, was built at the US Department of Energy's Burlington, Iowa, nuclear weapons assembly plant where some 3150 units of both the Mod 0 and Mod 1 were produced. All Mod 0 types were retired prior to the W25 entering Canadian service. Deployment of the W25 on the Genie began in 1957. Deployment of the W25/Genie on the VooDoo interceptor began after the USAF initiated the combination in 1959. The W25 was retired by the United States in November 1984 and final disassembly was done at Pantex in Texas in December 1984.

A properly cared for W25 had a reliability of 0.992 (high); and a properly-fired W25/Genie had a kill probability of 92%. This meant that with two W25/Genies per VooDoo the RCAF/CF was virtually assured of a hit and kill with a single interceptor, provided that the aircraft was well piloted.

All of the Canadian flight crews were instructed as to the reconfiguration of the weapons from "ferry" mode to armed mode. This was considered necessary, as it was thought that the crews might have to disperse to various locations with all of the weapons and no USAF technicians, but would have to carry them in an unarmed state. This meant that the pilot and navigator would have to crawl around underneath the VooDoo bomb bay, performing the delicate task of converting the W25 from the ferry to the armed condition.

The W25/Genie was a difficult weapon to use correctly. Only a very small envelope for the correct use of the weapon existed. Testing had revealed that an air defence nuclear weapon with a yield of less than 1 kt would not have a high enough yield to allow for a satisfactory kill radius (and therefore a larger allowable miss distance) at a range that would allow the interceptor aircraft time to escape after firing. The fighter would have to be so close to the bomber to ensure a near hit that the warhead could destroy the interceptor as well. The other end of the spectrum showed that yields above 2 kt would be lethal to the interceptor pilots at great distances and therefore also prohibitive. This all meant that the yield would have to be somewhere between 1.5 and 2 kt, and that the time of flight would have to be between four and five seconds. This envelope would allow the interceptor pilot to escape but still ensure a reasonable chance of destroying the bomber, crew, and bomb.

Nuclear blasts were not the big problem for the air defence pilots: nuclear *radiation* was the big problem. Testing had shown that a pilot would have to be at least 6.4 km away from the blast if a 2 kt device was detonated at 16 000 m to escape the lethal radiation. This distance dropped to only 3 km near sea level, but the corollary was that below 1000 m there was significant risk of residential damage from such a burst. However, environmental sensing devices were supposed to preclude such low-level detonations.

Another problem was that the US Air Force recognized that "the W25 was the most vulnerable of the Air Force's nuclear weapons to theft and full scale detonation."[13] This recognition led to increased security measures being taken, including the installation of the new PAVE SAFE preventive security system at the SAS, and the new deny/disable system for the warheads. However, as the USAF was uncertain as to the life expectancy of the F-101 aircraft (thinking them soon to be gone), the money was not spent on any of the Canadian sites.

The entire Genie/W25 combination was kept assembled in the SAS cells ready for transport and loading on a VooDoo in the QRA. It was common to keep two Genie/W25 units in a single SAS cell.

The W25 warheads were flown into the three VooDoo bases (Chatham, Bagotville, and Comox) and one deployment station (Val d'Or) by USAF transports. An exercise at CFS Val d'Or saw the unit practice to receive "4 Line One Items" from a nuclear resupply flight, leading to the possible conclusion that four W25 warheads were the number commonly resupplied to the VooDoo units and bases, or at least to the small detachment at Val d'Or. Records from CFB Bagotville indicate that two or three re-supply missions to remove older/time-expired warheads and bring in newly certified warheads was common.[14] Although lacking in context, it is worth noting that items were supplied to the SAS at Bagotville on both 10 January 1978 and 20 December 1978, and that there were three separate deliveries in 1983, the last full year of operation. This seems to demonstrate that there were two to three resupply missions per year. However, it is equally, if not more important to note that between 1981 and 1984 there were no new warheads supplied to CFB Comox. It is therefore likely that the resupply missions mentioned were only of non-war reserve items needed by the USAF detachment, and not of warheads. The final removal of all of the 24 or so warheads from Comox in 1984 seems to have taken place on two or three C-130 Hercules flights.

Detailed records[15] of a loading exercise at Val d'Or show the timing involved in the provision, loading and off-loading of a Genie rocket.

Tarmac Load Exercise
TIME ACTION
19:24 Convoy in progress
19:28 Convoy at QRA
19:51 Upload complete

20:15 Download complete
20:25 Convoy in progress
20:28 Convoy

From the time the convoy carrying the Genie arrived at the QRA, it took 23 minutes to place the rocket on the rotary bomb bay door under the VooDoo. It then took another 24 minutes to off-load the weapon and prepare it to be returned to the SAS.

THE ARROW, THE VooDoo, AND THE QRA

The Genie had originally been considered as the primary weapon for the Canadian A.V. Roe Company's new fighter/interceptor aircraft, the CF-105 Arrow. In an attack on the former Progressive Conservative Government of John Diefenbaker, Pearson stated that the nuclear commitment had been made after the destruction of the Arrow, and that "when the Arrow was constructed it was not suggested by those in charge at the time that the Arrow should carry nuclear weapons at all."[16] Again Prime Minister Pearson is guilty of significantly stretching the truth. As the document below shows, those in authority at National Defence were certainly thinking in terms of a nuclear Arrow.

DOCUMENT # 3
RCAF Programme of Activities, 1958–1962. Secret, Appendix D, Missiles and Weapons. Secret.

> Nuclear. The use of atomic warheads on air defence missiles would increase greatly their air defence operational effectiveness. The introduction of the MB1 as an air defence weapon for the Arrow is being studied.
> Unapproved

However, cancellation of the Arrow left Canada searching for a new all-weather fighter/interceptor. The offer by the US of the F-101 VooDoo still meant that the Genie might see Canadian service, as the VooDoo was considered most effective when utilizing the W25/Genie weapon. The Genie had almost been forgotten until the VooDoo appeared on the scene. Diefenbaker and his government approved the purchase of the VooDoo aircraft on 06 December 1960, but there was no talk of nuclear weapons at this time. However, the military was certainly not going to pass up the opportunity to arm their new aircraft with the nuclear Genie, and had begun planning for that weapon's arrival in Canada. At the time, there were still five full air defence bases scheduled to get the VooDoo, and by extension, the Genie. The RCAF planned to equip all the sites with the necessary facilities.

DOCUMENT # 4
Major RCAF Programs, prepared 29 June 1962, Vol 2. Program No. 11. Secret.

> Program: Quick Reaction Alert Facilities
>
> The construction of these facilities in Air Defence Command at RCAF Stations Bagotville, Chatham, Comox, North Bay, Uplands and Val d'Or, is essential to satisfy a requirement to provide facilities where aircraft armed with special weapons can be positioned and maintained on an alert status, while maintaining the security control demanded of the USAF custodial conditions.
>
> Total estimated cost of construction (of 6 QRA facilities and 5 fire hall extensions/constructions) is $2 162 300.00

DOCUMENT # 5
Major RCAF Programs, 04 December 1962, Vol 2. Program No. 10. Secret.

> Program: Special Ammunition Storage (SAS)
>
> 1. As a result of the Cabinet's decision of 06 Dec 60, to provide facilities for the possible acquisition of special weapons, and the introduction of the CF101B in the RCAF, a requirement exists to provide RCAF Stations Bagotville, Chatham, Comox, North Bay, Uplands and Val d'Or with special armament storage facilities to accommodate the ready-use weapon loads required by CF101 aircraft and to provide these bases with facilities for security control of such weapons.
>
> 2. The following cost of constructing the above facilities is as follows:

STATION	COST
Bagotville	$730 000.00
Chatham	$737 000.00
Comox	$803 000.00
Val d'Or	$754 000.00

[author's note: figures for North Bay and Uplands have been removed as the QRA/SAS sites were not completed for Canadian nuclear use]

CF-101B VooDoo

The McDonnell-Douglas VooDoo aircraft acquired by Canada, the CF-101B, was used as a long-range strategic bomber-interceptor and armed with nuclear air defence weapons for that task. Powered by two J57-PW-55 turbojet engines, the CF-101B could reach speeds of close to Mach 1.85 and fly 2500 km. The aircraft was 20.52 m in length and 5.48 m high, and had a wingspan of 12.05 m. This extremely heavy interceptor had a gross takeoff weight of 21.18 tonnes which tended to channel a great deal of pressure down through the four small wheels. The armament was carried both inside and out of the aircraft, with the conventional missiles recessed on the bottom of the VooDoo below the cockpit, and the nuclear Genie carried inside the bomb-bay on the rotating bomb-bay door.

The Canadian VooDoos came in two batches. The first of 66 aircraft arrived at CFB Namao, Alberta in October 1961. During their 10 year life with the Canadian forces, seven of the aircraft would be lost in crashes by the operational squadrons. In 1971, under Operation "Peace Wings", the USAF took back the remaining 56 aircraft and gave the CAF 66 newer VooDoos in return. These new VooDoos had been built between 1956 and 1957, but had remained in long-term storage and had very low hours on them. Pursuant to a Cabinet decision,[17] the 56 VooDoos in operational use were reduced to 44 aircraft. This decision would be reflected in the reduced squadron sizes, and in the denuclearization of CFB Chatham. Of the new aircraft, the three operational squadrons would crash 12 over the next 13 years: five from 409 Comox, four from 416 Chatham, and three from 425 Bagotville. By 1984 there were only 11 or 12 operational VooDoos in each of 409 and 425 squadrons, and 14 at 416 Squadron in Chatham.

AIR DEFENCE COMMAND

Air Defence Command (ADC) — formed at St. Hubert, Quebec, but moved to North Bay in August 1966 — was the military command responsible for the units in Canada having access to nuclear weapons. Both the BOMARC and the VooDoo/Genie were ADC weapons systems. The RCAF Air Defence Command had five VooDoo squadrons on alert in 1961, and three on alert in 1964–65 when the Genie/W25 was deployed.

The BOMARC system had come online with few problems, but that would not be the case with the VooDoo/Genie. The RCAF had signed a single service-to-service technical arrangement for the provision of warheads and support for both the BOMARC and the Genie, and therefore expected that as soon as one was in place, the other would proceed apace. But problems at the VooDoo squadrons left them unarmed with the for almost a year and a half after the arming of the BOMARCs.

Although it was realized that there were a number of deficiencies in the VooDoo/Genie programme, RCAF and USAF commanders decided to proceed with the Initial Capability Inspection at Station Comox on 15 December 1964. A total of eleven "limiting factors" for the base, the squadron, and the custodian forced the inspectors to conclude that Comox was "NOT READY" to receive nuclear weapons. With this disaster under their belt, the RCAF withdrew Bagotville and Chatham from the ICI schedule until full logistic and administrative support for the programme could be assured.[18]

After a great deal of work, the three VooDoo squadrons were brought up to standards acceptable to the USAF inspectors. Following another series of capability inspections and tactical evaluations which established each unit's operational capability, 409, 416, and 425 AW(F) (All-Weather [Fighter]) squadrons assumed a nuclear weapons quick reaction alert posture on 25 September 1965.[19] The final nuclear weapons site at Val d'Or, Quebec was finally accepted as "satisfactory" and became operational in February 1966.[20]

NORAD AND AUTHORIZATION

Like the BOMARC, the CF-101 squadrons fell under the operational control of the bi-national North American Air Defence Command HQ in the United States. Instructions on the use of the BOMARCs in an intercept mode would be issued from NORAD HQ in

Colorado Springs, or by the subordinate headquarters of 22nd NORAD Region at North Bay.

Authorization for the use of nuclear weapons by the Canadian VooDoo squadrons would come to the alert bases through two separate streams of the NORAD communications system. First, the USAF detachment had to receive authorization through US channels to release the weapons according to an order of the US National Command authority. In later years the US detachments would receive their orders from CINCNORAD through the Canadian base communications centre, thereby eliminating the secondary channel. The message was received by the one USAF Emergency Action Officer, and confirmed by a second Emergency Action Officer who was regularly tasked with other duties. At the same time CINCNORAD would be generating a high state of alert, and the nuclear-armed aircraft would be prepared for take-off.

Through Canadian channels, the Canadian commander at Northern NORAD Region (NNR) in the command centre (The Hole) at North Bay would transmit the Canadian authorization for the use of nuclear weapons to the various bases in Canada. Prior to the creation of Northern NORAD Region from 22nd NORAD Region, and greater Canadian control, this national authorization would have come from the NORAD Deputy Commander (who is always a Canadian) in NORAD Headquarters inside Cheyenne Mountain, Colorado Springs, Colorado. All Canadian communications would be received at the base through a secure telex system, and it is thought that such a system was also used by the US detachments in the early years. The messages arrived as a coded stream, and had to be decoded by their recipients. The message for the US detachment would note that CINCNORAD had authorized the use of nuclear weapons and then give some details.

After receiving these authorizations the war reserve W25/Genies would be loaded on the aircraft in a mass load setting and the aircraft directed to take off. With no PAL locks, the W25/Genie was armed once it was placed in the aircraft in a non-ferry configuration. The final check on its use was a two-man cockpit system involving the pilot and navigator. The two men would receive the final "go" code over the radio, and then each would independently break open a small plastic container they carried in their flight suit. If each man confirmed that the number in their sealed plastic container, the

CIS/24/51 matched the incoming "go" code, then they would proceed to use their two Genies if the target appeared. Each man had a physical veto over the firing, and both had to give consent for the ultimate use of the weapons in the bomb bay.

Formed in 1957 to protect the North American land-mass from a Soviet bomber attack, NORAD shrunk in importance as the threat of Soviet bombers receded through the 1960s. By 1974, the USAF ADC was fielding only 132 Unit Authorized (UA) aircraft, and Canada was fielding 48 VooDoos. There were 18 aircraft with each of 416 and 425 AW(F) Squadrons, and 12 aircraft at 409 AW(F) Squadron.[21] However, later duties included early warning of ballistic missile attack and possible coordination of ballistic missile defence efforts.

Notable NORAD incidents involving Canadian units armed with nuclear weapons included two rather serious alerts: one accidental, and one political. On 09 November 1979 a computer chip failure at the NORAD command post in Cheyenne Mountain, Colorado Springs. caused an increase in the alert level in anticipation of a Soviet bomber and missile attack. Canadian VooDoo units were generated to a higher alert posture. Another equally as frightening incident occurred in 1973 when US president Richard Nixon put all NORAD forces on a DefCon 3 alert level during another of the middle east crises. This NORAD action generated a response at various Canadian bases as the readiness posture was increased. The Canadian government moved quickly, and the three squadrons were returned to a normal alert state in a few hours.

INITIAL WARHEAD ARRIVAL

Although the Service-to-Service Supplementary Arrangement for the Genie had been made in October 1963, the Genie only reached operational status in June 1965.

RCAF Air Defence Command had been planning for nuclear weapons since the late 1950s, when they originally considered equipping the ill-fated Avro Arrow with two missiles per fighter. However, the early deployment of nuclear weapons in Canada after the agreement was signed was killed by the inability of the VooDoo squadrons and supporting bases to pass the rigorous US Air Force Inspector General's Initial Capability Inspection and Nuclear Safety Inspection. When the first squadron and base failed, the other two were removed from the inspection schedule. The idea that an initial "failure" was a standard procedure to curb complacency and underscore the seriousness of the task is belied by the fact that all previous Canadian nuclear weapons units passed the ICI on the first try.

When the RCAF finally did pass the required inspections, the deliveries to the three RCAF ADC Stations took place in May 1965, and all deliveries were completed before 01 June 1965.[22] In the House of Commons there was the almost inevitable question about the nuclear status of the VooDoo units. An MP stood up and asked the Minister of National Defence Paul Hellyer if the squadrons had become operational "in terms of being equipped with nuclear missiles". Hellyer, in what was called a smart-alec reply in the House of Commons, stated: "That is a fair interpretation."[23]

The fourth VooDoo/Genie site, used by 425 Squadron from Bagotville, received its nuclear weapons by air delivery at the end of November 1965. However, these weapons were kept locked in the SAS as Station Val d'Or was not considered satisfactory for the full operational deployment of nuclear-armed alert aircraft.[24]

W25 NUCLEAR WARHEAD ARRIVAL & DEPARTURE DATES

Base/Station	Arrival	Departure
Chatham	01–31 May 65	31 Mar–03 Apr 75
Comox	01–31 May 65	25–29 Jun 84
Bagotville	01–31 May 65	12–19 Apr 84
Val d'Or	23–30 Nov 65	15 Apr 75

CF-101B VOODOO/GENIE UNITS, SITES, OPERATIONAL DATES

Sqdn	Base/Station	Operational Dates
409	Comox	01 Jun 65–25 Jun 84
416	Chatham	01 Jun 65–31 Mar 75
425	Bagotville	01 Jun 65–11 Apr 84
425	Val d'Or	15 May 70–31 Mar 75

CFB COMOX

Comox was Canada's only nuclear weapons site west of Ontario. Although originally under the jurisdiction of Maritime Air Command, the station was transferred to Air Defence Command on 01 June 1964 to facilitate the acceptance of nuclear weapons by 409

AW(F) Squadron. Under Department of National Defence reorganization, RCAF Station Comox became CFB Comox on 13 April 1966.

Comox officials knew that their station and 409 Squadron would be the first to undergo the rigorous Initial Capability Inspection, and feverish preparations were made. Fifty-five airmen from the site were given nuclear weapons loading courses,* and security forces worked with the USAF custodians at the SAS and QRA compounds. With the completion of the SAS compound on 24 September 1964, and the completion of the QRA facility on 20 October 1964, the units seemed ready for the ICI.

The five-day Initial Capability Inspection began 14 December 1964 as a team from USAFHQ, USAF ADCHQ, CFHQ, RCAF ADCHQ, and 425 MMS arrived. The ICI was failed, and Comox did not receive nuclear weapons. The inspection regime revealed 11 limiting factors for the custodial unit, the base and the squadron, and ADCHQ choose to withdraw the two other VooDoo bases and squadrons from the inspection schedule. In fairness, however, it must be said that 8 of the limiting factors were judged against the custodial detachment.[25] The next six months were spent preparing all three sites for the repeat ICIs in the summer of 1965. When the ICI was finally passed that summer, Detachment 5 of the USAF 425th Munitions Maintenance Squadron was authorized to give full nuclear support to Comox.

Within months of the arrival of nuclear weapons, protesters were at the gates. At the end of August, a peaceful sit-in was violently broken up by RCAF military police and the RCMP. Non-participating witnesses said that the RCMP was arresting some people even before the protesters had taken any actions.[26] Despite some outcry, the nuclear weapons would stay in place until the summer of 1984. A few days before this incident, RCN sailors from HMCS Antigonish attacked peaceful protesters, destroyed their banner, and stole and destroyed personal property held by the group.[27] Officers present at the scene refused to restrain the men under their command, leading many observers to conclude that the entire incident may have taken place with the approval of the Comox base commander and the high command in Ottawa.

---

* A rocket is unguided, whereas a missile is guided.

At the end of 1984, after the departure of 409 Squadron, Detachment 5, and 60% of the base armament personnel, Comox was closing buildings and becoming a nuclear ghost town. The final report of the nuclear years notes with pride that Comox "was the last unit in Canada to have the vast responsibility for the direct security of nuclear weapons and components."[28]

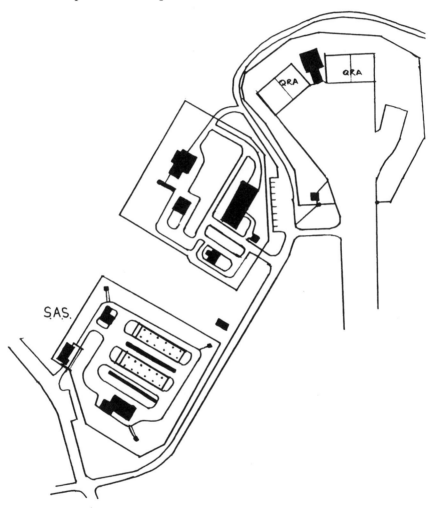

DIAGRAM #3
CFB Comox QRA and SAS.

409 ALL WEATHER FIGHTER SQUADRON

The 409 "Nighthawk" All Weather Fighter Squadron based at Comox flew the CF-101B VooDoo under the motto "Media nox meridles Noster" or "Midnight is our noon."

The unit converted to the VooDoo at Station Namao under the guidance of 425 Squadron from 05 February to 13 March 1962. It then moved into its permanent home at Comox in March 1962. After a considerable period of preparation — and one failed Initial Capability Inspection — the squadron stood alert in September 1965. For nearly 20 years 409 Squadron would have basically the same routine of alerts and exercises and springtime capability inspections.

There were opportunities to fire a live rocket whenever the unit sent a team to the annual William Tell air weapons competition in Florida, or when there were weapons tests in Canada. During two weeks in mid-September 1968 a CF-101B and crew were sent to the Cold Lake firing range to participate in the "CF-101B/AIR-2A Compatibility Verification Programme," which involved a number of live firings. The squadron was also noted for having won first place in the F-101/Genie weapons loading competition at William Tell 1970, and "the 409 team took an early lead in the competition with the spectacular achievement in successfully firing eight AIR-2A rockets in eight consecutive attempts."[29]

The following year was important for the aircraft fleet. In March 1971, serious engine flaws grounded the fleet. Then, in August and September, the entire fleet of CF-101s was flown to the US under the "Peace Wings" exchange programme with USAF. The USAF wanted to re-acquire the VooDoos they had originally supplied to Canada for their own use in Viet Nam, and were willing to exchange a newer model with infrared scopes for the older ones. Canada accepted the offer.

It seemed that Comox and 409 Squadron were plagued with certification problems. After the first ICI failure in 1964, one would expect that the units involved would be slightly more careful, yet in August 1973 it failed the Alert Force Capability Test (AFCT). They were able to recover from this setback, however, and the AFCT was successfully repeated in November. One year later, in November 1974, a no-notice QRA evaluation was sprung on the base. The squadron passed.

Less-than-stellar evaluations did not dampen the spirits of the unit, and it continued to participate in various exercises, and even fared well when representing Canada at various annual William Tell competitions. During June 1980 the squadron was able to fire six of the few remaining practice Genie rockets in Exercise Combat Pike at Tyndall AFB in the United States.

Due to both financial considerations, and the ongoing denuclearization of the Canadian Forces, 409 would be reduced in size and commitment over the years. The most dramatic change took place in January 1975 when Minister of National Defence James Richardson cut the number of aircraft at each VooDoo/Genie squadron and reduced the number of available aircrew. In addition, changes to the NORAD requirements meant that as of 01 April 1975, "the normal Alfa readiness posture for CF ADC was two conventionally-armed double-tanked interceptors on 5-minute alert" at the three bases.[30] The VooDoos were also equipped with two conventionally armed Falcon infrared missiles on the outside of the missile bay door.

The unit stood its last QRA on 28 June 1984, likely the last day nuclear weapons would have been present at Comox.

DULL SWORD

Like the other nuclear units, 409 would, from time-to-time, have a small accident. The document below is the finest example of a Dull Sword report currently available, and has therefore been included in this collection. It is worth noting that although the Genie in question appears to be an ATR-2L training rocket, the incident was considered serious enough for a Dull Sword report. It is instructive to note that the rocket was then returned to the SAS for a full check and re-certification.

DOCUMENT # 6
29 September 1967, 1850z, from CANFORBASE Comox, to RCCWC/ CANFORCEHED.
DULL SWORD — DULL SWORD.
    A 27 Sep 1855 zulu
    B Combat turnaround position number 9
    C ATR-2L trainer
    D 409 Squadron, CFB Comox ADC
    E Loading — Combat turnaround training
    F During loading operation steps 1 to 56 as per TO-1F-101B-16-2CL-1 had been completed. As C man commenced lowering of MF9 trailer lift arm, the weapon separated from the rack. Downward motion of lift arm was too rapid, and as a result the starboard

motor igniter lanyard was pulled before movement of the weapon could be arrested. However, lanyards did not separate from the weapon. Switch assy motor initiating, FSN-1340-00-672-1147 was replaced after a complete motor check had been carried out by SAS Maintenance. Weapon returned to storage as serviceable. MB1 rack inspection revealed it to be serviceable. Repeat loadings with inert weapon indicated no mechanical malfunctions.

Probable cause of incident.
1. Load crew error — Failure to ensure that rack was properly locked.
2. Main cause was failure of "C" man to comply with cautionary note in EO-05-185A-2NAB, Section III, step 28 (third caution).

Corrective action taken.
1. C man decertified.
2. Retraining and recertification of crew man to be carried out.
Load crews briefed on reason for cautionary note in T.O.

One of the only two bits of verbal artistry associated with Canada's nuclear weapons deployments came out of the Dull Sword and Broken Arrow exercises which were regularly held. The following poem, written by Airman 1st Class Gunn was dedicated to "all the stalwarts who are involved in this nefarious affair, and particularly to the chaps in Air Defence Command who contributed so much to the thoughts expressed therein."

Broken Arrow
The alarm had sounded, loud and clear,
To warm the chaps who were drinking beer
That a Broken Arrow was about to occur
Out on the airfield, I do aver.
As planned the response was quick and fast
Particularly by the boys in NAST

Who had trained and trained, then trained again
In doing their job, (except in the rain).
 At the incident scene the Controller was there,
Waving a flag, high in the air,
The firemen too were right at home
Fighting the fire (will they run out of foam?).
 The fire chief ordered the crew to withdraw
At just the right time, when a "torching" he saw:
All are accounted for in the hasty retreat
(But how about the man overcome by the heat?).
 A job for the check point, this surely is,
(Check each man through, know where he is.).
 The EOD first enters the scene
To clear the path of hazards unseen,
And then the Radmons, with PAC-IS
(Is their training sufficient to cope with the mess?).
 The alpha probe must be placed with care
Close to the surface, which may be bare
Of obstructions and points which damage the face
And punch small holes in the wrong place.
 "There's a high reading! A million 'Cs'",
And here we are, a long way down breeze.
It may be a hole letting in light
(Can the monitor check it to make sure it's right?)
 There is a hole, and we need a new face,
(Are they at the scene, or back at base?)
The On-Scene Controller is waiting for news
From the Radmons as the ground they peruse,
But no word he gets of the rad situation
(The 510s are good, but they're back at the Station).
 For hours and hours everyone waits,
It's almost time to change the dates
But then comes the Radmons with the information
Needed to restore the sad situation.
 Time to clean up and vacate directly,
So back to the hot-line, and undress correctly,
(Can they do it alone, they need help they say)
Should have thought of that — another delay.

Now they need water, and lots of it too
(For those who are scaled-Vehicle type 62)
Will help with the problem of cleaning the decks,
And runways and buildings, and faces and necks.
Bins for disposal, and bags for waste,
Some borrowed, some stolen, some gathered in haste;
Clearly the need can be seen in advance
(Then why must it wait? Why take a chance?).
Some wait for an issue, some bemoan their lot
While others know they must use what they've got.
So on with the job, and start to train,
For those Bs at Command will be back again!

DETACHMENT 5

Based at CFB Comox, Detachment 5 of the USAF 425 Munitions Maintenance Squadron supported 409 AW(F) Squadron beginning in 1965. This was the only USAF unit handling nuclear weapons on the west coast of Canada, and it was fully operational until the nuclear commitment was ended in 1984. Evidence indicates that the last 24 or so weapons left the base in the latter half of June. The last commanding officer, Major Ron Carlson, left Comox on 11 July following a 10–14 day cleanup period after the weapons had been shipped out. This would place the removal of the W25 warheads from the Comox SAS between Monday the 25th and Friday the 29th. The official history of the base shows that the security section was fully active until 01 July 1984,[31] and then dramatically reduced.

There are conflicting stories of the final removal of the W25s. Most seem to recall that the weapons were airlifted out of Comox on board a single flight of a specially-equipped C-141 Starlifter from Scott AFB to the nuclear weapons storage facilities inside the Sandia Mountains at Kirtland AFB in New Mexico. However, another recalls that the warheads may have left on two or three C-130 "Hercules" flights out of McChord AFB in Washington state and headed to either Kirtland AFB in New Mexico, or directly to Amarillo, Texas, and their ultimate destruction at the Pantex atomic weapons assembly and disassembly plant. The only mention of the detachment leaving in the base newspaper is a banner on the back page wishing them farewell on 28 June 1984.[32]

Under the command of Major R.L. Crutchfield, 6 officers and 35 other ranks saw the full activation of their unit when the alert facilities became operational on 30 September 1965.[33] Under the command of Major Carlson, Detachment 5 entered history as the last nuclear support unit in Canada.

In its latter years, the detachment had a total of about 48–50 staff, with seven or eight of them being officers. There were two safety staff, a maintenance team of seven or eight, and a quality assurance team of two. Most of the staff were assigned as custodial agents and security police, as there would have to be two custodial agents with each warhead when it was removed from the SAS. When the aircraft underwent a Mass Load, there would need to be two custodial agents for each weapon until the aircraft had been completely loaded and the Genies safely ensconced inside the bomb bays of the VooDoos. At this point two custodial agents could care for all the units loaded into the closely situated aircraft.

CFB CHATHAM

RCAF Station Chatham in New Brunswick was the second VooDoo operating base in eastern Canada. Supporting 416 AW(F) Squadron, Chatham accepted the completed SAS facilities and the new QRA buildings on 7 and 14 October 1964 respectively. Although the buildings were not completed until October 1964, by April 1963 a quantity of Genie rockets were already stored in the "O"-type weapons storage building. Although Comox and Bagotville were ahead of Chatham on the inspection schedule, Chatham became the first VooDoo base to be certified to load operational nuclear weapons on the aircraft.[34]

The nuclear commitment at CFB Chatham was the shortest of any of the three VooDoo bases. For various reasons both in Canada and especially in the US, the Genie nuclear commitment was being scaled back in the mid-1970s. The USAF was disenchanted with the crude Genie and had already developed far more advanced conventional and nuclear air-to-air missiles such as the nuclear Falcon and conventional Sidewinder. Chatham was then chosen to be stripped of its nuclear weapons. On 18 March 1975 the base practiced for a Dangerous Cargo Movement, and a base Nuclear Accident Response Exercise (NAREX) was held. Two weeks later, the joint Canada-US "Operation Starlifter" saw the removal of the 24–30 or so remaining W25 nuclear weapons from the Chatham SAS bunkers.[35] With the weapons gone, the US flag over the SAS at Chatham was lowered for the final time on 30 June 1975, as detachment commander Captain Ernest Daniels and the remainder of his unit prepared to leave.

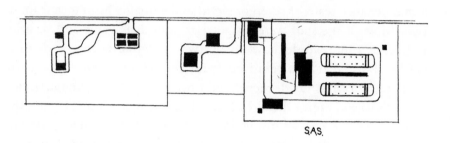

DIAGRAM #4
CFB Chatham SAS.

416 ALL WEATHER FIGHTER SQUADRON

The "Black Lynx" squadron was formed at Station Bagotville on 01 January 1962. They converted to VooDoos under 425 tutelage at Station Namao in January, and from February through July were based at Uplands in Ottawa. They then moved to Bagotville for the July through November 1962 period, finally settling at Chatham in November. The crews first scrambled on 05 July 1962 in what turned out to be a test. Days later they would put a VooDoo in the air in 1 minute 30 seconds to intercept a USAF SAC B-52 bomber.[36] Soon they would be regularly intercepting Lufthansa flights and other stray airliners coming over from Europe. The unit moved to Station Chatham on 16 November 1962, but would not receive nuclear weapons until May 1965. A Tactical Evaluation test on 28 January 1964 would have both alert aircraft airborne within three minutes.

Although based at Chatham, the squadron moved about quite a bit. In July 1968 they were deployed to Bangor, Maine while the Chatham airport was refinished. Then in the summer of 1972 the whole squadron stood alert at Val d'Or as their home runways were being repaired. This happened again the following summer, causing the unit to move to Shearwater, Nova Scotia.[37]

In 1971 the unit exchanged all its VooDoos for new USAF VooDoos under the "Peace Wings" programme, but this did not affect the nuclear alert status.

416 Lynx, along with 425 at Bagotville, was originally formed as an 18 aircraft unit establishment, tasked with having two VooDoo on 5-minute alert, and two VooDoos on 15-minute alert. Financial considerations at NDHQ led to the 10% reduction in all flying time, and the requirement that the 15-minute alert become a one-hour alert. After two years this was accepted by NORAD and written into the NORAD regulations.[38]

On 17 January 1975, the Minister of National Defence announced that for economic reasons the number of operational CF-101B VooDoos would be cut from 56 to 44 within a few months. This meant that 416 would be reduced by 6 VooDoos and 20 aircrew. Later that year, with no warheads at Chatham, and one-third fewer aircraft and crews, 416 managed to pass their Tactical Evaluation on 02 October 1975.

During what was probably their final QRA scramble of the nuclear period, two conventionally armed VooDoos were sent aloft on 23 September 1974 to find and intercept a large four-engined propellor-driven aircraft (which would have appeared much like the Soviet long-range air force Tu-95 bomber). What the pilots found was a distressed C-121 Super Constellation cargo aircraft near Sable Island.

Because they did not have nuclear weapons of their own, 416 had to rely on CFB Bagotville across the Quebec/New Brunswick border for their nuclear support. On a regular basis aircraft from Chatham would proceed in groups of three or four to Bagotville for the "inevitable" Mass Load exercises and checks.[39]

Despite having lost their nuclear weapons in the mid-1970s, 416 was the last squadron to operate the CF-101B as an interceptor. This last operational VooDoo squadron ceased operations on at 21:00 GMT, 31 December 1984.

DETACHMENT 4

Based at CFB Chatham, Detachment 4, whose motto was "Up First," supported 416 AW(F) Squadron beginning in April 1965. Although formed at Chatham in late 1964,[40] lack of authorization for the deployment of nuclear weapons kept the unit idle. Full nuclear support was only provided after the Inspector General's nine day visit, 18–27 July 1965, which cleared the way for the operational deployment of the warheads.[41]

This was the shortest-lived Genie support detachment, as the Chatham nuclear storage site was emptied in April 1975, and the last representative of the detachment departed his quarters in the SAS compound on 30 June 1975. Although not long-lived, the detachment did manage to be awarded the USAF Outstanding Unit Award three times.[42]

During their 10 years at Chatham, Detachment 4 donated close to 2000 books to the base library. However, when the news came that they were leaving, the base library was told to prepare all books donated by the detachment for immediate shipment.[43] It is likely that these instructions came not from the detachment, but from National Defence Headquarters in Ottawa.

If 416 AW(F) Squadron required access to the W25/Genie, they would fly to Bagotville and be armed by Detachment 3.

CFB BAGOTVILLE

The SAS bunkers at CFB Bagotville were the second-last places in which the Canadian military had nuclear weapons. After spending $903 954.25 on the SAS and QRA facilities, CFB Bagotville was physically ready to store and deploy nuclear weapons.[44] The W25 warheads for the Genie rockets arrived at Bagotville between 25 May and 01 June 1965,[45] thus paving the way for 425 Squadron to stand QRA.

Aside from having to support a full squadron on site, Bagotville also assisted the alert site at Val d'Or, Quebec, which was assigned to cover the Ottawa region. Sometimes the nuclear certified personnel were called upon to serve at other locations. OPLAN 3000, a NORAD document, called for Bagotville to send a nuclear weapons loading crew to CFB North Bay to support the forward deployment of the USAF 147 Fighter Interceptor Group under Operation Limp Hand or Chess Set, and to support VooDoos sent to North Bay from Bagotville.

In the spring of 1984 Mobile Command soldiers from CFB Valcartier moved up to Bagotville to provide a security force for the final removal of the Genie warheads from the SAS facility. This final nuclear support operations occurred between 12 and 19 April 1984, when their last W25 warheads were removed.[46] All base security personnel were used to ensure the secure transfer of nuclear weapons from the SAS to the waiting USAF transporter. With the final weapon gone, and after close to 20 years of uninterrupted nuclear security duties, the Central Security Control site was closed, and all nuclear-related security work was terminated. Most of the combat arms personnel used as SAS and QRA guards were then transferred to CFB Valcartier.[47]

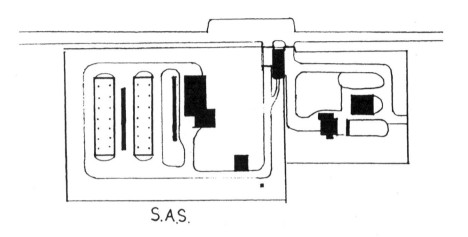

S.A.S.

DIAGRAM #5
CFB Bagotville SAS.

425 ALL WEATHER FIGHTER SQUADRON

"Les Alouettes" Squadron, flying under the motto "Je Te Plumerai" ("I Shall Pluck You") was reformed in the summer of 1962 after converting to VooDoos at Station Namao in October 1961. They arrived at Bagotville, their permanent home, on 10 July 1962. They became the first operational squadron, without nuclear weapons, on 01 October 1962, and spent their first operational month in a state of high alert due to the Cuban missile crisis.[48] 425 was the only nuclear unit in Canada to be visited by the man responsible for bringing nuclear weapons to the Canadian military, Prime Minister Pearson.[49]

425 AW(F) Squadron had to be in two places at once, as they were responsible for providing the VooDoos and crew to operate at CFS Val d'Or in northern Quebec. To accomplish this the unit was divided into four operational flights and one Z flight (Command).

Each operational flight alternated one week on Bagotville alert then one week on Val d'Or alert, and then the third week at other duties and training. This meant that there would be 4 aircraft on alert at Bagotville and two on alert at Val d'Or. Between 01 July and 07 October 1974, 425 had to deploy every VooDoo they had, and many more Genies, to Val d'Or as the runways at Bagotville were undergoing repair. One can only conclude that the Val d'Or SAS site had never seen so many nuclear weapons.

As one of the two squadrons originally formed as an 18-aircraft unit establishment, 425 was tasked with having two VooDoo on 5-minute alert, and two VooDoos on 15-minute alert. However, in September 1972 CF ADC lowered the two 15-minute alert aircraft requirements to one-hour alert status due to a directive to reduce the monthly flying rate at all squadrons by 10%. This short term action was extended indefinitely in 1973. To make the situation appear better, NDHQ appealed to CINCNORAD to change the requirements for alert posture at 18 UE squadrons to the new Canadian reality of two aircraft at five minutes and two aircraft at one hour. In February 1974 CINCNORAD concurred.[50]

THE FOUR FLIGHT SYSTEM

FLIGHT	WEEK 1	WEEK 2	WEEK 3	WEEK 4
A	FLYING DUTIES	EXTRA DUTIES	VAL D'OR ALERT	OFF
B	OFF	FLYING DUTIES	EXTRA DUTIES	VAL D'OR ALERT
C	VAL D'OR ALERT	OFF DUTIES	FLYING DUTIES	EXTRA
D	EXTRA DUTIES	VAL D'OR ALERT	OFF	FLYING DUTIES
Z	ADMINISTRATION, OPERATIONS, TRAINING, BACK-UP			

With both the squadron and CFB Bagotville holding an important position as the nuclear support site for two squadrons and a northern alert location, inspections and exercises were very important. In October 1979 the Alert Force Capability Test (AFCT) took many personnel by surprise as a Mass Load was being conducted at the same time.[51]

The squadron was cut by half on Canada Day, 01 July 1982.[52] Flying under the new Operation "Cold Shaft", 425 started holding one hour alerts instead of the previous five-minute alerts. They also continued to provide the nuclear support for CFB Chatham, and would provide five-minute QRA if Chatham was fogged in, but were generally reduced to one-hour alerts until operations ended on 30 June 1984.

DETACHMENT 3

Based at CFB Bagotville, Detachment 3 supported the VooDoo-flying 425 AW(F) Squadron beginning in 1965.

This was the second longest serving USAF nuclear support unit in Canada. On 19 April 1984 the last member of Detachment 3 boarded a USAF transport and departed Bagotville.

DOCUMENT # 7
1964, Stn Bagotville Historical Report. Appendix. B, page 12, section 11, Detachment 3. Secret.

The mission of the detachment is to offer munitions support to the CF-101B aircraft. Initially much training had to be accomplished to familiarize the personnel on a weapon which in some cases was new to them. Training progressed slowly at first due to the non-availability of certain regulations, manuals, and pamphlets. The Security Maintenance and Loading sections were hampered in their training due to the fact that the SAS area had not been completed.

Problem areas encountered by this detachment could be divided into three areas.

(a) Non-availability of Air Force Manuals and Regulations.

(b) Completion dates of the SAS and QRA were rolled back several times.

(c) Non-availability of essential supplies (furniture, safes, locks).

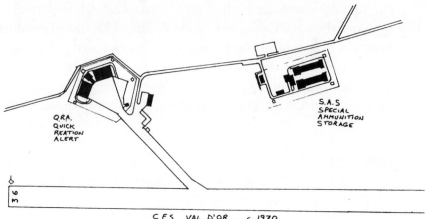

QRA.
QUICK
REATION
ALERT

S.A.S
SPECIAL
AMMUNITION
STORAGE

C.F.S. VAL D'OR , c. 1970.

DIAGRAM #6
CFS Val d'Or QRA and SAS.

CFS VAL d'OR

"As a flying unit with a nuclear capability, (and alert facilities) but no aircraft of its own, Station Val d'Or was unique in the RCAF."[53]

> "The initial concept required that the unit provide facilities for CF101B aircraft from Stn Bagotville to hold 5 minute and one hour readiness, plus a requirement for a nuclear weapon storage and handling capability. The monumental task facing all personnel was to transform a small detachment with negligible facilities into a fully operational unit with a nuclear capability, but having negligible facilities."[54]

The government had taken a lot of heat for its nuclear stand, and ministers were starting to lash out for lack of better arguments. When the member representing the Val d'Or region questioned the need for the nuclear weapons site, Minister of National Defence Hellyer suggested that this was a kind of gift to the constituency. He then sneered at the MP and called into question the member's commitment to his own constituents.[55] To add to the contempt shown, Hellyer later revealed that the local authorities had not been consulted at all about the nuclear deployments and the government's intention "to build storage facilities for special weapons" at Val d'Or.[56]

Various teams held Pre-Initial Capability Tests at Val d'Or on

8–12 February 1965, 25–28 May 1965, and 12–15 October 1965. The real ICI occurred on 31 October to 05 November 1965,[57] and "acquisition of nuclear warheads quickly followed."[58] The site was authorized to receive the nuclear warheads, but limiting factors prevented their operational deployment from Val d'Or. Due to lack of facilities for vehicles, ground equipment, and petroleum products, the warheads were being stored and maintained in one of the alert hangars. This created a potential fire and explosive safety hazard which prohibited loading and storage of primary armament in the QRA area.

The lack of a suitable separate maintenance hangar made it necessary to perform aircraft maintenance in one of the alert hangars, especially in the winter. These factors were enough to prevent the USAF from allowing the nuclear weapons to be used to the site.[59] The problem was that the RCAF had planned on only being able to reach full operating capacity with both the fighters and the number of nuclear weapons if they used Val d'Or.[60]

The RCAF high command had anticipated a failure at Val d'Or, and during the summer decided to emplace the Genie warheads at the site in an interim "storage only"[61] posture. Therefore, the primary weapons capability would initially be limited to storage of a full complement of primary weapons available for use during an air defence emergency, a limited loading capability comprising three certified loading crews, and Practice/Proficiency loadings which would be accomplished using training weapons only. Tactical weapons were not to be removed from SAS unless required for the destruction of invading Soviet bombers.[62]

In fact, this state of affairs continued for years, forcing the RCAF/CF to make contingency plans. Air Defence Command Operational Order 6/70 on "Clearzones" and "Rummage" would allow the mass load of the VooDoos at Val d'Or during a sustained emergency situation, such as existed during the Cuban Missile Crisis in 1962. The Director of Nuclear Weapons stated that the unit could be at a fully armed alert state within three hours in such a situation.[63]

Although planned for the summer of 1965,[64] deliveries of the W25 warheads began on 23 November 1965.[65] Over the years, deliveries would take place at least annually, and more probably twice per calendar year. The only open records of such deliveries are for 17/18 October 1966,[66] 03 June 1968,[67] and 24 July 1969.[68]

With only an interim posture possible at Val d'Or due to the limiting factors, the RCAF commanders decided to ask for money to bring the site up to required standards. They felt that it was "considered that the requirement for proper support facilities at this airfield is sufficiently urgent to warrant immediate attention by Defence Council."[69] When the Defence Council decided to spend the money is unclear, as the construction of an aircraft maintenance hangar did not begin until 04 June 1973, only two years before closure.

The site was finally cleared of limiting factors by a combination of small construction and rewriting of regulations and operational orders. The May 1970 Capability Inspection determined that "the unit demonstrated a satisfactory warhead/weapons capability," and that "there were no limiting factors."[70] Until this time the site had only a storage capability for the Genie warhead, and an operational capability only at DEFCON 1 or a state of AIR DEFENCE EMERGENCY. Under the new Operational Order "Chainsmoker 6/70" of 4 May 1970, and as applied 13 May, the limiting factors were lifted.

Chainsmoker, or Air Defence Command Operational Order 6/70, had been revised to enable the QRA hangars to be set up as a "Mass Load" area after a "Clearzone" of nuclear safety/security procedures had been set up to handle from two to four alert aircraft. This procedure could be further extended by "Rummage" to establish a peacetime QRA situation in cases such as the continuing DEFCON 3 state which lasted for 23 days during the Cuban missile crisis. With "Clearzone" the aircraft could be alerted and armed with nuclear Genies within three hours.[71]

DOCUMENT # 8
01 June 1970, ADC S3350-4165/VI(DCOCOps), draft, secret,
Operation Order __/70 — "CHAIN SMOKER".

    1. Val d'Or was reactivated as a peacetime alert/wartime dispersal base and upgraded to a self-accounting unit on 1 Dec 64. A full complement of primary weapons is stored and maintained ready for immediate use. The use of the QRA hangar as an aircraft maintenance facility prohibits the loading of primary weapons and standing alert under normal

QRA posture (and is) therefore limited to loading primary weapons under Mass Load conditions when required for an increased DEFCON/Alert State, for NORAD/Region generated Fairkick II exercises, for authorized evaluations and inspections, and for training exercises generated by the CO. Should the operational situation require standing alert with primary weapons, the CO is to take action to convert the area from Mass Load Area standards to QRA standards as soon as possible.

2. MISSION To locate four CF101 aircraft at CFS Val d'Or on a DEFCON 5 ALPHA Alert posture and operate six CF101 aircraft during simulated or actual DEFCON 3 conditions.

3.a.(1) CFB Bagotville and 425 AW(F) Sqn shall provide operational aircraft and combat ready crews to meet the following alert commitments:

(c) CFS Val d'Or shall be required to combat load four aircraft within 3 hours with primary and secondary weapons under Mass Load conditions when required for an increased DEFCON/Alert state.

3.c.(1) During an air defence emergency CFS val d'Or shall be prepared to operated with a minimum of six CF101 aircraft.

3.d. NUCLEAR. (3) The USAF Custodial Detachment Commander of Det 6 of the 425th MUM Squadron will be responsible for the USAF nuclear safety programme pertaining to the USAF weapon maintenance area.

With Operational Order Chainsmoker in place, the unit could finally function nearly as it was originally intended. The following document demonstrates how Val d'Or was to function in an advanced state of readiness, and also shows the times necessary for readying, loading and unloading the VooDoos. In this case, two VooDoos are brought to full alert posture with nuclear weapons for a period of about 30 minutes as an exercise. Although it was an exercise, it does serve to show the reaction times and operational capabilities of the unit and the crews from 425 Squadron. Normal Mass Loads would involve placing four aircraft in a tight formation near the QRA shelters so that two MPs could be present to guard the VooDoos while nuclear weapons were present.

DOCUMENT #
19 September 1974, Val d'Or Combat Air Control log book, (all times Zulu)

> 1031 Weapon ordered for Tarmac 2
> 1050 SD advised of Mass Load
> 1052 A/C to loaded. 005-038-
> 1054 5 min A/C to North Ramp
> 1140 Convoy terminated
> 1210 A/C 038 on 5 min 1205
> 1211 A/C 005 on 5 min 1208
> 1213 038-005 downloading at this time
> 1225 Downloading commencing
> 1255 Download completed — prepare for convoy
> 1320 Mass Load terminated

DULL SWORD

There are only two open records of accidents at Val d'Or. On 12 March 1971, at 1930 GMT, there was a static electricity incident which involved a W25 nuclear warhead. Information about the incident has never been declassified.

The second known incident occurred on 05 July 1974, at 22:15 GMT when the base personnel, possibly Explosive Ordnance Disposal, firefighters, and armament technicians, supplied what the USAF calls a "Helping Hand" at storage igloo #20.[72] A Helping Hand is extended when there is an incident involving nuclear weapons which is not serious enough to warrant being declared a Dull Sword, or worse. There are also no public details about this incident, but it is noteworthy that it happened in the SAS storage cells and not in the QRA.

SPYING

The one openly recorded spying event against the VooDoo/Genie nuclear sites happened in Quebec, and involved embassy staff from Poland, a member country of the Warsaw Treaty Organization. In

May 1965 three persons were found in an RCAF parking lot outside the airfield, having with them a camera and binoculars. The base security officer questioned them and discovered that they were from the Polish Embassy. What they would discover about Canada's northern air defences by sitting outside the dual military and civilian airfield at Val d'Or, Quebec, is anyone's guess. Having diplomatic immunity, they were simply told to leave the area, and they presumably returned to Ottawa.

DOCUMENT # 9
-10 May 1965, 1730z, priority, secret, to CANAIRDEF and D/Security, from Stn Val d'Or.

> At approx 1315 hrs 9 May 65 a 1964 Valiant sedan licence number CD630 was observed parked in the RCAF-Only parking lot at entrance to this unit. Three persons — two male and one female in vehicle. This unit requested the occupants of the vehicle to identify themselves. The vehicle was registered to "Kazimierz, Kopec of 27 Henderson, Ottawa (Embassy of Poland): was operated by Kruczek, Zenon, 397 Millcraft Cres, Ottawa, Operators licence number K7644-79502-60331 Ontario. Passengers in vehicle were identified, after a discussion in a language not understood by RCMP or SSECO, verbally as Mr Vashos phonetic Stanislaw and his wife. The SSECO observed a camera and a pair of binoculars in the front seat, (they were) directed to leave. The vehicle entered Park de la Verendrye at 1500 hrs heading toward Ottawa.

QUEBEC SEPARATION

With the growth in Quebec separatist sentiment in the 1960s, the military became worried that some militant group would try to attack one of the three nuclear sites in Quebec, and possibly try to steal a warhead. In 1967 the Director of Security was confident enough to write that the threat was difficult to assess, but that "according to reliable sources no indication of separatist demonstrations or other hostile activity planned in Val d'Or area. While recent occurrences may be cause for concern, this HQ does not consider situation warrants more than increased state of vigilance at Val d'Or."[73]

The increased tensions between Quebec and the federal government in Ottawa resulted in the formulation of "Operation Rivet" in the late 1960s. The premise was that Val d'Or was a particularly sensitive area and a possible target for popular anti-nuclear demonstrations by certain factions of the populace. In the event of some form of threat or direct attack, the base personnel would be issued a gun and 50 rounds of ammunition. Mobile Command would also send reinforcements to the site if ADC made a proper request. In a worst case scenario, the commanding officer would be the sole authority, and base personnel and FMC reinforcements could open fire only on his direct order.[74]

None of these procedures ever had to be used. The violence used by the RCMP and base security personnel at other nuclear weapons sites ensured that people would be wary of making trouble.

DETACHMENT 6

Based at CFS Val d'Or, Detachment 6 supported the VooDoo-flying 425 AW(F) Squadron from CFB Bagotville from 1965 until 1975. This comparatively northern location lacked many basic facilities, and was used by VooDoos from 425 AW(F) Squadron from CFB Bagotville on a rotational basis. Unfortunately for the detachment staff, they had to stay on a permanent basis.

CLOSURE

As the Canadian military establishment contracted in the mid-1970s, the closure of Val d'Or was assured. It was planned that the VooDoos of 425 Squadron would be repatriated to Bagotville or stand off-site alerts at CFB North Bay.[75] The small USAF Munitions Maintenance Detachment (#6) at the site would also be redeployed or closed out under a separate CF-USAF arrangement.

The SAS area was cleared out during the first half of April 1975, and on 25 April the bunkers were closed.

DOCUMENT # 10
Jan 75, ADC 1920-24194(COMD), Annex A, Cloba Val d'Or, Major
Milestones.

START	ACTIVITY	COMPLETE
1 Feb 75	Disassemble primary weapons	1 Apr 75
23 Mar 75	Cease military flying	1 Apr 75
1 Apr 75	Airlift primary weapons, missiles and explosives.	15 Apr 75
25 Apr 75	Close SAS	25 Apr 75

Primary military activity, also known as flying, at Val d'Or came
to an end at 23:12 GMT on 23 March 1975, and the duty officer
wrote in the Val d'Or Combat Air Control log book: "2312 'The End
of an Era'"[76]

RETIREMENT

As the end of the Canada's VooDoo/Genie era approached, the
politicians were once again called upon to dance around the nuclear
weapons subject. It was an open secret that the VooDoos were
equipped with nuclear weapons, but members of the Trudeau
Government worked hard to sidestep that fact.

On 25 February 1982, the Minister of National Defence, Gilles
Lamontagne and also a former 425 Squadron member, told a member
of the Standing Committee on External Affairs and National Defence
that "with the new F-18 there will be no need for any kind of nuclear
weapon. The position of Canada on that is that we do not possess any
nuclear weapons, factually, in Canada. The first F-18 will be arriving
in October of this year, and I think that will be the start of the time to
get rid of the last remnant of some of the nuclear weaponry that was
legated to us when we bought the VooDoo. So, my answer will be: as
soon as we can get rid of whatever agreement we might have on this
question, I think the better it will be."[77] He went on to state that "in
NORAD of course we have the commitment right now that requires
us to have nuclear weapons on our soil." Of course, this answer was as

disingenuous as Pearson's statement almost twenty years earlier that Canada had not "acquired" nuclear weapons, even though they were being deployed for more than one hundred-fifty RCAF aircraft at the time.

On the same day to the same committee, the Secretary of State for External Affairs, Marc MacGuigan, stated "we shall no longer require or have access to any nuclear weapons for use by the Canadian Forces as soon as the CF-101 interceptor is replaced with the CF-18A."[78] He went on to admit that it was "perhaps less readily explainable that we have a fighter plane which can use only nuclear-tipped weapons, but that was a decision that was made in the sixties, and with the phasing out of the plane, the CF-101, we will not have any nuclear weapons ourselves."[79]

DOCUMENT # 11
Minutes of AIR2A Nuclear Weapons System Project Officers Meeting, Kirtland AFB (22–24 May 1984)
"Action Item Number 83-1-1, Subject: Cancellation of Engineering Support with Canada."
Discussion: The POM felt that engineering support should continue until CF101 aircraft and AIR-2A rockets have been phased out. Canada requested termination of support, end of 84. The AFWL representative took a few minutes to echo appreciation of the entire US nuclear community in the successful achievement of this precedent setting milestone in the continental nuclear defence. A hearty three cheers for the CF support. Action Item: Closed.

By the time Canada sent back the final 48 or 54 Genie warheads, the United States Air Force had little time for the ancient weapon system. This was clear from the almost off-hand manner in which the warheads were packed for removal as demonstrated by the following document. Note that Sandia is recommending the use of crumpled-up newspaper as packing material for nuclear weapons.

DOCUMENT # 12
27 March 1984, Sandia National Laboratories, file 6-9, W25. re: W25 Warheads for Retirement.

W25 Special Retirement Procedures.
For all W25 warheads being returned to the DOE for retirement, prior to shipment accomplish the following additional procedures:
1. Remove the MC1274 Firing Set and Pressure Cover using applicable procedures,
2. Tuck detonator cables down between sphere and case. Using any available pressure sensitive adhesive tape, secure the detonator cables so as to prevent excessive movement during shipping. If desired, any suitable packing material such as crumpled newspaper may be stuffed on top of cables in place of using tape.
3. Reinstall firing set and pressure cover using applicable procedures in TP W25-1 with the following exceptions: Do not perform a continuity test, pressurize the warhead, or perform a pressure test.

Canada maintained three operational VooDoo/Genie bases, but by 1984 only two still had nuclear weapons. CFB Chatham, New Brunswick, had seen the removal of their W25 Genie warheads to Bagotville between 31 March and 03 April 1975. The joint Canada-US "Operation Starlifter" brought together the talents of Base Security and Base Armament personnel for the shipping of about 24 W25 warheads from the Chatham SAS compound.

The last nuclear weapons to leave Canadian service were the W25 Genie warheads standing alert at CFB Bagotville, Quebec, and CFB Comox, British Columbia, in 1984. The open documentation shows that the last nuclear weapons were flown out of Bagotville in April 1984. This left only the Genies at Comox as the last remaining nuclear weapons on Canadian soil in Canadian service. During the week of 12–19 April 1984, a specialized USAF transport squadron from Scott Air Force Base airlifted the Bagotville warheads away from Canada. However, the USAF detachment at Comox remained in place until the beginning of July. Comox can claim the curious historical distinction of being the last nuclear base in the Canadian military, having shipped its 24 weapons out between 25 and 29 June.

In one of the only direct statements on actual nuclear weaponry ever provided by the Liberal governments over a twenty-year period,

Jean Chretien stood up in the House of Commons and stated that "The last piece of nuclear armament was withdrawn from Canadian soil last July," (meaning July 1984).[80] Declassification has now given us those dates, and the future prime minister was only off by a week.

DOCUMENT # 13
Annual Historical Report 1984, CFB Bagotville, Base Operations Officer, 25 March 1985.

> 12–19 April 1984 — End of our nuclear capability with the departure of the American Detachment (425 MUNS).

DOCUMENT # 14
Annual Historical Report 1984, CFB Comox, Base Security Section, A/B Secur O, 16 January 1985.

> This unit was the last unit in Canada to have the vast responsibility for the direct security of nuclear weapons and components.

The quiet removal of the last Genie warheads in June 1984 signalled the end of direct Canadian participation in the field of nuclear weapons. There would be no more "buckets of instant sunshine" carried by the Canadian military.

CHAPTER 7

ANTI-SUBMARINE WARFARE

Both the Royal Canadian Navy and the Royal Canadian Air Force, at the urging of their maritime patrol arms, considered acquiring airborne nuclear depth charges for use against Soviet Northern Fleet, Baltic Fleet, and Pacific Fleet submarines operating off the coasts of North America. This was a nuclear commitment which was never to be a reality for the Canadian military. The origin of the naval nuclear episode goes back to an approach made by the US government in mid-1958. Cabinet then approved, on 15 October 1958, the opening of negotiations for the "storage of nuclear anti-submarine weapons for Canadian and United States use from Canadian bases."[1] and within two months negotiations had already begun at the highest levels, with the US Secretaries of State and Defense in attendance.[2] The RCN traced the origin of their formal interest to the Cabinet meeting of 06 December 1960, but the roots go back another two years.

The RCAF, in an effort to keep its options open regarding nuclear weapons for maritime roles, had adopted a low-key but determined approach to the subject as soon as the initial US approach was heard. At that time, the RCAF was already proposing that their anti-submarine patrol aircraft eventually be armed with a nuclear depth charge. Although this went unapproved, it was not disapproved, and the requirement stayed on the books.

DOCUMENT # 1
RCAF Programme of Activities, 1958–1962. Appendix D, Missiles and Weapons, Secret.

> 3. Nuclear. (b) To increase the effectiveness of maritime patrol, atomic weapons are required.
> Unapproved

With constant, low-key, pressure from the militaries on both sides of the border, it was almost inevitable that this question make its way into discussions at the leaders' level. At the US presidential retreat at Camp David in 1958, Cabinet members from both countries got as far as mentioning the emplacement of ASW nuclear weapons for Canada, but the Canadian delegation was initially only willing to accept ASW weapons for US Navy ASW forces stationed in Newfoundland.

DOCUMENT # 2

Ministerial Meeting Canada - United States, Camp David, 8/9 November 1959. Top Secret.

ATOMIC STORAGE

Mr. McElroy (Secretary of Defense) pointed out that there were four types of atomic storage under consideration.

(c) Anti-submarine forces of Canada and the US. Both Mr. Pearkes and Mr. Green foresaw no difficulty for anti-submarine weapons in Argentia.

Whether through pure hope or for another unknown reason, the RCAF soon came to prepare for the day it would have nuclear anti-submarine weapons. Money for facilities was budgeted, and planning began for the construction of special weapons storage bunkers at Maritime Air Command sites such as Comox, British Columbia, Summerside, Prince Edward Island, and Greenwood, Nova Scotia. The RCN was also interested in nuclear weapons storage, or "stowage" in navy parlance, at RCN Air Station Shearwater. In the end, only the massive storage bunkers at Comox would be used to house the W25 warhead for the Genie rocket used by Air Defence Command.

DOCUMENT # 3

27 April 1961, RCAF Defence Programme 1962–1963, RCAF file S-000-115-62, Vol 1.

Facilities for Special Weapons M.A.C.
1962–63   1963–64   1964–65
$50 000. $800 000. $1 400 000.

During the Diefenbaker years the prospect of arming the airborne anti-submarine warfare forces of the RCAF was seriously considered, and documentation to this effect made it all the way to the Cabinet Defence Committee. Minister of National Defence George Pearkes briefed the CDC in December 1959 that the draft agreement with the United States for the acquisition of nuclear weapons for Canadian forces would include a provision for consultation with SACLANT, the Supreme Allied Commander Atlantic (always a US Navy admiral), on the placement of weapons in Canada.[3] This was the first sure sign that the Diefenbaker Cabinet was giving real consideration to the prospect of nuclear ASW capabilities for the RCAF and RCN. Almost five years later, SACLANT was once again prepared to restate his requirement that Canada arm its ASW aircraft with nuclear depth bombs.[4]*

Aside from this early and brief mention, there was virtually no talk of the proposal, and by early 1963 Pearson had set aside all such talk by saying that there was no record of a firm commitment in this weapons system. At exactly this time, the NATO military authorities urged the changing government of Canada to "take steps to modify anti-submarine warfare aircraft to carry nuclear weapons."[5] What is interesting is the process by which nuclear weapons were NOT acquired for a naval role in Canada, despite significant preparations having been made by the RCAF and RCN for their operational deployment.

The new Pearson Cabinet was given the full five-item list for the annex which included the BOMARC, the CF-101, the CF-104, the Honest John, and the "Air-dropped anti-submarine weapons for the RCN and RCAF." Soon many were questioning of the inclusion of ASW weapons, as they had pledged to honour four nuclear commitments, and there had been no public mention of ASW weapons. The Cabinet members agreed that there was no evidence of this Canadian commitment, and that they were not willing to extend their credibility that far, especially as theirs was a minority government.[6]

---

* 25 May–18 Dec 64, ten nuclear weapons loading courses given to 55 airmen.

DOCUMENT # 4

09 May 1963, Cabinet Conclusions, #7-63, Report of Cabinet
Defence Committee; nuclear weapons agreements.

During the discussion on the scope of the
proposed agreement, it was noted that this was
governed, under paragraph (1) by an annex listing five
weapons or weapons systems.

Some questioned the inclusion of anti-submarine
weapons. The government had pledged itself to
honour four nuclear commitments, but there had
been no public mention of anti-submarine weapons,
nor had Cabinet been given any evidence of a
Canadian commitment to use such weapons.

Others felt that the inclusion of the anti-
submarine weapons, which was only permissive, made
for a sensible package. The Minister of National
Defence said that a number of Canadian anti-
submarine aircraft had already been modified to
permit the use of these weapons and he had military
advice that it would soon be impossible to perform
Canada's anti-submarine role effectively without
nuclear weapons.

The Cabinet agreed, that the Minister of National
Defence inquire into and report on the anti-
submarine weapon requirements of the RCN and
RCAF with specific reference to, — (i) modification
of ASW aircraft, undertaken or programmed, to
permit the use of air-dropped nuclear weapons; (ii)
whether any commitment had been made to use
nuclear weapons, and, if so, how it had been made;
(iii) whether a requirement for air-dropped anti-
submarine nuclear weapons is likely to develop in the
near future, and the probable urgency of such a
requirement.

However, some members thought that the item should be kept as
a prudent planning item for the future. They noted that the MND
had reported that "a number of Canadian anti-submarine aircraft had
already been modified to permit the use of these weapons and he had

military advise that it would soon be impossible to perform Canada's anti-submarine role effectively without nuclear weapons."[7]

Cabinet then directed the MND to make inquiries into the ASW requirements of the RCAF and RCN, and to look into the "modification of ASW aircraft, undertaken or programmed, to permit the use of air-dropped nuclear weapons." The Cabinet also wanted to know from the MND "whether any commitment had been made to use nuclear weapons, and, if so, how it had been made; (and) whether a requirement for air-dropped anti-submarine nuclear weapons is likely to develop in the near future, and the probable urgency of such a requirement."[8] There is no record of Hellyer ever returning to Cabinet with an answer to those questions. However, it is clear now that the aircraft in question were the Neptunes on the west coast, for in the spring of 1963, the Argus had not yet been "modified for nuclear weapons."[9] The Royal Canadian Navy was also involved by this time, having modified their small Tracker aircraft for nuclear carriage.

The reality was that the previous government, with the full knowledge of the prime minister and the active participation of the MND and SSEA, had drafted and undertaken negotiations on a document providing for nuclear ASW weapons for the Canadian forces. By the summer of 1962 a schedule had already been drafted covering the "Stockpiling of Nuclear Anti-Submarine Weapons for the RCN and RCAF Maritime Command."[10] This schedule included the provision that special stowage areas in HMC Ships would be built for nuclear weapons storage. The RCN recognized that a full deployment of nuclear ASW weapons would require special weapons stowage facilities to be built into seven St. Laurent Class destroyers,[11] two Mackenzie Class destroyers,[12] the aircraft carrier HMCS Bonaventure, and the fleet replenishment ship HMCS Provider.[13] It would also require shore stowage in Shearwater and Comox. But hardware and ships were not the end of it: each ship would require a USN nuclear weapons detachment for maintenance and custodial purposes, as would each shore stowage site.

During the Pearson-Kennedy meeting in Hyannis Port, the two leaders agreed that the "treaty would be in general form, and would not go beyond the four weapons or weapons systems to which Canada was committed."[14] Pearson was undoubtedly pleased that it would not include nuclear anti-submarine weapons, but may have been worried that the question of storing USAF and USN nuclear weapons in Canada would be a difficult one with which to deal.

The next Cabinet meeting opened with a row between the two Pauls. In a Memorandum to Cabinet written by Paul Martin for the 14 May Cabinet meeting, the SSEA said that he wanted to re-insert the annex, but with the exception of the reference to ASW nuclear weapons. He told Cabinet that "the object of the change was to confine present action to 'commitments' undertaken by the previous government in order to facilitate the handling of the problem in Parliament. In my view there would be important advantage in this regard in being able to state, if questioned, that the agreement itself makes clear that this limitation exists."[15]

Paul Hellyer came out against the change, instead preferring to widen the possible scope of the agreement by deleting the annex altogether. He felt that specifying the weapons systems in advance "would rob it of the desirable element of flexibility and would necessitate an elaborate and expensive procedure to bring other weapons within the scope of the agreement." Hellyer felt that the mere fact that only four systems had been mentioned did not mean they were the only commitments to be met. Pearson sided with Martin.[16] In this case the political considerations were primary over the military considerations. Pearson was aware, as Paul Martin noted, that "the Parliamentary division on nuclear weapons policy might be the most difficult to be faced by the government,"[17]and would not risk his government on one extra nuclear duty.

SSEA Paul Martin wrote to Cabinet that they should seriously consider eliminating the ASW nuclear weapons from the annex to the proposed agreement, as there seemed to be no record of any such commitment having been undertaken by the previous government.[18] After a great deal of debate, Cabinet sided with Martin on the basis of the argument that there had been no previous commitment, and that it would be politically difficult for the government to be seen as extending nuclear weapons use in Canada.[19] After all, this was a minority government, and Pearson would not risk his political future on a single nuclear commitment.

At the next Cabinet meeting Martin suggested that the annex be reinstated, and that the reference to nuclear anti-submarine weapons simply be omitted. This would allow the government to say that the agreement was limited to the four weapons systems publicly discussed.

However, the MND, Paul Hellyer, "said that he would prefer not to make the proposed change," as it would result in increased costs if, in the future, new types of weapons were to be deployed. He argued that "The fact that only four weapons systems had been mentioned publicly during the election did not mean that they represented the only commitments to be met" and that "the role of the R.C.N. was involved, since without nuclear weapons the existing role seemed likely to become nonsensical." At this point Pearson stepped in and stated his preference: he favoured the more limited provisions proposed by the SSEA, and at the same time said that the role of the RCN would require reassessment and that such a review would cover the prospective need for nuclear anti-submarine weapons.[20]

The nuclear anti-submarine warfare issue would not die, and Pearson recognized that this would be a problem when the final agreement was announced. Pearson wanted to be able to tell the press that the agreement was limited to the four stated systems, and that "no extension of the agreement beyond the four existing commitments would be contemplated until the government had completed its review of the defence programme." Paul Hellyer was still fighting for the maritime commitment, and continued to argue that the ASW commitment "was almost a commitment comparable with the others." The full Cabinet shot him down by saying that "it had not been identified publicly as a commitment."[21]

Even after the question appeared to be settled, and the final agreement signed, the military would not give up. Paul Hellyer again went back to the Cabinet and stated that there was still a possibility that Canada would need nuclear ASW weapons in the future. In a last valiant attempt, Hellyer mentioned "the possible need by both Canadian and US forces in Canada of anti-submarine nuclear weapons, but (that) this should not be proceeded with until the review of Canadian naval policy had been concluded."[22] The question was never raised in Cabinet again. All future discussions of nuclear weapons for ASW purposes centred on their deployment to Newfoundland for the US Navy VP squadrons at Naval Air Station Argentia.

That was the more-or-less public side of the nuclear commitment. What has only recently emerged was that Hellyer asked the Chairman of the Chiefs of Staff to direct the Naval Staff to prepare a set of studies on providing nuclear ASW weapons capability for the Canadian Maritime Forces. The Naval Staff responded with

"Acquisition of Nuclear Anti-Submarine Weapons for Canadian Maritime Forces"[23] on 06 March 1964, and "Methods of Providing Nuclear Weapons to Canadian Maritime Forces"[24] that same day. The draft documents went before the Naval Policy Co-ordinating Committee on 3 and 4 March, where the former paper, with changes, was recommended to the Naval Board, and the latter paper was deferred pending further discussions with the RCAF.

Within the week, Rear Admiral K.L. Dyer, VCNS, was forwarding the papers to the Naval Board with recommendations for immediate action on the first and discussion with the RCAF on the second.[25] Three days later the Naval Board met. The record of the discussion was so secret that it had been removed from the record normally available to only senior officers, and was instead held only for those who had been at the Board. Vice Admiral H.S. Rayner, along with Rear Admirals Dyer, Dillon, and Stirling, decided that the paper would form the basis of a submission to the Chiefs of Staff committee, and that the RCN should proceed with nuclear acquisition. The lingering question is why this was happening after Cabinet had formally ended the naval aspect of nuclear armament for the Canadian military, and why it was done at the request of the Minister of National Defence.

Most disappointing for Maritime Air Command must have been the news that after all those years of hoping and planning, and after the news that nuclear weapons would be provided for the VooDoo, Starfighter, BOMARC and Honest John, nuclear anti-submarine weapons would never arrive. Cabinet deliberations had centred on the fact that there was no stated commitment for nuclear ASW weapons, and that with a delicate balance of votes in the House of Commons, the government would not support the military's request.[26]

AIRCRAFT:

Argus
One of the unanswered questions of Canadian maritime nuclear history is why the RCAF had the Argus modified to carry nuclear weapons *after* the government of Lester Pearson had ruled out the acquisition of nuclear depth charges for Canada. The Neptune was nuclear-capable prior to the election of the Liberal Government in 1963, yet military documentation indicates that the Argus was not

converted for nuclear use until at least the spring of 1964.[27]

In the early and mid-1960s this long-range maritime anti-submarine patrol aircraft was modified with the internal racks and bombing equipment necessary for the aircraft to utilize either the Mk 101 "Lulu" or B57 nuclear anti-submarine depth bombs. The RCAF Maritime command had modified the wiring and bomb bay systems of 33 Arguses for a total of cost of $204 000.00 by the spring of 1963.[28] However, they had not yet acquired the weapons control units which had already been provided for the Neptunes.

The Argus was a massive, four-engined, long-range, aircraft built by Canadair. It was a derivative of the Bristol Britannia, but with a Canadian fuselage and US powerplants.

Length	*39.09m*
Wing span	*43.38m*
Weight	*67 tonnes loaded*
Bomb load	*1.815 tonnes in each of 2 bomb bays.*
	3.450 tonnes on external hard points.
Endurance	*24 hours*
Range	*6 600–8 000 km*
Engines	*Wright R-3370 TC981 EA-1 , 18 cylinder radial*
Crew	*15 men*

The original conventional weapons load of the Argus was comprised of the Mk 43 Mod 3; the Mk 44 Mod 1; and the Mk 30 anti-submarine torpedoes. It also carried the Mk 54 depth charge. Submarines would be detected by the AN/ASR-3 "Sniffer"; the AN/AQA-3A and modified AN/AQA-5 "Jezebel"; the "Julie and AN/AJH-301 Recorder; and the AN/ASQ-8 Magnetic Anomaly Detector (MAD). Radar sensors on board were the AN/ASV-21 and the AN/APS-20 for surface searches.

The RCAF Argus fleet was divided into three squadrons sited at two bases on the east coast:

404   "Buffalo" Squadron, CFB Greenwood, NS, from April 1959 until the introduction of the Aurora in 1980.

405   "Eagle" Squadron, CFB Greenwood, NS, from August 1958 until the introduction of the Aurora in 1980.

415   "Swordfish" Squadron, CFB Summerside, PEI, from May 1961 until the introduction of the Aurora in 1980.

The conventional weapons storage areas at both Greenwood and Summerside were never converted to hold nuclear weapons even though these were the designated Maritime Air Command nuclear depth bomb sites. It is rumoured that during the Cuban missile crisis various Canadian personnel were dispatched to these sites in anticipation of nuclear use. However, the compounds remained single fenced and lacked the enclosed double gates and enhanced security features associated with nuclear storage sites. Special Ammunition Storage bunkers and maintenance facilities for nuclear weapons, and support buildings for the US military custodial and maintenance personnel are not to be found at either of these sites. It is therefore safe to conclude that nuclear weapons were never present in a long-term deployment sense, although there is no reason to rule out a temporary passage of USN nuclear systems on similar aircraft through either site.

The manuals for the use and maintenance of the Argus[29] clearly show the features built in for the intended nuclear weapons. Most important were the additions made to the tactical navigators' station for nuclear weapons control and use. At this station in the aft port cabin of the aircraft, the tactical navigator would select and arm the nuclear weapon or weapons to be used against a submarine. In the manual, photographs and diagrams shows the Armament Panel in the Tactical Navigator's Station. Please see the end of the photo section for a picture of the Armament Panel.

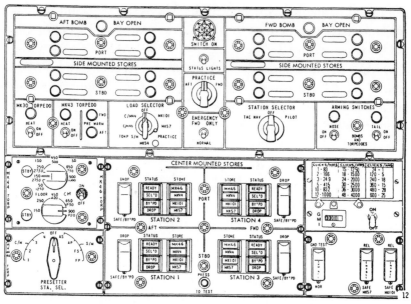

DIAGRAM #1
Argus nuclear weapons armament panel.

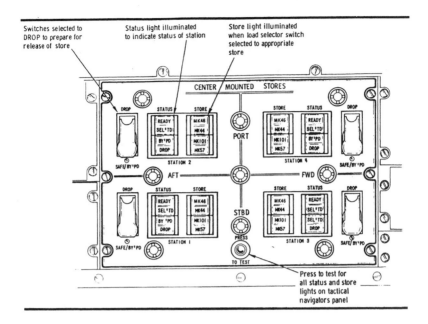

DIAGRAM #2
Argus Center Mounted Stores control panel.

The small sub-panel just up-left of centre labelled "LOAD SELECTOR" contains a dial with eight selections, the top being "OFF," and those from 6 o'clock to 11 o'clock being conventional torpedoes and depth charges/bombs. The 4 o'clock position has a "PRACTICE" setting. At the 1 o'clock position is the "MK 101" setting, and at the 3 o'clock position is the "MK 57" setting. It is not possible to accidentally dial in to either of these selections without first depressing a small safety button below the selector dial which allows the dial to be turned to the right.

The small sub-panel at bottom right is unlabelled, but contains the "ENABLE" switches. There is one switch for the Mk 57 (left) and one switch for the Mk 101 (right). Each switch is marked "SAFE" (bottom) and "REL" meaning release circuits (top). These were built in to control safety features in the release circuits of the Mk 57 and Mk 101 nuclear depth charges.

The central sub-panel on the lower half of the Armament Panel is labelled "CENTER MOUNTED STORES." In the centre there are four sets of lights, one for each of the four stations (two per bomb bay). Each set of lights indicates the type of weapon stored, choosing from the Mk 44 and Mk 46 torpedoes, and then the Mk 101 and Mk from the Mk 44 and Mk 46 torpedoes, and then the Mk 101 and Mk 57 nuclear depth bombs. Beside each column of store lights is the column of status lights labelled "READY," "SEL'D," "BY'PD," and "DROP." Beside each station indicator light is a switch. In the down position the switch is at "SAFE/BY'PD," and in the up position the switch is at "DROP."[30]

In order for the nuclear depth charge to be used, both the tactical navigator and the cockpit crew would have to perform a series of release procedures. At least two men in opposite ends of the aircraft would have to select the arming option on their bomb control panels, and only then could the nuclear stores be dropped. In the cockpit the arming switch would have been sealed with wire and lead, necessitating the purposeful cutting of the seal.

The Argus at the National Aeronautical Collection in Rockcliffe, Ottawa, was donated by the CAF in whole, and retains all of the nuclear release equipment in place.

Neptune

There was another, though smaller, maritime patrol aircraft available to the RCAF. The Neptune was also capable of carrying nuclear weapons, and was the only maritime patrol aircraft based on the west coast. The first of 25 aircraft built by Lockheed was delivered to the RCAF at Station Greenwood in 1955. The Neptunes used by the RCAF were not only theoretically nuclear-capable, they were technically equipped as such by December 1962. A test aircraft and crew were sent to the Special Weapons facility at Kirtland AFB, New Mexico, for initial safety inspections and certification in the final week of November 1962.[31] The RCN referred to these RCAF aircraft as having "a nuclear weapon capability" which the Argus did not yet have at all.[32] The RCAF Maritime Command had modified the wiring and bomb bays of 24 Neptunes for a total of cost of $48 000.00 prior to the spring of 1963,[33] and by the spring of 1964 had procured 26 weapon monitor and control units for 13 aircraft.

The P2V-7 Neptune was a medium, four-engined, long-range aircraft built by Lockheed in the USA.

Length	*27.84m*
Wing span	*31.64m*
Weight	*34.35 tonnes (max. T.O.)*
Endurance	*20 hours*

Range	*3 660 km*
Engines	*Wright R3350-32V, radial (x2)*
	Westinghouse J34 Turbojet (x2)

The weapons and sensors capabilities are roughly the same as on the Argus, simply on a smaller scale.

By the time nuclear weapons became a possibility for maritime use, the RCAF operated only one Neptune squadron: 407 Squadron at Station Comox, British Columbia, from May 1958 to January 1968.

The RCAF was actively planning on a nuclear maritime role at Comox, and the Neptunes of 407 Squadron would be the delivery vehicle. Their only other choice of carrier would have required the redeployment of an Argus squadron to the west coast, but this would have significantly degraded their ASW abilities in the crucial North Atlantic theatre of military operations. The RCAF considered the move, but this would have involved massive costs, and would have degraded the operational capability of 409 AW(F) Squadron which was holding its NORAD nuclear duties with the VooDoo and Genie out of the main hangar, #7, and QRA facilities on base. So, although there were nuclear-capable facilities at Comox, they were already committed to NORAD duties: any use of them for ASW storage would have degraded the NORAD capabilities of the site, and this was unacceptable to the RCAF, NORAD, and the government.

The Neptune became operational with nuclear weapons in the US Navy in 1950, and would carry both the Mk 101 "Lulu" and the Mk 105 "Hotpoint" beginning in 1958, and then of the new Mk 57 in 1964. Twenty-four Canadian Neptunes were altered for nuclear weapons carriage of the Mk 101 and Mk 57, but only 13 had the full operational capability to carry and use nuclear depth charges, and both ground and air crew were provided with manuals[34] and some training to that end. However, it was not actually easy to make the transition. Although the aircraft made for the US Navy were nuclear-armed, the Canadian ones lacked the proper electrical circuitry. The RCAF then found out that they could no longer get the required electrical connectors for nuclear weapons from Lockheed, and so began a hunt using the Canadian Joint Staff in Washington for appropriate wiring to allow the RCAF to mate a nuclear depth bomb to the Neptune.[35]

There were multiple steps necessary to drop either the Mk 101 or received and verified, the pilot, using the Pilot's Armament Control Panel, would move the "MASTER ARM" switch from off to on, and move the "SELECT STORES" switch to "BOMB."

The navigator, using the Navigator's Armament Control Panel, would turn the Armament Selector dial to "BOMB OR TORPEDO," and select either the "RIGHT" or "LEFT BOMB BAY STORES SECTION SELECTOR" switch. He would then move the "STORES ARMING" switch away from off.

DIAGRAM #3
Neptune DCU-77/A Mk 101 bomb arming panel.

The final unlocking of the nuclear system took place in the cockpit with identical dual control systems provided to both the pilot and the co-pilot. Two small DCU-77/A electronic control boxes sat on top of the instrument panel. Both men would cut off the wire and lead seal, thus allowing the dial to be turned from "OFF" to "SAFE" and then to "ARM." The pilot would turn the dial first, and then the co-pilot would activate his DCU-77/A. This box was originally designed to control the final arming of the Mk 101 weapon, but was later extended with minor modifications to provide positive control for the Mk 57 as the electronics were similar.

If need be, a crew member could arm the bomb with an H-3133 manual safety switch wrench by rotating the manual safety switch 90 degrees from "SAFE" to "ARM." However, this would normally have degrees from "SAFE" to "ARM." However, this would normally have been done on the ground by the US armament personnel prior to flight.

Then, once either the pilot or co-pilot had opened the bomb bay door, the depth charge could be released. The navigator needed only to depress the "STORES RELEASE" button on his Armament Control Panel to effect the drop and eventual detonation of either the Mk 101 or the Mk 57.

THE AIRBORNE NUCLEAR DEPTH CHARGES

From the late 1950s through to the end of the 1960s, the only weapons Canada could possibly have received from the US Navy for anti-submarine warfare tasks were the Mk 101 "Lulu" depth bomb, the Mk 105 "Hotpoint" depth bomb, and the Mk 57 depth bomb. The Lulu and Hotpoint entered service in 1958, and the Mk 57 became operational in 1963.

Mk 101 "LULU"

The Mk 101 bomb was developed due to the shortcomings of the earlier, and oversized "Alias Betty" nuclear depth bomb. So large was this early design that only a tiny handful of aircraft could carry the weapon, and then only after major modifications to their bomb bays. The Lulu would remedy that problem, and make it possible for most aircraft-carrier-based planes to utilize the weapon.

The RCAF purchased a set of Mk 102 reusable practice bombs for the Lulu at a cost of $50 000.00. It was expected that each bomb could be used up to three times, and was therefore much more economical than the Hotpoint practice weapons.[36] This stock was to last one year.

Initial design concepts were tested during Operation Teapot in 1955, and final design tests were the Erie and Seminole shots of Operation Redwing. The final product was proof-fired in the summer of 1957 during Operation Plumbbob.

The Mk 101 "Lulu" nuclear depth bomb was carried internally on ASW patrol aircraft of the US Navy. The 546 kg snub-nosed bomb was 2.35 m long and 0.46 m in diameter. Armed with the W34 warhead, the Lulu would have a yield of about 10 kilotons. The bomb was nothing more than a cylindrical atomic bomb device with a hollow aft-body, and four fins with a ring of sheet steel surrounding their ends.

Lulu also carried a small retardant parachute for drops from higher speeds, which fell off as it entered the water.

Fuzing was both by hydrostatic depth fuzes, and by a backup timer fuze should the primary system fail. Although short on safety devices, the Lulu would not detonate until after it had sunk more than 25 m into the sea. In addition, the bomb would automatically detonate if it struck the seabed in less than 230 m of water.

Approximately 2000 W34 warheads were built for Lulu bombs between August 1958 and late 1962 by the General Mills company. The US Navy began to replace the Lulus with B57 bombs starting in July 1964, with the final Lulu being withdrawn from service in 1971, as the B57 nuclear depth bomb had completely taken over the nuclear ASW job. A Lulu can be seen at the National Atomic Museum at Kirtland AFB, New Mexico.[37]

Mk 105 "HOTPOINT"

The Mk 105 bomb was the first multi-role modular package bomb used by the USA. With various noses and tails, this small bomb could be carried by any US naval aircraft either internally or externally.

Although the RCAF spent $120 000.00 on Mk 106 expendable practice bomb for the Mk 105,[38] there is no evidence that either the Argus or the Canadian Neptune were built to carry, arm and drop this weapon. All Neptune and Argus manuals and electronic control panels refer only to the Mk 101 and Mk 57 nuclear depth bombs, and no mention is made of the weapon in official documents. This training drop shape was probably purchased on behalf of the RCN who had converted their CS2F-2 Tracker aircraft for single weapon carriage.

The Mk 105 weighed 682 kg, and was 2.39 m long and 0.457 m in diameter. Armed with much the same W34 warhead as the Lulu, it had a yield of about 10 kilotons.

Fuzing was both by hydrostatic depth fuzes, and by a backup timer fuze should the primary system fail. In addition, the bomb was originally designed to have a "laydown" capability, but this was not necessary for submarine hunting.

Approximately 600 W34 warheads were built for Hotpoint between June 1958 and September 1962 by the General Mills company. The US Navy replaced all Hotpoints with both Lulus and

B57s by the end of 1964. A Hotpoint, complete with modular noses and tails, can be seen at the National Atomic Museum at Kirtland AFB, New Mexico.[39]

B57

The B57 was designed and used as an anti-submarine depth charge and was an internally or externally carried free fall or parachute-retarded nuclear weapon. As it was a Navy weapon, it was also equipped with hydrostatic detonators, giving it an anti-submarine capability. Although not to the US Navy's liking, the weapon had a Permissive Action Link. The W57 bomb was a "nominal yield" weapon, of less than 20 kt. It was originally developed for the US Navy and US Marine Corps in response to their request for a small (size and yield) tactical bomb.[40] More complete information is contained in Chapter 3, as this weapon type was ultimately deployed by the RCAF on the CF-104 Starfighter strike aircraft in NATO Germany.

The RCAF purchased a set of BDUC 20 (sic) reusable practice bombs for the Mk 57 at a cost of $105 000.00. It was expected that each bomb could be used up to three times.[41] The RCAF expected to go through all of these shapes in the first year of training. After this, the total cost of practice weapons would fall from $275 000.00 to about $117 000.00 annually.

THE ROYAL CANADIAN NAVY

Although there have been rumours over the years that the RCN had been equipped with nuclear weapons at some time in the 1960s, there is no proof of this curious assertion. What is true is that the RCN did seriously consider the acquisition of major weapons systems for its surface fleet which could have used nuclear warheads.

The weapon most commonly associated with the RCN when nuclear issues come up is the ASROC, or Anti-Submarine Rocket. The ASROC was a quick-reaction, ship-launched, short-range ballistic rocket which would fling an homing torpedo or a nuclear depth charge towards a submarine. First deployed in 1961, the ASROC came to Canadian ships in 1968.

The solid-fuelled ASROC is 4.57 m long with a body diameter of 30 cm. Most importantly, the ASROC is a dual-capable weapon, carrying either a conventional homing torpedo or a nuclear depth charge. To have ASROC is not necessarily to have nuclear weapons.

The nuclear weapon for ASROC was the Mk 17 depth bomb which utilized the W44 warhead. This 1 kt warhead weighed less than 130 kg. The bomb would be dropped into the water when a small explosive charge severed the steel band holding the body together in flight.

The RCN recognized that the ASROC, even using the Mk 46 homing torpedo, was hopelessly inaccurate. The naval staff noted that with a Kill Probability (Pk) of 0.23, the system "falls below Staff requirements", and that "with two salvoes, kill probability is acceptable". However, they also noted that the overall reliability was high, and that it could carry nuclear depth bombs if needed.[42]

In the end, the ASROC launcher and rockets were a whole lot cheaper than converting these ships to helicopter destroyers (DDHs), and the naval staff decided on the ASW rocket. ASROC launchers cost $825 000.00 without the sensor equipment. Each ASROC rocket cost $ 8 800.00, and the Mk 46 homing torpedoes cost $57 000.00 each. A full ships complement of twenty ASROC cost $177 600.00. The RCN thought that the nuclear depth bombs (the W44) would cost $330 000.00 each. This meant that a complete ship's outfit based on the Mk 46 torpedo would cost $1 140 000.00, while the same based on nuclear deployment would cost $6 600 000.00. Of course, the RCN would not have had to buy the nuclear depth bombs had such arrangements ever been made.

In the late 1950s the first of seven Restigouche Class ships was commissioned. The ships were 113 m in length, with a beam of 13 m, and a top speed of 28 knots. They carried a crew of 12 officers and 237 men in the 2390 tons displacement. The curious aspect of deploying the ASROC on this class of ship was that it was not even on the original Naval Board list of ships to be converted for nuclear carriage.

By 1967, the first of four Restigouche Class ships to be converted to the ASROC system was sent for a major refit. The Terra Nova (hull #259) was rebuilt between 1967 and 1968 to accommodate the new ASROC launcher. Fitting the massive structure meant the removal of the aft twin gun mount. Following this initial emplacement, the Gatineau (hull #236) was rebuilt in 1970–71; the Kootenay (hull #258) was rebuilt in 1970–72; and the Restigouche (hull #257) was rebuilt in 1970–72: all outfitted with ASROC. As these ships were coming back on line, the reorganization of the fleet caused their movement from the east coast to the west coast. Only the Terra Nova*remains in use, the others having been decommissioned** or put on long term ready use without crew.***

In addition to the ASROC system, the RCN did acquire two other nuclear carrier systems. These two were aircraft: because the RCN had aircraft carriers, they also had their own fleet of aircraft separate from the RCAF. In the late 1950s the RCN had bought the Tracker anti-submarine aircraft to be operated from their aircraft carriers in the Atlantic. And for added protection of the surface fleet, the Sikorsky Sea King ship-borne helicopter was acquired.

TRACKER

The last of the nuclear-capable aircraft in Canada did not belong to the RCAF, but rather to the Royal Canadian Navy.[43] The RCN had acquired 100 Tracker CS2F-1 and CS2F-2 from Toronto-based DeHavilland Canada (which built them under licence from Grumman Aircraft) as anti-submarine patrol aircraft to be based on the RCN aircraft carrier based in Halifax. Long after the last Canadian aircraft carrier, HMCS Bonaventure, had left the fleet, the Trackers continued in service with the CAF. Having passed its initial safety study in December 1961, the Tracker was the first nuclear ASW aircraft in Canada, beating the Neptune which had its initial safety check in November 1962.

The CS2F-2 Tracker was a twin-engined, medium-range aircraft. The initial lot was delivered in October 1956, with 43 Mk 1 aircraft and 57 Mk 2 aircraft eventually being produced. The RCN had 38 of the 55 CS2F-2 aircraft modified for nuclear carriage of the Mk 101, and were preparing to further modify the Trackers to carry the Mk 57.[44]

Length	*12.88m*
Wing span	*21.24m*
Bomb load	*2.18 tonnes (internal)*
Bomb Bay	*4.03m x 0.65m*
Weight	*13.22 tonnes (max. T.O.)*
Endurance	*9 hours*
Speed	*240–300km/h (cruise)*
Engines	*Wright R-1820-82, radial (x2)*

---

* HMCS Terra Nova retains the ASROC system.

** HMCS Kootenay and HMCS Restigouche have been decommissioned.

***HMCS Gatineau is ready to sail on 180 days notice: her crew having been sent to other assignments. However, this ship may soon face the scrap-heap.

(Pratt & Witney Canada)

Being a small carrier-based aircraft meant that there was little room in the Tracker for the bomb, and the aircraft was limited to a single nuclear depth bomb in its left-of-centre, 4.03m long bomb bay.[45] The earlier "Alias Betty" nuclear depth bomb would not have fit into the tiny Tracker bomb bay, and was therefore never considered.* Lulus have been described as being "shoe-horned" in that minimal space.

Little is publicly known about the Tracker nuclear weapons preparations, code-named "Snowflake".[46] What is known is that the RCN had originally modified six Trackers to carry the Lulu nuclear depth bomb, and that two RCN Trackers** with crews, led by Lt. Seth Grossmith and Lt. A.T. Houston, were tested at the US Special Weapons Center on Kirtland Air Force Base, New Mexico[47] the week of 07 December 1961. During this series of capability and safety reviews and tests, the RCN crews dropped test shapes of the Mk 101 Lulu at the weapons range near Socorro, New Mexico. A year later, LCdr S.M. "Shell" Rowell and his Tracker proceeded back to Kirtland for Phase Two of Snowflake: the finalization of the circuitry modifications necessary for operational carriage of the Lulu.[48]

For the initial capability review and safety studies, the RCN received a single Mk 101 test shape (the Mk 102) which included all the internal electrical circuits and connections. It arrived at Shearwater by train from the US, marked "VX-10 Commanding Officer Eyes Only." Since ordnance usually arrived by special shipment, the Ordinary Seaman who opened the crate was more than a little surprised to find a large bomb-shaped object in a crate not bearing explosives markings.

Since the commitment was never formalized by the Pearson government in 1963, the Tracker nuclear programme simply died away. Although the Mk 57 NDB came into the US inventory after the RCNs capability and initial safety studies were completed, the RCN had planned on using and tested the Tracker with the TX57.***

At the time of the modification and testing, the RCN had the following squadrons which could have operated the converted aircraft.

---

* Janes' *All the World's Aircraft* originally referred to the carriage of a Betty bomb, but in all subsequent issues dealing with Tracker noted carriage mainly of one Mk 101 and later one Mk 57 nuclear depth bomb internally. Since the bomb bay was only about 3.7 m long, it was impossible to carry two nuclear depth bombs internally.

** The lead nuclear-capable Tracker was #1545.

*** The TX57 was the test and experimental version of the final Mk 57 nuclear depth bomb for the USN and USMC.

VX 10   "Superbia in Progressum"
VS 880   "Reperer et Detruire"
VS 881   "Ense Constanter Alato"

Only a handful of crews from VX 10 knew the basic nuclear procedures, and only a small number of VS 880 crews had even the informal nuclear briefing and basic handling training from the USN. The USN had provided, free of charge, loading and delivery training to a number of Canadian crews in the hope that the Canadians would soon be joining the USN in nuclear operations following a formalized arrangement.

By the time of the Cuban missile crisis in October 1962, the RCN had modified six Trackers, and all were held ready during the mobilization for possible nuclear use. The special aircraft and crews were sent to wait out the crisis at the Yarmouth, Nova Scotia airfield, and would proceed to hand over their modified Trackers to US Naval aviators at the USN nuclear shore stowage facility at Quontset Point.

Additionally, since the Trackers were aircraft-carrier-based planes, there were plans to modify the aircraft carrier Bonaventure for the stowage of nuclear depth bombs. Although it would have been comparatively easy to fit a US Navy-standard special weapons stowage locker in a lower deck during one of the frequent visits to the shipyard for refit and maintenance, there is no evidence that this was ever accomplished. After the removal of the Banshee attack aircraft from the Bonaventure, a great deal of weapons storage space was freed up. This could have been used for nuclear depth bomb storage had the ship sailed south to the USN Quonset Point site in Rhode Island to pick up the weapons. Although retired RCN members like to intimate this happened, it was never done.

SEA KING

The CHSS-2 Sea King ship-borne helicopter is the only weapon system still in Canadian service which was planned by the RCN to carry a nuclear weapon. Experimented with by the RCN VX-10 Squadron, the Sea King would theoretically have been able to carry a Lulu or Hotpoint nuclear depth bomb on the right forward store. As the 1960s progressed, the B57 bomb would be added to this list, but only for the US Navy Sea Kings. The first Sea King came into RCN service in May 1963, and the Naval Staff told the high command that the Sea King was already wired for nuclear carriage.[49]

The RCN decided in the spring of 1962 that they would seek approval to build shore-based nuclear weapons stowage facilities at both RCN Air Station Shearwater, Nova Scotia, and at RCAF Station Comox, British Columbia. It was planned to have bunkers capable of holding "up to fifteen nuclear weapons" for use by the ship-based Sea King helicopters of the RCN.[50] Since there was to be a US custodial detachment based at Comox for the Genie weapons, this extra commitment would have been a relatively minor addition. However, a nuclear stowage site at Shearwater would have necessitated the stationing of a complete US Naval custodial detachment at great cost to the RCN. It was then realized that such a commitment would require at least an additional 80 RCN members and some 240 RCAF members, and that this could cost $1.6 million per year. The Naval Board was recommended to approve construction of the stowage at Shearwater for a cost of $500 000.00 in 1962.[51]

With the ending of the maritime nuclear option by Cabinet in early 1963, the naval aspect slowly disappeared, and the Sea Kings continued to operate with conventional torpedoes and depth bombs.

CONCLUDING THOUGHTS ON THE MARITIME WEAPONS

Neither the RCAF, nor the RCN, nor the Canadian Forces ever received anti-submarine warfare nuclear weapons, whether air-dropped or ship-deployed. The most persuasive argument against this notion is the fact of the deployment of the other systems for the RCAF and Canadian Army. It is instructive to note that these four weapons systems came to Canada only after great debate, the signing of diplomatic notes, the signing of various service-to-service technical arrangements, and the stationing of US military nuclear custodians at all Canadian nuclear sites here or abroad. Given that all of this happened, and given that this is the standard means of providing nuclear weapons to US allies, there is no real compelling reason to believe the rumours of nuclear weapons being aboard Canadian ships.

In the end, only the US Navy would deploy any ASW nuclear weapons in Canada, and that was not until after new government-to-government and service-to-service agreements had been negotiated and signed in the summer of 1967.

CONCLUDING THOUGHTS

It was a cold night when the first nuclear warheads arrived in North Bay on 31 December 1963. Canada, with that single shipment of seven nuclear weapons, had joined the small but growing group of nuclear-armed states.

It was a hot day in The Hague on 08 July 1996 when the International Court of Justice delivered their ruling on the legality of the use of nuclear weapons. The court, in a non-binding, split decision of eight to seven, found that "the threat of use of nuclear weapons would generally be contrary to the rules of international law applicable to armed conflict, and in particular the principles and rules of humanitarian law." This decision, for which many had waited years, would have called into question the entire strike programme NATO and Canada had in Europe.

However, the divided court was less condemning about the use of defensive nuclear weapons. They wrote that it was not possible to conclude whether it would be lawful or unlawful to use defensive nuclear weapons "in an extreme circumstance of self-defence, in which the very survival of a state would be at stake." This part of the decision would have left plenty of room for the government of the day to justify the BOMARC and the Genie rocket.

The Justices stated that world leaders should deal with the threat of nuclear war by immediately moving to negotiate the disarming of the nuclear arsenals. Canada, which now has a self-serving tendency to see itself as a nuclear virgin, will support this position and not look hypocritical. However, had this decision been handed down in 1963 when Prime Minister Pearson was acquiring nuclear warheads at home and abroad, and at the same time supporting useless multilateral negotiations on disarmament, the result would have been to place his minority government in an even more perilous position with regards to public opinion.

Canada is no longer in a position to acquire nuclear weapons of any type or for any purpose. The climate of the 1950s, the "Pentomic Era," is long passed; and the sole supplier, the United States, has been denuding its own forces of tactical nuclear weapons since 1991. In addition, the years have seen Canadians become more and more anti-nuclear, and hardly likely to accept such a role for the Department of National Defence. Even the suggestion that a new weapon system, the submarine, was to be powered by a nuclear reactor, brought all the anti-nuclear sentiments of Canadians to the surface and effectively scuttled the dream of the navy.

This was a unique period of Canadian military history, and it is most unlikely ever to be seen again.

THE AGREEMENT, ARRANGEMENTS, AND COMMANDING OFFICERS

This section is purely documentary, and includes the final government-to-government agreement, never before seen by the general public. Also here are the three service-to-service technical arrangements which were used to bring the actual nuclear weapons into the Canadian military establishment.

THE AGREEMENT: 16 AUGUST 1963

It was never intended that the agreement Canada signed with the United States to provide nuclear weapons for Canadian forces be made public. In fact, it was never to be seen by Parliament. Pearson and Martin assured the United States government that the document would be considered privileged information, and not presented to Parliament. The only access Parliament would have would be to a statement by the Prime Minister explaining his nuclear policy. Pearson noted that Parliament would then have a chance to debate the issue, but that this would not interfere with the signing and implementation of the agreement. The draft of this document came to light when the copy presented to the Governor General for signature was turned over to the National Archives, and transferred to microfilm in the early 1980s. The actual signed agreement and US response were not declassified until 1995.

Privy Council 1963-1224, 16 August 1963. Secret, "Draft Canadian Note Concerning Nuclear Warheads for the Canadian Forces" as given under the Deputy Governor General's signature, 16 August

1963, and returned to External Affairs with all papers. SECRET July 11, 1963 "Draft Canadian Note Concerning Nuclear Warheads for the Canadian Forces"
(NOTE: the draft is identical to the final signed version of Note 125)

Note No. 125   Ottawa, August 16, 1963.
Excellency,

I have the honour to refer to Articles 20 and 21 of the communiqué issued by the North Atlantic Council on December 19, 1957, and to appropriate authorities of the Canadian and United States Governments regarding the general principles under which nuclear warheads will be made available for the Canadian Forces.

It is the understanding of my Government that in the course of these discussions agreement was reached regarding these general principles. In order to implement this agreement my Government suggests the following arrangements:

(1) The United States shall provide and maintain stockpiles of nuclear warheads for the use of the Canadian Forces in respect of the weapons and weapons systems shown in the attached Annex, which may be amended from time to time by agreement between the two governments. In this agreement the expression "nuclear warhead" includes the associated weapon where the two cannot practically be considered as physically separate components.

(2) Stockpiles of nuclear weapons, to meet the needs of approved defence plans, will be established at locations to be determined by the Allied Commanders concerned in accordance with their approved plans and in agreement with Canadian and U.S. military authorities, or as determined by the U.S. and Canadian military authorities when appropriate.

(3) Except as otherwise agreed, the costs of construction, administration and maintenance of the storage sites and associated facilities, including those required for the support of the United States custodial and support personnel, shall be borne by Canada. Provision, without cost to the United States, of land required will be the responsibility of Canada. To the extent that the North Atlantic Council approves the establishment of nuclear stockpile sites under NATO common infrastructure, the apportionment of costs will be subject to NATO infrastructure procedures. Installations and facilities for nuclear warhead storage and maintenance will be built and

maintained to satisfy NATO or U.S. standards and criteria as applicable. Installations and facilities for normal logistic support (housing, messing, offices, etc.) which may not be specified under NATO criteria, will be provided and maintained as mutually agreed.

(4) It is recognized that the custody of any stocks of nuclear warheads provided by the United States will be the responsibility of the United States and that United States personnel will be provided for this purpose. The status of such personnel in Canada will be governed by the provisions of the NATO Status of Forces Agreement and any supplementary arrangements which may be agreed upon.

(5) The release of nuclear warheads to meet operational requirements will be the subject, where practical, of prior inter-governmental consultation. They will be used, when authorized by both Governments, only in accordance with procedures established by the appropriate Allied Commander or by the Canadian and United States military authorities as applicable.

(6) The United States shall be responsible for the maintenance, modification and assembly of nuclear warheads, including the provision of personnel and technical equipment for the performance of these functions.

(7) External security for all nuclear warheads in storage or during actual movement is the responsibility of Canada within Canada and, except as otherwise agreed between the appropriate authorities of the two Governments, elsewhere where there are nuclear warheads for the support of the Canadian Forces. The details of external security arrangements will be determined by the United States and Canadian military authorities and in accordance with the directives of the Allied Commander, where appropriate.

(8) The United States shall be responsible for the movement, in accordance with agreed procedures and in conformity with applicable Canadian laws and regulations, of the nuclear warheads between the United States and points of entry in Canada. Subject to the provisions of Article (4) above, Canada will be responsible for the transportation of nuclear warheads between points in Canada, and elsewhere as may be agreed. In respect of Europe, the United States will be responsible for the movement of nuclear warheads into and from the countries within the ACE area. Subject to the provisions of Article (4) above, the Canadian Forces, except as otherwise agreed between the appropriate authorities of the two Governments, will be responsible

for the movements of the weapons within countries in the ACE area.

(9) Except as otherwise agreed by the appropriate authorities of the two Governments, a reliable system of signal communications will be provided by the Government of Canada where necessary to meet the purpose of this agreement.

(10) Canada will be responsible for providing reasonable administrative and logistic support for the United States personnel described in Articles (3) and (4), and their dependents.

(11) Where Canada is a joint user, with other members of NATO, of storage facilities in Europe, the division of responsibilities for the support and external security of such facilities will be as agreed between the governments concerned and the appropriate Allied Commander.

(12) The safety procedures for storage, maintenance, transport, loading, delivery and salvage of nuclear warheads will be at least equivalent to U.S. standards and will be the subject of arrangements between the appropriate authorities of the United States and Canada taking into consideration classified (atomic) information which may be transferred under agreements between the two governments and the interests of other allied governments, as applicable.

(13) Supplementary arrangements required to implement this agreement will be negotiated between the appropriate military authorities of the United States and Canada.

(14) Canada and the United States will consult with regard to any notification or other form of diplomatic communication addressed to a third government concerning the proposed establishment of any stockpiles of nuclear warheads on its territory for possible Canadian use. Agreement on the location of stockpile sites will be obtained from the appropriate authorities of any third country in which stocks are to be maintained.

(15) Publicity concerning this agreement and its implementation shall be governed by the Exchange of Notes of February 19 and 24, 1951 concerning publicity relating to joint Canadian-United States defence plans and operations.

I propose that if the foregoing is acceptable to your Government, this note and your reply indicating such acceptance will constitute an agreement between the two Governments on this subject, the agreement to enter into force on the date of your note in reply.

Accept, Excellency, the assurances of my highest consideration.

signed
Paul Martin
Secretary of State
for External Affairs

ANNEX
WEAPONS AND WEAPONS SYSTEMS
1) The IM99B (Bomarc)
2) Air-to-Air missiles for the CF-101
3) Air-to-Surface weapons for the CF-104
4) The 762mm Rocket (Honest John)

SECRET Ottawa, August 16, 1963 Note No. 58
Sir:

I have the honor to refer to your Note 125 of August 16, 1963 and the Annex attached thereto proposing on behalf of the Government of Canada certain arrangements under which nuclear warheads will be made available for the Canadian Forces.

I am pleased to inform you that the arrangements set forth in your Note and Annex are acceptable to my Government. My Government further agrees that your Note and this reply shall constitute an agreement between the two Governments, effective to-day.

Accept, Excellency, the renewed assurances of my highest consideration.

(signed)
W.W. Butterworth
US Ambassador to Canada
The Honorable
 Paul Martin, P.C., Q.C.,
  M.P., M.A., LL.M., LL.D., D.C.L.,
   Secretary of State for External Affairs,
    Ottawa.
    SECRET

AUTHORIZATION FOR THE OPERATIONAL USE OF NUCLEAR WEAPONS
10 July 1964, US State Department Letter No. 138 of 27 January 1965 from Washington, Secret, Draft.

Sir:

1. I have the honour to refer to the Exchange of Notes of August 16, 1963 between our two Governments; in particular to paragraph 5 of the Secretary of State for External Affairs' Note No. 125 of that date; to the Letters of understanding of the same date, concerning consultation prior to the release of nuclear warheads top, and authorization for their operational use by NORAD forces in Canada; to the Exchange of Notes of September 28 and 30, 1963; in particular to paragraph 6, of the Secretary of State for External Affairs' Note No. 162 of September 28; and to the review by officials of the two Governments of existing arrangements between our two Governments providing for certain measures which might be taken when hostilities involving North America appeared likely or possible and for various forms of consultation concerning situations which might lead to the outbreak of such hostilities.

2. The general pattern reflected in these various arrangements is that the measures envisaged require governmental authorization, which normally would be given only at the time and following inter-governmental consultation. The possibility of surprise attack is reflected by the qualification, explicit or implied, that the time factor might not always permit prior inter-governmental consultation and might in certain circumstances require some of these measures to be undertaken on the basis of prior authorization.

3. The Canadian Government wishes to propose the conclusion of a comprehensive Agreement with the United States Government, in the terms set out below, both concerning bilateral consultation between the two Governments with regard to situations which might lead to the outbreak of hostilities involving North America, and hence might call for the release of nuclear warheads to NORAD forces, and concerning procedures relating to the authorization to CINCNORAD for operational use of nuclear

weapons. The object of this agreement would be:

(a) to consolidate relevant provisions of existing agreements and to define more precisely (1) the relationship between such consultation and measures relating to North American defense which might be undertaken in a situation of rising tension or to prepare for possible war, and (2) the procedural arrangements and channels of communication applicable to such consultation;

(b) to specify the procedures for authorizing CINCNORAD to use operationally forces equipped with nuclear weapons.

CONSULTATION

4. (a) As the NORAD Agreement recognizes that the air defense of North America is single and indivisible, there is a special obligation of both Governments to maintain the closest consultation in any situation which could develop into a direct military threat to North America and consequently would lead to such precautionary steps as the raising of NORAD's state of readiness. It is agreed that in a situation of increasing international tension which could give rise to hostilities involving North America, a meeting of representatives of our two Governments will be convened, on the initiative of either Government, (1) to examine jointly that situation in both its political and military aspects, and (ii) to consider, and to coordinate as appropriate, the courses of action which the two Governments might decide to undertake in relation to that situation.

(b) In a situation involving so urgent a risk of hostilities involving North America that is not considered practicable to convene such a meeting, either Government may initiate consultations concerning that situation through the medium of telecommunications, this to be known as "emergency consultation."

(c) Rapid and reliable telecommunications facilities will be provided which will, with due regard for security, permit the simultaneous participation in such emergency consultation of the President, the Secretary of State, the Secretary of Defense, and the Chairman of the Joint Chiefs of Staff for the United States, and the Prime Minister, the Secretary of State for

External Affairs, the Minister of National Defence, and the Chief of the Defence Staff for Canada, and the Commander-in-Chief, NORAD (CINCNORAD).

(d) Consultation between our two Governments in a situation of increasing international tension will be fully effective only if each has an adequate understanding of the views of the other concerning the background of that situation. Accordingly senior civilian and military representatives of our two Governments shall be prepared to meet at intervals of approximately six months to discuss situations which, in the view of either Government, might so develop as to lead in due course to a risk of hostilities involving North America. These discussions will be informal and exploratory and will not be regarded as involving or implying any commitment on the part of either Government as to the action it would take or the position it would adopt in particular circumstances not yet arisen.

PREPARATORY MEASURES

5. (a) In the course of consultation undertaken as provided in 4(a) or 4(b) above consideration shall be given to the advisability of implementing measures which might be proposed by either Government or by CINCNORAD in preparation for possible hostilities involving North America. Such measures could include:

    (i) the institution by either country of military or civil alert measures on a national basis,

    (ii) the increase by CINCNORAD of the state of readiness of the North American Air Defense Command,

    (iii) measures by national authorities preliminary to operational use of nuclear weapons by NORAD forces,

    (iv) the release of by the United States Government of nuclear weapons to Canadian forces committed to NORAD, and the concurrent authorization by both Governments to CINCNORAD for the operational use of nuclear weapons.

(b) Except as provided in 5(c), 5(d), and 9 hereunder, measures of a joint nature such as those listed in 5(a), (ii) and (iv) above shall not be undertaken until they have been discussed and agreed in the course of inter-governmental consultation as provided in 4 above.

(c) If an attack on North America appears imminent or probable in a matter of hours rather than days inter-governmental consultation between CINCNORAD and the two Governments might, of necessity, coincide with or even follow certain actions of a preparatory nature such as those listed in 5(a) above. In that event, the other parties concerned will immediately be informed of the action taken, and consultation will take place as soon as possible.

(d) Where time or other factors preclude his first consulting national authorities, CINCNORAD's authority, as set out in his terms of reference, to increase the state of readiness of his forces is reaffirmed, and his authority in an emergency to authorize the use of nuclear warheads is affirmed in the manner hereinafter prescribed.

(e) In a situation in which general war appears likely or imminent, certain other preparatory measures, not relating directly to the air defence of North America but nevertheless of concern to both Governments, would probably be considered. It would be appropriate that such measures be discussed in the course of the inter-governmental consultation for which provision is made in this agreement.

PROCEDURES

6. (a) When time permits and communications and other facilities are available, the normal channel for the initiation by either Government of consultation as provided in 4(a) and (d) above shall be between the United States Department of State and the Canadian Department of External Affairs via the Canadian Embassy, Washington. procedures already established to permit rapid communication between our two Governments at any time by this channel may be used for this purpose.

(b) In addition to the channel indicated in 6(a) above, channels which may be used to propose emergency consultation as provide in 4(b) above include President-Prime Minister, Secretary of State-Secretary of State for External Affairs, Secretary of Defense-Minister of National Defence, Chairman of the Joint Chiefs of staff-Chief of the Defence Staff or between designated officials of the Department of State and of the Department of External Affairs. Such emergency consultation may be initiated at the suggestion or request of CINCNORAD and, in such circumstances, CINCNORAD should normally be invited to participate in any discussions bearing on North American defense and involving other senior military advisers of the two Governments.

(c) Each Government shall establish and maintain such internal arrangements as will permit it to participate, at any time and on short notice, in such emergency consultation. Each Government shall inform the other of the nature of those internal arrangements, to the extent that such information would facilitate the prompt and effective conduct of such emergency consultation.

(d) Arrangements will be made to provide for periodic exercises to test and practice the procedures for initiating and conducting such emergency consultation, such exercises to be held on occasion in conjunction, with appropriate military and civil defense exercises.

AUTHORIZATION FOR THE OPERATIONAL USE OF NUCLEAR WEAPONS BY NORAD FORCES

7. (a) Both Governments have placed nuclear armed Air Defense Forces under the operational control of CINCNORAD. Elements of these forces might be required to undertake Air Defense operations either in the event of a strategic attack upon North America or in connection with hostilities not involving such an attack but nevertheless involving the vital interests of either Government.

(b) USA authorization for the release of nuclear weapons to Canadian Forces under the operational control of CINCNORAD, and Canadian and USA authorization for the use of nuclear weapons by forces under the operational control of CINCNORAD, including the cross-border deployment of nuclear armed forces and their employment in the airspace of both countries, will be effected upon declaration of Defense Condition one (strategic attack against North America is occurring) or in emergency circumstances as indicated in 8 below.

(c) Authorization for use of nuclear weapons in connection with hostilities in the North American area but not necessarily involving a strategic attack against North America will be effected as indicated in 9 below.

STRATEGIC ATTACK AGAINST NORTH AMERICA

8. (a) In the case of a gradual build-up in international tension, the inter- governmental consultative machinery, both political and military, would be active. By this time, as international situations develop, NORAD readiness and defense conditions could be changed to any of the defense conditions, or air defense emergency, as may be appropriate considering the seriousness of the situation.

(b) To provide for the emergency circumstances set forth in (e) below in which prior consultation is not practicable it is agreed that the President of the USA will provide for the timely release of nuclear warheads to Canadian NORAD Forces, and that the Prime Minister, acting on behalf of the Government of Canada, and the President, acting on behalf of the Government of the USA, will provide for the timely authorization to CINCNORAD to employ operationally nuclear armed forces.

(c) Nuclear weapons thus made available upon a declaration of Defense Condition one or Air Defense Emergency by CINCNORAD, either under emergency circumstances or through the consultative process covered by 4 above, will be used in accordance with the approved NORAD rules of interception and engagement (NORAD Regulation 55-6) and NORAD Nuclear Weapons Employment Procedures.

(d) Measures of a precautionary nature, the movement of forces in accordance with national preparedness procedures, and special deployment procedures applicable in areas such as Alaska where the period of warning could be very short may be undertaken as necessary in either country on the authority of the government of that country.

(e) The following circumstances referred to in this paragraph are as follows:

(i) A surprise attack in force against targets in Canada, or the

USA, or both. In the absence of any advance warning that such an attack was imminent, or of any indication that large scale hostilities had started or were imminent in other theatres where USA or Canadian forces were involved, direct and unequivocal evidence that an attack in forces had begun would be required. (Examples of developments which would be considered an "attack in force" would include the actual entry of substantial numbers of bombers into Canadian or USA sovereign airspace, or the detection of several missiles on trajectories originating from the USSR and terminating in North America, or a combination of several missiles and bombers penetrating the BNEWS and DEW Lines, respectively, on flight paths patently directed towards North America.)

(ii) Several nuclear bursts of unknown origin occurring in the space of a few minutes within the confines of the USA or Canada.

(iii) Reliable evidence that a large number of bombers had taken off or several ICBM's had been launched from bases in the USSR in circumstances preceded by a period of increased international tension.

(iv) A properly authenticated communication form any major NATO or USA commander clearly indicating that attacks involving the use of nuclear weapons had been launched in at least one theatre directly involving NATO or USA forces.

(v) Any circumstances in which in CINCNORAD's judgement a strategic attack against North America or an attack against Alaska, is imminent or occurring and in which delay might seriously prejudice the defense of the area involved.

GENERAL CONDITIONS

9. (a) In view of the possibility that situations might arise not involving a strategic attack against North America but nevertheless involving the vital interests of either government, each government shall, notwithstanding the other provisions

of the agreement, retain for purposes of its own defense the freedom to take measures, at home or abroad, not inconsistent with the sovereignty of the other. Such measures would include the employment, under national control and not subject to any restrictions arising from this agreement, of forces otherwise under the operational control of CINCNORAD. In the event such forces are so employed, the other government concerned will be informed immediately of the action taken.

(b) In the circumstances envisaged in 9(a) above, each government shall be entitled to make use of the NORAD command and control facilities to the extent necessary for the effective employment of its forces.

10. This agreement when it comes into forces shall supersede the existing Agreements listed in Annex A.

11. This Agreement may be reviewed by the two governments at the request of either government, and after such review may be terminated upon six months' notice. It may be modified or amended at any time, by agreement, upon the proposal of either government.

12. If the foregoing is acceptable to your government, I propose that this Note and your reply thereto shall constitute an Agreement between our two governments on this matter which comes into effect on the date of your reply.

ANNEX A

I. On the date on which it comes into force the agreement to which this is annexed shall supersede the following earlier agreements concluded between the Governments of the United States of America and of Canada:

A. The agreed minute dated June 14, 1951 concerning frequent special consultations on mutual defense arrangements and related matters.

B. The Agreement relating to consultations respecting the alerting of the North American Air Defense System set out in the following four notes:

(1) Note of May 14, 1956 from the Canadian Ambassador, Mr. ADP Heeney, to the Secretary of State, the Hon. John Foster

Dulles.

(2) Note of December 4, 1956 from the Deputy Under Secretary of State, Mr. Robert Murphy, to the Canadian Ambassador, Mr. ADP Heeney.

(3) Note of March 1, 1957 from the Canadian Ambassador, Mr. ADP Heeney, to the Secretary of State, the Hon. John Foster Dulles.

(4) Note of November 10, 1958 from the Deputy Under Secretary of State, Mr. Robert Murphy, to the Canadian Ambassador.

C. The so-called MB-1 agreements relating to authorization for United States interceptor aircraft under the control of NORAD to carry nuclear air-to-air defense weapons over Canada, set out in the following exchanges of notes:

(1)(a) Note of February 19, 1957 from the Secretary of State, the Hon. John Foster Dulles to the Canadian Ambassador, Mr. ADP Heeney.

(b) Note No. 91 of February 19, 1957 from the Canadian Ambassador, Mr. ADP Heeny, to the Secretary of State, the Hon. John Foster Dulles.

(2)(a) Note of June 28, 1957 from the Acting Secretary of State, Mr. Christian Herter, to the Canadian Ambassador, Mr. Norman A. Robertson

(b) Note No. 362 of June 28, 1957 from the Canadian Ambassador, Mr. Norman A. Robertson, to the Acting Secretary of State, Mr. Christian Herter.

(3)(a) Note of May 12, 1958 from the Acting Secretary of State, Mr. Christian Herter, to the Canadian Ambassador, Mr. Norman A. Robertson.

(b) Note No. 262 of May 12, 1958 from the Canadian Ambassador, Mr. Herbert A. Robertson, to the Secretary of State, the Hon. John Foster Dulles.

(c) Note of May 12, 1958 from the Canadian Ambassador, Mr. Herbert A. Robertson, to Mr. MG Parsons of the Department of State,

(d) Letter of May 14, 1958 from Mr. MG Parsons of the Department of State, to the Canadian Ambassador, Mr. Herbert A. Robertson.

(4)(a) Note of June 20, 1959 from the from Mr. Robert Murphy, to the Canadian Ambassador, Mr. ADP Heeny.

(b) Note No. 390 of June 30, 1959 from the Canadian Ambassador, Mr. ADP Heeney, to the Secretary of State, the Hon. Christian A. Herter, and subsequent notes on this subject up to and including the exchange of notes of June 30 and July 5, 1964 between the Canadian Ambassador, Mr. CSA Ritchie and the Secretary of State.

D. The agreements relating to increases in CINCNORAD's status of readiness, as set out in the following exchanges:

(1)(a) Letter of September 30, 1959 from the Canadian Ambassador, Mr. ADP Heeney, to the Secretary of State, the Hon. Christian A. Herter.

(b) Letter in reply of October 2, 1959 from the Secretary of State, the Hon. Christian A. Herter, to the Canadian Ambassador, Mr. ADP Heeney.

(2)(a) Letter of June 11, 1960 from Mr. Saul F. Rae, Minister of the Canadian Embassy, to Mr. Woodbury Willoughby of the Department of State.

(b) Letter in reply of January 14, 1951 from Mr. Woodbury Willoughby of the Department of State to Mr. Saul F. Rae, Minister of the Canadian Embassy.

II. On the date on which it comes into force, the agreement to which this is annexed shall modify the exchanges of letters of August 16, 1963 between the Secretary of State for External Affairs, the Hon. Paul Martin, and the American Ambassador, Mr. W. Walton Butterworth, relating to their exchange of notes Nos. 125 and 58 of the same date, regarding the provision of nuclear warheads for Canadian forces, as follows:

"The reference on the first page of Mr. Martin's letter to Paragraph 5 of the exchange of notes concerning consultation which was to be understood to be in accordance with the procedures set out in the secret exchange of letters dated September 30 and October 02, 1959 and supplementary exchanges, all of which are now superseded. This reference shall now therefore be understood to refer to consultation in accordance with the procedures set out in the agreement to which this is annexed."

III. On the date on which it comes into force, the agreement to which this is annexed shall modify the agreement on the storage of nuclear air-to-air defensive weapons at Goose Bay and Harmon Air Force Base for United States forces, as set out in the exchanges of letters of September 28, 1963 (Note No. 162 from the Secretary of State for External Affairs, the Hon. Paul Martin, to the American Ambassador, Mr. W. Walton Butterworth) and September 30, 1963, (Note No. 112 from the American Ambassador, Mr. W. Walton Butterworth, to the Secretary of State for External Affairs, the Hon. Paul Martin), as follows:

Paragraph 6 of Mr. Martin's Note No. 162 stated that:

"The release of warheads to meet operational requirements will be the subject, where practicable, of prior intergovernmental consultation. They will be used, when authorized by both governments only in accordance with procedures established by CINCNORAD. The MB-1 Agreements, of June 30, 1959 and June 1, 1962, shall apply to the removal of these weapons for operational reasons from areas utilized by US forces at Harmon and Goose Bay under existing agreements between the two Governments."

This paragraph shall now be understood to read:

"The release of warheads to meet operational requirements will be the subject, where practicable, of prior intergovernmental consultation. They will be used, when authorized by both governments, in accordance with the provisions of the agreement to which this is annexed. They will be used, when authorized by both Governments through the consultative procedures or in the emergency circumstances set out in the agreement to which this is annexed and only in accordance with procedures established by CINCNORAD."

THE SERVICE-TO-SERVICE ARRANGEMENTS:

Bomarc and Genie

The BOMARC and Genie were covered by the same document, originally signed in October 1963. This original arrangement, the first to be signed, remains hidden: however, the renewed service-to-service arrangement covering only the BOMARC has been declassified. Given that all of the arrangements are very similar, it is highly likely that the Genie arrangements were virtually identical to those of the BOMARC. It was the original arrangement which cleared the way, operationally, for the first importation of nuclear weapons into Canada on 31 December 1963.

19 February 1970, Service-to-Service Agreement Between the United States Air Force and the Canadian Armed Forces on a Supplementary Arrangement for the Canadian CIM-10B (Formerly Designated IM-99B) to Implement the Government-to-Government Agreement of August 16, 1963 Concerning Nuclear Weapons for Canadian Bases.

The Chief of Staff, United States Air Force and the Chief of the Defence Staff, Canadian Armed Forces (CF) agree to the provisions contained herein.

SECTION I — GENERAL

1. Purpose: The purpose of this CF/USAF Supplementary Arrangement, hereinafter referred to as "this agreement", is to establish and describe the procedures governing the receipt, storage, maintenance, transport, loading, delivery, salvage, custody, security, and control of the nuclear warheads for the CF CIM-10B squadrons, in order to provide an operational capability while ensuring compliance with applicable United States laws and regulations, such as the United States Atomic Energy Act of 1954, as amended, and applicable Canadian laws and regulations.

2. Authority: This agreement implements and draws its authority from the Canada/United States agreement effected by the exchange of Canadian note 125 and U.S. note 58 dated 16 August, 1963, and pertinent letters of understanding of the same date.*

3. Policy: This agreement prescribes the procedures necessary for both the USAF and CF to exercise their respective responsibilities under the aforementioned Government-to-Government agreement. This agreement further establishes procedures to insure nuclear safety, which is of a paramount interest to both the Unite States and Canadian Governments. The CF and USAF each assume responsibility for insuring compliance with the terms of this agreement by their own personnel and any non-CF/USAF personnel sponsored by them, respectively.

4. DEFINITIONS:

a. Access — Physical proximity or contact in such a manner as to allow the opportunity to activate, tamper with, or bypass critical components of a nuclear weapons system so as to cause, then or later,

---

* The USN operated Sea King helicopters with B57 NDBs until after 1984.

premature arming, detonating, launching, firing or releasing.

b. Custody — Maintaining care of United States materiel designated Restricted Data or Formerly Restricted Data and all components of that materiel.

c. Custodian — The qualified USAF individual exercising the authority to maintain custody delegated by the USAF Detachment Commander.

d. Entry — The physical act of going into a controlled area. It implies compliance with the administrative controls required to be eligible to enter the area.

e. Material — Documents and printed-matter.

f. Materiel — Equipment, apparatus, and Supplies (does not include printed-matter).

g. Security — A condition which results from the establishment of measures which protect designated information, systems, components, and equipment against hostile persons, acts, or influences.

5. PROCEDURES:

a. The United States Air Force will provide:

(1) Nuclear Warheads for the CIM-10B missile in Canada.

(2) Custodial detachments necessary to insure conformance with United States law. These detachments will be provided with necessary warhead technical support equipment.

(3) Communications equipment required for United States purposes exclusively.

(4) Peculiar support requirements, such as clothing sales, court-martial jurisdiction, administrative procedures, etc. The USAF ADC Commander will conclude necessary arrangements and required agreements with the CF and appropriate USAF agencies.

b. The Canadian Armed Forces will provide:

(1) Suitable and secure maintenance and storage facilities for the purpose of maintaining the warhead.

(2) Support to United States personnel and their dependents such as messing, housing, etc., to the same standards and on the same basis as that provided to comparable Canadian personnel.

(3) Base security, including protection against sabotage, espionage, subversion, and attacks by hostile persons or forces.

(4) A reliable system of signal communications as required to meet the purposes of the Government-to-Government agreement,

except as may be otherwise provided for in any existing or future Canada-United States agreements dealing with the provision of communications.

6. OPERATIONAL USE: The Canadian CIM-10B weapon system will be used, when authorized by both Governments, only in accordance with procedures established by CINCNORAD and approved by the appropriate Canadian and United States authorities.

SECTION II — MISSION AND ORGANIZATION

1. United States Air Force Detachments: A USAF Detachment is established at each Canadian BOMARC site.

a. Mission:

(1) exercise and maintain custody as defined in Section I.

(2) Establish, operate, and maintain control of a United States cryptographic system.

(3) Receive, store, maintain, and supervise/monitor the handling of all nuclear warheads.

(4) Assure compliance with the approved United States Safety Rules for the CF CIM-10B/weapon system.

(5) Comply with all applicable CF directives provided such directives are not in conflict with, or prevent the exercise of, the above mission responsibilities. The USAF Detachment Commander will provide personnel support to accomplish warhead maintenance and custody functions that only USAF personnel can perform on a basis that will permit the CF SAM Squadron Commander to meet his missile maintenance schedules.

(6) Custodial Responsibility is assigned to the Commander of the USAF Detachment through a United States chain of command, and will be exercised twenty-four hours a day by the USAF Custodial Detachment prior to warhead release by the appropriate United States authority.

b. Organization: The size of the USAF Detachment will be kept to a minimum required to provide custody as specified by United States law and to support CF maintenance operations. Personnel will be assigned in accordance with currently established Unit Detail Listings.

2. Canadian Armed Forces: A CF Surface-to-Surface Missile Squadron is established at each BOMARC site.

a. Mission:

(1) The Canadian CIM-10B weapon system will be used, when

authorized by both governments, only in accordance with procedures established by CINCNORAD and approved by the appropriate Canadian and United States authorities.

(2) Security of all base facilities, consistent with custodial responsibility of the USAF Detachment Commander, is assigned to the CF SAM Squadron Commander. Base security responsibilities shall be established in CF directives and orders and exercised so as to be at least commensurate with USAF security for similar United States installations.

(3) Assist the USAF Detachment in receiving, storing and handling of nuclear warheads.

(4) Assure compliance with United States approved weapon safety rules through appropriate direction in authorized Canadian publications.

(5) Comply with all technical and operational procedures required for use with the CIM-10B weapon system.

b. Organization: The size of the SAM Squadron will be sufficient to fulfil its NORAD mission. Personnel will be assigned in accordance with current Canadian Forces Organization Orders (CFOO's).

SECTION III — PROCEDURES

1. General: The Canadian BOMARC Squadrons are a part of the North American defence complex, under the operational control of CINCNORAD. NORAD Rules of Engagement apply and lines of communication are established from NORAD to the respective SAGE sectors and, thence, to the Canadian BOMARC Squadrons.

2. Receipt: Nuclear warheads will be shipped to the USAF Custodial Detachment by USAF airlift. Loading and unloading of the aircraft in Canada will be accomplished by the aircraft personnel. Loading and unloading of the convoy vehicles will be accomplished under the supervision of USAF Detachment personnel. Nuclear warheads will be receipted for by a Munitions Accountable Supply officer or his designated representative.

3. Transportation: The United States Air Force will be responsible for the movement of the nuclear warheads between the United States and points of entry in Canada in accordance with approved procedures and, while in Canada, in conformity with applicable Canadian laws and regulations. The CF will be responsible for the transportation of nuclear warheads between points in Canada under USAF custody, and in a manner consistent with applicable United

States laws and regulations.

4. Storage: all storage functions of warheads in the USAF Maintenance and Storage Area will be performed by CF/USAF armament personnel under the direction and control of USAF personnel.

5. Maintenance:

a. All maintenance functions on the warhead will be accomplished solely by United States Air Force personnel in the USAF Maintenance and Storage Building.

b. At least one USAF Custodian will accompany CF maintenance crews at any time they enter a shelter which contains a warhead. USAF personnel will remain in the shelter to insure armament access panels remain in place. USAF personnel will insure that the shelter is locked and surveillance returned to the intrusion alarm system upon leaving the shelter. Joint USAF/CF working procedures will insure that this requirement does not hamper CF missiles, launcher, and shelter maintenance.

c. all missile and launcher equipment maintenance will be accomplished in accordance with applicable USAF Technical Orders.

6. Loading: The loading and unloading of warheads will be performed by CF crews under the observation of a technically qualified USAF custodian. CF crews will consist of a minimum of one supervisor and two crew members.

7. EOD: Explosive Ordnance Disposal is a CF responsibility. USAF EOD personnel will be furnished to perform and actions that require access to Restricted Data materiel. USAF EOD personnel may participate in EOD operations not involving Restricted Data materiel at the request of the CF providing CF personnel maintain responsibility for and supervision of the operation. should an incident involving nuclear materiel requiring EOD action occur on, or in the vicinity of, a CF CIM-10B base, the USAF Detachment Commander will be the designated USAF "on-the-scene" representative for the purpose of the "Service-to-Service Agreement between the USAF and the CAF on the Responsibilities for Response to Nuclear Weapon Incidents Involving Canadian Territory", dated 20 August 1968.

8. Training: Training will be conducted in accordance with current CF/USAF directives to insure that all operations are conducted by qualified personnel.

9. Publications: Publications will be obtained through CF, USAF or

jointly approved administrative procedures.

10. Facilities:

a. site facilities will be in conformance with current jointly approved drawings to include a United States maintenance and storage area with space for the following:

(1) The Commander's office.

(2) Cryptographic Room.

(3) Toilet.

(4) Security Lobby.

(5) Intrusion Alarm monitoring panels.

(6) Warhead Storage.

(7) Warhead Maintenance.

(8) Storage of Restricted Data documents.

(9) Supply Office.

(10) Administrative Office.

b. The site intrusion alarm system will be in conformance with USAF security standards with the master monitor panel located in Central Security Control and will be continuously monitored in the USAF maintenance and storage area by means of a remote monitor panel.

c. Each launcher shelter that contains a nuclear warhead will be locked with a secure key lock to which only USAF personnel will have the key.

11. Security: The CF will provide and employ such facilities, equipment, and personnel as required for the protection of classified CIM-10B weapon system components in Canada. Security of all base facilities, consistent with the custodial responsibility of the USAF Detachment Commander, is assigned to the CF SAM Squadron Commander.

a. USAF Aerospace Defense Command and Canadian Forces Air Defence Command will coordinate to insure compatibility of CF security directives with USAF security criteria.

b. The USAF Detachment Commander will:

(1) Control Entry into the USAF Maintenance and Storage area.

(2) Establish and certify to the CF and the eligibility of those USAF or USAF-sponsored personnel who have a requirement for entry into CF SAM Squadron restricted areas and access to classified information.

(3) Permit entry of CF and CF-sponsored personnel, to the shelters of the United States Maintenance and Storage Area,

consistent with custodial responsibility as defined in Section I, subject to prior receipt of certification by the CF.

(4) Determine, in conjunction with the CF, which CF security regulations, practices, and procedures are applicable to USAF and USAF-sponsored personnel operating on CF SAM Squadron installations and issue such instructions as required to insure compliance therewith.

(5) Process in accordance with USAF administrative regulations, reports of violations of CF security regulations committed by USAF or USAF-sponsored personnel and advise the CF of action taken in each case. Report immediately to the CF any violation of security agreements, regulations, practices, or procedures coming to the attention of the USAF.

(6) Insure internal security of the USAF Maintenance and Storage Area. Armed support will be provided by the CF.

c. The CF SAM Squadron commander will:

(1) Provide security for all base facilities consistent with the custodial responsibility of the USAF Detachment Commander.

(2) Permit entry of USAF and USAF-sponsored personnel, subject to prior receipt of certification by the USAF, provided that no operational objection exists.

(3) Establish and certify to the USAF the eligibility of those CF or CF-sponsored personnel who have a requirement for entry into CF SAM Squadron shelters or U.S. Maintenance and Storage Area.

(4) Establish and provide to the USAF those CF security regulations, practices, and procedures requiring conformance by USAF or USAF-sponsored personnel operating at CF SAM Squadron installations.

(5) Establish and provide to the USAF, in writing and on an as required basis, a guide for security classification of information concerning the operation of the Canadian CIM-10B program.

12. Communications: The USAF Detachment will establish a normal off-line cryptographic account under the provisions of applicable USAF regulations and manuals.

a. CF teletype facilities will be utilized for transmitting and receiving encrypted traffic and unclassified traffic. Enciphering and deciphering will be accomplished with off-line cryptographic systems located in the USAF Maintenance and Storage Area.

b. Message routing procedures for both classified and unclassified communications will provide the USAF Detachment Commander with the means of communicating United States classified information, including TOP SECRET, with any Air Force installations within North America.

SECTION IV — SAFETY

1. General: Compliance with applicable Canadian laws, regulations, Nuclear Weapons Instructions and with approved U.S. Nuclear Safety Rules is mandatory at all times by both USAF and CF personnel.

2. Procedures: The USAF Detachment commander will appoint a USAF Nuclear Safety Officer. The Det. Commander and the USAF/NSO will, in conjunction with the Canadian Nuclear Safety officer, advise the CF Base Commander on matters pertaining to nuclear safety. The authority of the USAF Det. Commander with respect to non-adherence to Nuclear Safety Rules and procedures is final. Whenever he determines that a nuclear hazard exists, he will immediately remove the shelter plugs or take such other appropriate action, then notify the CF SAM Squadron Commander of the situation. The safety procedures for storage, maintenance, transport, loading, delivery, and salvage of nuclear warheads will be at least equivalent to U.S. standards and will be the subject of arrangements between the appropriate military authorities of the United States and Canada, taking into consideration classified nuclear information which may be transferred under agreements between the two governments.

3. Human Reliability Programme: The CF and the USAF are responsible for establishing agreed standards for evaluating personnel who handle or have access to nuclear weapons, devices, or controls, and for eliminating personnel who are incompatible with assignment in these sensitive areas. The CF and USAF will establish appropriate directives and checklists to ensure that this programme is implemented and continuously maintained.

4. Radiological Hazards: Protection from warhead radiological hazards, including detection and decontamination is the responsibility of the CF SAM Squadron Commander. The USAF Detachment Commander will be responsible for providing the necessary information on the nature of hazard to the CF SAM Squadron Commander, and for detection of radiological hazards in the USAF Maintenance and Storage Area.

5. Explosive, Ground and Industrial Safety: Explosive, ground and industrial safety procedures will be in accordance with current CF

directives or with current jointly approved directives.

SECTION V — INSPECTION

1. Capability Inspections: Capability Inspections of CF BOMARC units will be a joint responsibility of the USAF and CF and will be conducted in accordance with applicable USAF/CF directives at prescribed intervals. Full CF participation as authorized in all areas, except those prohibited by United States law, or which are the exclusive responsibility of the Detachment Commander.

2. Spot Inspections: Spot inspections of functions controlled by the USAF Detachment Commander will be the responsibility of USAF (ADC). Spot inspections of all other functions will be the responsibility of the CF. In areas of mutual responsibility and interest, a joint USAF (ADC)/CF team will be formed.

3. Re-inspections: Re-inspection of functions controlled by the USAF Detachment Commander will be the responsibility of USAF (ADC). Re-inspections of all other functions will be the responsibility of the CF. Where areas of mutual responsibility and interest are involved, a joint USAF (ADC)/CF team will be formed.

4. Reports: Reports and reporting of corrective action taken as a result of these inspections will be as provided for in applicable USAF/CF regulations. The CF report of corrective action taken will be forwarded to Headquarters USAF from the highest echelon deemed appropriate by the CF. Information copies of these reports will also be furnished to USAF ADC.

CF-104 Starfighter

The service-to-service arrangement for the Canadair CF-104 Starfighter was the only arrangement to equip the RCAF in Europe with nuclear weapons. The second of all the arrangements, it involved the RCAF and the USAF Europe, and is the longest and most detailed of the documents. Although the arrangement does not specify the type of weapon involved, the USAFE would supply the RCAF with three different types of nuclear gravity bombs. This was the last text of the arrangement to be released by the Canadian government. The arrangement for the Starfighter is very close in structure to the other arrangements, although much longer. In fact, the arrangements for both the BOMARC and Genie, and the USAF squadrons at Goose Bay and Harmon Field, are modelled upon each other for ease of negotiation and clarity of meaning. It can therefore be concluded that the military simply took a workable arrangement and copied it, with minor variations for the individual weapons systems, for all necessary documents.

The main body of the arrangement, called the "agreement" in the text, and Annex B dealing with Alert Procedures, are reproduced here. The annexes dealing with security and inspections have been deleted for the sake of brevity.

31 January 1964, Service-to-Service Technical Arrangement between the United States Air Force Europe (USAFE) and the Royal Canadian Air Force (RCAF) for the Canadian CF-104 Weapon System to Implement the Government-to-Government Agreement of August 16, 1963 Concerning Nuclear Weapons for Canadian Forces.

SECTION I INTRODUCTION
1. PURPOSE.
The purpose of this Royal Canadian Air Force (RCAF)/ United States Air Force in Europe (USAFE) Arrangement, hereinafter referred to as "this agreement", is to establish and describe the procedures governing the receipt, storage, maintenance, transport, loading, delivery, salvage, custody, security and control of nuclear weapons for RCAF CF-104 strike squadrons assigned to the Supreme Allied Commander Europe (SACEUR), in order to provide an operational capability while ensuring compliance with applicable United States laws and regulations, (such as the United States Atomic Energy Act of 1954, as amended), the Allied Commander Europe Plan for the NATO Special Ammunition Storage Program dated 30 Mar 61, and applicable Canadian laws and regulations as well as the provisions of applicable United States and Canadian agreement with the Host Nation.

2. AUTHORITY.
This agreement implements and is subject to the provisions of the Canada/United States agreement effected by the exchange of Notes 125 (Canada) and 58 (United States) dated 16 Aug 63, and support the North Atlantic Council Declaration and Communiqué (Document PC/10, NATO Ministerial Meeting of 16–19 December 1957).

3. POLICY.
This agreement prescribes the procedures necessary for both the USAFE

and RCAF to exercise their respective and joint responsibilities under the aforementioned Government-to-Government agreement. The RCAF and USAFE each assume responsibility for insuring compliance with the terms of this agreement by their own personnel and any non-RCAF/USAFE personnel sponsored by them, respectively.

SECTION II GENERAL

1. STATIONING OF FORCES.

In the implementation of this agreement, the USAFE will station custodial detachments comprising a mutually agreed number of military personnel and personnel serving with, employed by, or accompanying the forces (dependents), equipment and other material on agreed Royal Canadian Air Force (RCAF) bases or elsewhere in Allied Command Europe (ACE) area made available by the RCAF, and will use such agreed bases and facilities for agreed military purposes. These USAFE forces will hereinafter be referred to as the Custodial Detachments.

2. CUSTOMS.

The RCAF will arrange for customs formalities to be carried out on the Canadian bases for US personnel and materiel in accordance with applicable intergovernmental agreements.

3. NUCLEAR WEAPONS SUPPORT AND CONTROL.

a. Nuclear weapon support will be provided to RCAF nuclear delivery units in support of NATO defence plans. The time of deployment of custodial detachments to custodial storage sites will depend upon the attainment of operational readiness by RCAF delivery units and the availability of adequate storage and administrative facilities and other support as mutually agree herein.

b. The US forces will retain custody of all US nuclear weapons and will release US nuclear weapons to the RCAF only in accordance with NATO defence plans, SACEUR directives, and US national control procedures. Custodial and operational procedures for U.S. owned training weapons will be as prescribed by USAF.

4. COMMAND JURISDICTION.

The presence of the USAF at the agreed bases will not alter the command responsibility and authority of the RCAF Base Commander; but with respect to the custodial detachment, all functions of command will be the sole responsibility of the Custodial

Detachment Commander. The Custodial Detachment Commander will ensure compliance with all applicable RCAF directives provided such directives are not in conflict with or prevent the exercise of the Custodial Detachment Commander's responsibilities.

5. SUPPORT AND COSTS.

a. The RCAF will provide at no cost to the United States or personal cost to the individual US personnel, all land, facilities, services, supplies, and other logistic and administrative support required by this agreement unless otherwise specifically stated therein. The cost of salaries and allowances of US military personnel and such equipment and training as the United States has agreed to furnish will be borne by the United States Government.

   b. Common items of administrative and logistical support, such as billeting, messing, transportation, mail service, etc., will be provided by the RCAF to United States personnel and their dependents to the same standard and on the same basis as that provided for equivalent Canadian personnel. USAF peculiar support requirements, such as clothing sales, court-martial jurisdiction, administrative proceedings, etc., will be provided from USAF sources. The responsible USAF Commander will conclude necessary arrangements and required agreements with the RCAF and appropriate USAF agencies.

SECTION III COMMUNICATIONS
1. GENERAL.

a. All point-to-point communications will be through NATO/national channels, except that the USAF will, at its own expense, install, equip, maintain and operate a communications facility for separate US National channels.

   b. Nuclear weapons will not be made available on the storage site until communications consistent with SHAPE criteria are available, and above cited US communications are operational.

   c. All communications equipment and services (telephone, teletypewriters, cable, longlines and like facilities) will be arranged for by the RCAF, except as otherwise provided herein.

   d. US personnel will be assigned as part of the custodial detachments for the equipment, operation, and maintenance of US communication facilities for use of the custodial detachment. Cost of this US provided equipment and its installation and maintenance will be borne by the US.

2. RESPONSIBILITIES.

a. The USAFE will provide, operate, and maintain US communications facilities, together with the US national cryptographic equipment and documents required for the cryptographic section of these facilities for use of the custodial detachment.

b. The RCAF will provide, operate, and maintain:

(1) Speech communications between the storage site, the alert area, and the custodial detachment administrative area on the associated RCAF base, including all required terminal equipment.

(2) Teletypewriter communications through prescribed NATO/National channels for access into higher echelon NATO channels and into a US military communications station at a designated transfer point. These facilities will be made available for utilization by the Custodial Detachment Commander as required.

(3) Mobile communications equipment as required in paragraphs 7 and 14 of Annex A.

(4) Long distance official telephone service for the custodial detachment through NATO/National channels. Where NATO/National facilities will not provide required service, such official calls, if deemed urgent by the Custodial Detachment Commander, may be placed for the USAF element through existing civil facilities, and charges so incurred will be paid by the RCAF. The USAF signatory to this agreement gives assurances that such calls placed through civil facilities will be restricted to occasions of real urgency and will investigate fully and evidence indicating that such restriction is not being observed.

c. The RCAF will ensure that all communications facilities are available to coincide with the installation and operational dates of the US element at the selected RCAF base.

d. The RCAF will provide and maintain an operating area for the USAF cryptographic facility physically secured in accordance with existing NATO standards. This area must be collocated with the administrative area of the custodial detachment.

SECTION IV SUPPORT
1. INSTALLATIONS.

a. The RCAF will be responsible for obtaining and making available without cost to the US all land areas required by the USAF, and will assure that provision is made for the construction of required structures and facilities in accordance with NATO criteria. To the extent that North Atlantic Council approves the establishment of nuclear stockpile sites under NATO Common Infrastructure, the apportionment of costs will be subject to NATO Infrastructure procedures.

b. Buildings and facilities not scheduled by NATO but required by the USAF to fulfil the terms of this agreement will be provided by the RCAF. These will be provided in accordance with standards agreed by the Custodial Detachment Commander and the RCAF Base Commander and use will be made of existing RCAF buildings to the maximum extent possible.

2. MATERIEL.

a. Technical tools and equipment required by the USAF custodial detachment to perform its mission will be provided by the USAF.

b. For items of equipment other than those covered by "a" above, the USAF will provide a list of applicable items to be supplied by the RCAF. These will include all furnishings and equipment required in the facilities provided. This list will be subject to agreement between the RCAF and USAFE. The items supplied will remain RCAF property and be subject to RCAF materiel accounting procedures.

c. Replacement items of equipment, when required, will be provided through the same procedures used in obtaining original items as outlined in paragraph "a" and "b" above.

d. Support services required by the custodial detachment, such as laundering and dry cleaning of organizational property, maintenance, fuels, lubricants, and repair of vehicles and equipment, will be provided by the RCAF.

3. TRANSPORTATION.

a. The RCAF will provide:

(1) the following vehicles in operational condition for continuous use outside the ammunition storage area, on and off base, in support of the custodial detachment. The custodial detachment will provide drivers for these vehicles.

1 ea auto, motor sedan, 4-door

2 ea 1/2-ton pick-up truck,

1 ea approximately 15 passenger bus

1 ea EOD vehicle, 4-wheel drive

(2) The following vehicles in operational condition for continuous use within the ammunition storage area. The custodial detachment will provide drivers for these vehicles.

2 ea 1/2 ton pick-up truck

1 ea forklift, 6000 lb minimum capacity

2 ea trailer stake body, 4' x 8' bed

(3) Permission and licensing of custodial detachment personnel in accordance with RCAF regulations to drive RCAF vehicles.

(4) When available other such vehicle support as required.

(5) On request of the USAFE but at no cost to the USAF, freight shipment within ACE area of military equipment associated with USAF nuclear support of RCAF Strike Units. This will include all loading, unloading, packing, unpacking, and temporary storage of such freight shipment.

(6) Payment of transportation costs for official travel of custodial detachment personnel on temporary duty related to USAF nuclear support of RCAF Strike Units.

(7) Daily transportation for dependent children to locally operated US or Canadian dependent schools on the same basis as that provided for Canadian dependent children.

b. The USAF will provide:

(1) Shipments of personal effects of USAF personnel and dependents arriving at or departing from agreed bases.

(2) Transportation for USAF personnel arriving at or departing from the agreed bases on permanent change of station.

4. PERSONNEL SUPPORT.

a. Personnel Supplies: Items of personal supplies and equipment not otherwise provided for under para 2, above, including weapons, ammunition, and clothing, for USAF personnel, shall be the responsibility of the USAF.

b. Housing:

(1) Bachelor Officers, NCO's and Airmen or those not accompanied by dependents will be provided furnished quarters without cost to the individual or to the U.S. Government.

(a) Officers will be provided billets in the RCAF BOQ on the same basis as that provided equivalent Canadian personnel. Service charges such as for laundry may be assessed at the same rates as for Canadian personnel.

(b) NCO's and Airmen will be billeted in the assigned USAF barracks.

(c) U.S. and Canadian authorities recognize that the above facilities do not meet NATO criteria for dormitory and administrative facilities. Should these facilities not prove sufficient due to an increase in the size of the custodial detachment, a requirement for use of these facilities by Canadian Forces, or other pertinent reason, the RCAF will apply for NATO common infrastructure funding for Type "C" dormitory and administrative facilities authorized.

(2) The RCAF will provide furnished quarters to US personnel accompanied by dependents to the same standard and on the same basis as that provided for equivalent Canadian personnel. The total cost of rental charges to USAF personnel for RCAF controlled housing will not exceed the current USAF housing allowance.

c. Recreation Facilities: The RCAF will:

(1) Permit USAF personnel to use all existing athletic and recreational and day room facilities.

(2) Make available to USAF personnel the privilege of membership in all RCAF clubs and messes for officers, NCO's, and others, according to rank. USAF membership in messes, clubs and or institutes will be in accordance with RCAF regulations governing such membership, including mess and club dues.

d. Schools: Dependent children of US personnel will be permitted to attend RCAF dependent schools on the same basis as dependent children of RCAF personnel. Where an RCAF dependent school does not exist, adequate school facilities, including maintenance and custodial services, utilities and other operating costs, will be provided by the RCAF. Administration of the dependent school or schools so provided will be the responsibility of the US.

e. Medical Support: The RCAF will provide:
Medical support to USAF personnel and their dependents in accordance with existing arrangements.

f. Food Service: The RCAF will provide messing on a repayment basis to US personnel on ration strength (not separate rations) to the same standard and on the same basis as that provided to comparable Canadian personnel. US personnel not on ration strength (on separate rations) will pay scheduled meal prices.

5. MAINTENANCE AND UTILITIES.

a. The RCAF will provide all necessary maintenance of land areas, roads, utilities, structures, and facilities occupied by the USAF, and will furnish and operate all civil engineering services required by the USAF, including but not limited to utilities (such as electricity, heat, water, gas, and sewage disposal), janitorial service, trash disposal, and snow and ice removal.

b. The RCAF will make minor modifications and alterations to structures and facilities to meet USAF requirements as mutually agreed between the Custodial Detachment Commander and the RCAF Base Commander. Major modifications, alterations, or additions will be as mutually agreed between the USAFE and the RCAF. Restoration, rehabilitation, and repair of structures and facilities as required upon termination of occupancy by the USAF, will be a RCAF responsibility, except that the USAF will reimburse the RCAF for willful or negligent damage over and above fair wear and tear caused to such structures and facilities by US personnel.

6. FIRE PROTECTION.

a. The RCAF will furnish fire protection, including fire fighting personnel and equipment, for USAF material and personnel. Except as indicated below, fire prevention measures and inspections will be the responsibility of the RCAF.

b. The RCAF will provide crash and rescue equipment and personnel trained for fire protection within the USAF restricted areas and in the proximity of nuclear weapons particularly those weapons under conditions of alert or transport. The USAF will be responsible for fire prevention methods and inspections in the areas described above and will provide to the RCAF personnel, in accordance with US disclosure procedures, special information and instructions necessary for performance of their duties. The RCAF will implement USAF provided procedures for preventing and combating fires that might threaten nuclear weapons.

SECTION V INFORMATION ACTIVITIES
1. GENERAL.

Publicity relating to joint Canadian-US defence plans and operations will be governed by the provisions of the US-Canadian Notes of 19 and 24 February 1951, except that access by members of press or other news media to areas containing nuclear weapons will be jointly approved by the appropriate RCAF and USAF commanders.

2. RELEASE OF NEWS.

a. The RCAF Base Commander, prior to releasing any information concerning the USAF or its personnel at the agreed bases, will obtain clearance from the Custodial Detachment Commander. If the information is of possible general interest, (i.e., other than "spot news" as defined in the aforementioned notes of 19 and 24 February 1951) clearance will be obtained through the AOC 1 Air Division, RCAF, who will coordinate such request for clearance with the Commander-in-Chief, United States Air Force in Europe, with Supreme Allied Commander, Europe, and with the appropriate Canadian government agencies as applicable.

b. The Custodial Detachment Commander, prior to releasing any information concerning the RCAF or its personnel at the agreed bases, will obtain clearance from the RCAF Base Commander. If the information is of possible general interest, clearance will be obtained from Headquarters USAFE, which will coordinate such request for clearance with the AOC 1 Air Division, RCAF, and with SACEUR.

SECTION VI — SAFETY
1. NUCLEAR WEAPONS.

a. The USAF will provide all necessary information pertaining to safety rules and procedures governing nuclear weapon operations in accordance with US National disclosure policy and established transmission or retransmission channels. The RCAF Base Commander will furnish the Custodial Detachment Commander any pertinent Canadian safety regulations. When such regulations are made available they will be forwarded to appropriate US agencies for evaluation.

b. The USAF and the RCAF will be responsible for compliance with United States Nuclear Weapon System Safety Rules and procedures for nuclear weapon operations. The USAF and the RCAF also agree to comply with any non-inconsistent Canadian safety regulations and with any provisions of Annex B, hereto, entitled "Alert Procedures for RCAF Nuclear Strike Forces", for each weapon system-bomb combination.

c. The RCAF will certify to the Custodial Detachment Commander that the armament system of each delivery vehicle meets the standards prescribed and approved by the USAF. Such certification will be made by the RCAF Base Commander or his designated representative prior to placing the delivery vehicle on Quick Reaction Alert and at any time that the armament system is modified or affected by other changes in the delivery vehicle configuration subsequent to original certification. No modification will be made to the weapon control, monitor suspension or release system without USAF approval. The RCAF will report any failure of weapon control, monitor, suspension or release system to appropriate USAF agencies.

d. The RCAF and the USAFE will establish a nuclear safety inspection system. (see Annex C) USAF assisted by the RCAF will conduct inspections in accordance with Annex C to insure that nuclear safety rules and procedures are being followed.

e. The Custodial Detachment Commander will designate an USAF Nuclear Safety Officer who, in conjunction with the RCAF Nuclear Safety Officer, will advise the RCAF Base Commander on matters pertaining to nuclear safety. However, any documents pertaining to nuclear safety and containing Restricted Data or Formerly Restricted Data will be passed to the RCAF in accordance with procedures established under "The Agreement Between the United States of America and the Government of Canada for Co-operation on Uses of Atomic Energy for Mutual Defence Purposes", dated 22 May 1959 as amended. The authority of the Custodial Detachment Commander with respect to the determination of the non-adherence to United States Nuclear Weapon Safety Rules and procedures is final. Whenever he determines that a nuclear hazard exists, he will immediately notify the RCAF Base Commander of the situation, then place in storage the weapon involved, or take other appropriate action until the situation is corrected.

f. Protection from weapon radiological hazards, including detection and decontamination (exclusive of the nuclear weapon storage area which is the responsibility of the Custodial Detachment Commander) is the responsibility of the RCAF Base Commander. The Custodial Detachment Commander will be responsible for providing the necessary information on the nature of the hazard to the RCAF Base Commander.

g. USAF and RCAF personnel who control, handle, have access

to, or control access to nuclear weapons, or nuclear weapon control systems, must be certified as acceptable in accordance with the criteria of the Human Reliability Programme (HRP) as specified in respective USAF and RCAF orders.

2. MUNITIONS DESTRUCTION, NEUTRALIZATION, OR DISPOSAL.

a. The USAF will be responsible for destruction, neutralization, or disposal of all US munitions which may be provided within the framework of this agreement and which require the services of qualified technicians.

b. The RCAF will provide assistance as requested by the Custodial Detachment Commander.

c. Recovery of nuclear weapons, including warhead sections, will be accomplished by USAF personnel with the RCAF furnishing movement security as provided in Annex A, para 14, as appropriate.

SECTION VII — SECURITY
1. GENERAL.

Minimum security standards and basic security responsibilities as set out in Annex A are established in accordance with the overall security plan for nuclear weapons and are contained in Annex C, SHAPE 6430/20 "Allied Command Europe Plan for the NATO Special Ammunition Storage Programme". The Custodial Detachment Commander and the RCAF base Commander will maintain contact, exchange releasable regulations and security procedures and keep fully informed of all matters affecting security of the base and of US and Canadian property and personnel connected therewith.

a. USAF Responsibility: The Custodial Detachment Commander will maintain custody of and control access to the nuclear weapons and US owned training weapons, and will establish exclusion areas, to which only designated US personnel will normally be admitted. As used in this agreement, custody is defined as the guardianship and safekeeping of nuclear weapons and their components, including source and special materials. This includes:

(1) Accountability for warheads and materials classified Restricted Data or Formerly Restricted Data which remain with the US as US property.

(2) Control of access to the warheads or material classified Restricted Data or Formerly Restricted Data in that it would take an

act of force against a US National, and therefore against the US Government, to obtain or use the warheads or materials classified as Restricted Data or Formerly Restricted Data, or obtain information concerning them.

b. Royal Canadian Air Force Responsibility: The RCAF is responsible for the general security of the agreed bases and external security of all land areas, structures, and other facilities made available by the RCAF for the use of the USAF. External security, for the purpose of this arrangement, is defined as protection against enemy forces, saboteurs, para-military forces or other unauthorized personnel.

2. LAW ENFORCEMENT.

The RCAF will be responsible for all normal military police activities involving Canadian or US military personnel. Security violations or other offenses will be investigated and handled in accordance with the NATO SOFA or any subsequent inter-governmental agreement which may supplement or supersede it. Copies of base regulations of a police or security nature applicable to US personnel will be furnished for dissemination to all US personnel.

3. EMERGENCY PLANS.

The RCAF commander responsible for the security of an area in which US nuclear weapons are located will prepare, in coordination with the US custodial detachment commander in the area, plans for the evacuation of all nuclear weapons with minimum delay in event of subversive activity, disaster, civil riot, or any similar emergency.

a. Such plans will indicate the conditions in which an emergency may be considered to exist. Regardless of the condition or the type of the emergency, nuclear and US owned training weapons will remain under US custody until release is authorized in conformance with R-Hour or S-Hour release procedures.

b. US personnel are responsible for destruction of US nuclear weapons when such action becomes necessary. Destruction orders issued by US custodial detachment commanders will be in accordance with joint plans.

SECTION VIII CLAIMS

Claims for property loss or damage, personal injury or death, in connection with the operation of this agreement, shall be dealt with in accordance with the provisions of the NATO SOFA or any other subsequent intergovernmental agreement which may supplement or supersede it.

SECTION IX ANNEXES

Attached hereto are Annexes A, B and C, which form an integral part of this agreement.

Annex A — Minimum Security Standards.

Annex B — Alert Procedures for RCAF Nuclear Strike Forces.

Annex C — USAFE and RCAF Nuclear Safety Inspection System.

SECTION X — ENTRY INTO FORCE.

The present agreement enters into force upon signature.

(signed by)

G.P. Disosway   D.A.R. Bradshaw

General, USAF   Air Vice Marshal

Commander-in-Chief   for Chief of the Air Staff

United States Air Force Europe   Royal Canadian Air Force

31 January 1964   31 January 1964

ANNEX B
ALERT PROCEDURES FOR RCAF NUCLEAR STRIKE FORCES.

Certain SACEUR designated RCAF strike squadrons will have US nuclear weapons readily available for use in accordance with procedures established by SACEUR and subject to USCINCEUR custody and release. Such squadrons are required by SACEUR to provide a specific number of aircraft on Quick Reaction Alert (QRA). The agreement establishes those responsibilities and procedures which must be followed to effect proper safety, custody and release for SACEUR committed RCAF units. These procedures will assure compliance with US Nuclear Weapon System Safety Rules and are considered the minimum essential to safeguard and control the nuclear weapons involved. However, both the USAF and the RCAF will comply with any additional restrictions or temporary limitations involving the weapon system when such are imposed by competent authority.

1. GENERAL.

The storage, handling, maintenance, loading, downloading, access or any other operation involving US nuclear weapons will be governed by the approved US Nuclear Weapon System Safety Rules as augmented by USCINCEUR/ CINCUSAFE and associated technical documents. Both USAFE and the RCAF will comply with and abide by these safety rules and the associated weapon system technical orders, checklists, or equivalents thereof approved by the USAF.

a. USAFE will provide the safety rules and appropriate technical publications as early as possible to facilitate the training of RCAF strike unit personnel and in no case later than assignment to QRA status.

b. The RCAF will insure expeditious distribution of these documents or changes thereto through national channels to the strike units.

2. ALERT POSTURE.

A portion of the SACEUR-committed RCAF force will be placed on QRA during peacetime conditions in order to provide SACEUR with a capability to launch high priority strikes in a minimum of time. During periods of increased international tension, SACEUR may declare conditions of advanced alert which require increased numbers of aircraft on QRA. The number of aircraft committed to QRA and the rate of force generation required by SACEUR announced alerts will be as specified in the SACEUR NSP.

3. TRAINING

a. **Practice Alerts.** Those weapon systems and crews which are on normal peacetime QRA will be subject to "no-notice" peacetime alert exercises at periodic intervals. Such exercises will be held to a minimum consistent with the maintenance of the required readiness posture. The purpose of these practice alerts is to check the reaction time of the crews and custodial detachment personnel and to train them for safe and rapid response to an actual alert situation. During these exercises all actions required up to, but not including, connecting external power or turning on internal aircraft power may be performed. No change will be made to the alert configuration of the weapon and no power will be applied to the weapon system. All procedures for starting the aircraft engines and subsequent actions required will be simulated unless such action is specifically permitted in the approved US Nuclear Weapon System Safety Rules.

b. **Operational Readiness, Exercises, inspections, and Tactical Evaluations**: To develop and maintain the capability to met SACEUR's force generation requirement (increased readiness), periodic full scale Emergency War Plan operational readiness exercises, inspections, unit tactical evaluations involving the weapon system, crews and custodial detachment personnel who are not on QRA will be conducted. Through these exercises weapon ground transportation and loading personnel are trained to perform safely and quickly tasks which would be required to generate additional forces under increased readiness conditions. During these exercises, inspections or evaluations, training weapons, inert practice bombs or war reserve weapons may be used.

(1) If war reserve weapons are used, the following criteria will apply:

(a) The procedures contained in paragraph 4 of this Annex which are applicable to a particular phase of the operation will be implemented.

(b) The weapon will be downloaded as soon as practicable.

(c) Adequate security will be provided all weapons.

(d) The "ARM-SAFE" switch, or the "READY-SAFE" switch will remain in the safe position.

(2) In all such exercises, regardless of the type of weapon or trainer used, security and access requirements will be the same as for war reserve weapons.

4. PROCEDURES AND RESPONSIBILITIES UNDER CONDITIONS OF QUICK REACTION ALERT:

a. During any operation involving US nuclear weapons or weapon loaded aircraft minimum of two (or more if specifically directed) authorized persons will be present. In each instance personnel must be capable of detecting incorrect or unauthorized procedures with respect to the task to be performed and familiar with pertinent safety and security requirements. The total number of personnel performing these functions will be held to a minimum consistent with the operation being performed.

b. Appropriate commanders will ensure that rigid administrative and security control procedures are constantly and vigorously enforced for all areas containing weapons.

c. **Weapons Storage**: Custodial detachments will store, maintain, inspect, modify and checkout all nuclear weapons and US-owned training weapons in accordance with approved US technical publications. Only approved test equipment and procedures will be used to perform electrical tests on such weapons.

d. **Weapons Maintenance and Configuration**:

(1) At any time a decrease in weapon reliability is suspected the weapon will be returned to the storage area for verification or maintenance.

(2) The Custodial detachment will thoroughly check all nuclear weapons to be placed on alert prior to delivery to the alert site.

(3) The RCAF will have no responsibility for maintenance of weapons other than final load checks and settings.

e. **Weapons Loading and Downloading**:

(1) The Custodial detachment will:

(a) Respond to the NATO formal and military alert requirements.

(b) Not apply power from the aircraft or external source to any loaded weapon prior to receipt of the SACEUR/ USCINCEUR RH-1A or SU-1A message or receipt of instructions from an authorized source for the purpose of weapon maintenance, test, checking or setting, or as authorized in the US Nuclear Weapon System Safety Rules.

(c) Monitor all weapon loading and load checks.

(d) Brief all alert aircrew, loading crews, USAF technicians and USAF custodians on the hazards associated with the inadvertent application of power and improper weapons handling.

(e) Provide a minimum of one USAF Weapon Custodian for each weapon/weapon system during ground transportation, loading, downloading and alert operations.

1. One custodial agent may have custody of two nuclear weapons provided they are not separated by more than 100 feet (30m), there are no intervening obstacles and visual and physical surveillance of each weapon or weapon system is possible.

(f) Monitor compliance by RCAF of applicable US approved safety rules and procedures.

(g) Provide a qualified weapon technician to monitor and assist RCAF during each weapon loading/downloading.

(2) The RCAF will:

(a) Provide only properly certified aircraft for loading of nuclear weapons or US-owned training weapons.

(b) Accomplish all loading, downloading and post load check procedures in accordance with approved USAF technical instructions and checklists or USAF approved RCAF equivalents.

(c) Keep to a minimum the towing of weapon loaded aircraft. During this operation the cockpit will be manned by the aircraft commander.

(d) Assure that no one is allowed entry to the QRA No Lone Zone or access to a weapon loaded aircraft unless accompanied by the assigned aircraft commander, designated weapon technician and a USAF custodian. A No Lone Zone is defined as the area clearly designated and lettered when no lone (single) individual is permitted access. The No Lone Zone is generally a circle around the weapon loaded aircraft of sufficient size to ensure that no part of the aircraft extends beyond that circle. In no case will the No Lone Zone be smaller than an area bounded by lines drawn between wing tips, tail, and nose of the aircraft.

(e) Insure that a qualified crew member checks the weapon for readiness prior to scramble.

f. **Weapons Release:**

(1) The Custodial detachment will provide an Alert Duty Officer on duty at all times that the RCAF strike unit is on QRA. The Alert Duty Officer will:

(a) Receive and authenticate the USCINCEUR portion of the SACEUR/USCINCEUR release message, then release US atomic weapons to the strike unit in conformance with SACEUR/USCINCEUR implementing instructions. It is mandatory that the SACEUR/USCINCEUR RH-1A or SU-1A release message be received in its entirety and authenticated prior to release of atomic weapons. If the SACEUR/USCINCEUR release message is received by the custodial detachment prior to receipt of this message by the RCAF Strike Unit through NATO National channels, the entire message will provided by the custodial detachment to the RCAF duty officer.

(b) Personally notify the USAF custodian(s) at the alert aircraft of the authority to release weapons.

(c) Notify the duty custodians at the storage area of the authority to release the remainder of the weapons assigned to the strike unit.

(2) When requested, the RCAF will assist in security and access control of the US Nuclear Release Materials Safe. The RCAF guard will ensure that access to this safe is gained only in the presence of a minimum of two US personnel, one of which must be a commissioned officer or warrant officer. A US Nuclear Release Materials Safe is a combination lock safe which contains US nuclear weapon release materials. When this safe is in position it will be in the centre of a clearly marked US Exclusion Zone.

g. **Evacuation or Destruction of Nuclear Weapons**: The custodial detachment will:

(1) Prepare necessary plans in coordination with the RCAF to provide a capability for the evacuation or destruction of US nuclear weapons to prevent their loss by enemy action or any other unauthorized action.

(2) If required, supervise and execute the evacuation/destruction of US nuclear weapons.

(3) If required, recall previously released weapons for evacuation/destruction as directed by USCINCEUR or as deemed necessary.

Honest John

The arrangement for the Honest John was written by the British and US governments in 1961 to cover the provision of warheads to the British Army's 50th Regiment Honest John unit at Hemer-Menden. As they were using the same site and same SAS bunkers and same US custodial detachment, the Canadian Army Commander in Europe simply signed the UK-USA document, thereby acquiring access to nuclear warheads for Canadian Honest John rockets. This was the last arrangement, and the only one to cover army nuclear weapons which Canada signed. This was also the only arrangement to be signed at a time when nuclear warheads were already present in the bunkers. However, the Canadian unit still had to receive further training and nuclear certification before having wartime access to the Honest John warheads.

The full Heidelberg Agreement, as signed by the British and the US Army, remains classified. What is available to us is the Canadian sections of the document which in detail lay out the Canadian and US Army responsibilities at Hemer. The UK/USA agreement remains a secret of those two countries, and given the British fetish with nuclear secrecy, it is doubtful they would agree to a public release even all these years after the weapons have been stood down, decommissioned and dismantled.

18 June 1964, Secret, Arrangement between the Designated Military Representatives of the United States Army, of Her Majesty's Secretary of State for Defence of the United Kingdom of Great Britain and Northern Ireland, and the Designated Representative of the Canadian Army for the Application to the Canadian Army of the Service-to-Service Technical Arrangement between the Designated Military Representatives of the United States Army and of Her Majesty's Secretary of State for Defence Department of the United Kingdom of Great Britain and Northern Ireland for Atomic Warhead Support of United Kingdom Atomic Delivery Units Dated 30 Aug 61 (Hereinafter referred to as The Heidelberg Agreement).

1. To implement the "agreement between the government of the United States and the government of Canada regarding the establishment by the US Forces of stocks of special weapons in Germany for support and utilization by Canadian Forces assigned to NATO" signed in Ottawa on 16 Aug 63, it is agreed as follows:

a. The Heidelberg Agreement of 30 Aug 61, as amended on 26 Feb 62 and 11 Jul 63, will apply mutatis mutandis in respect to operational Canadian Army delivery units equipped with Honest John weapon system and designated as users of the custodial Type A special ammunition storage (SAS) site at Hemer in the Federal Republic of Germany deployed in support of forces assigned or earmarked for assignment to SACEUR. It is understood that the Canadian Army Forces will carry out those provisions of the Heidelberg Agreement which pertain to the handling of stocks of special weapons furnished for utilization by them at Hemer.

b. In accordance with the policy guidance outlined in the letter from the Supreme Headquarters, Allied Powers Europe, dated 14 Aug 59, concerning the "support for NATO special ammunition storage sites where the site provides support to more than one user nation", the United Kingdom and Canada, as joint users, will divide responsibilities for support of the custodial Type A SAS site at Hemer. At this site the United Kingdom will be the sponsor nation. Sponsor nation is defined as that nation assuming responsibility for the operation, administration, and maintenance of a SAS site serving more than one user nation. Separate arrangements will be made between the British Army and the Canadian Army to determine the extent to which the Canadian Army will participate in the administration, security and maintenance of the site and the cost-sharing or such responsibilities.

2. Among the requisite changes in applying the Heidelberg Agreement to the Canadian Army Forces, those listed below are matters concerning which the Canadian Army may deal directly with the US Army or other appropriate agencies.

2.a. WARHEAD SUPPORT Nuclear warhead support will be provided to operational Canadian Army delivery units deployed to the continent of Europe in support of forces assigned, or earmarked for assignment to SACEUR. The time of deployment of US Army support units, and of the nuclear warhead sections, will be dependent upon the attainment of operational readiness by Canadian Army delivery units, the availability of adequate storage and administrative facilities, and other support as mutually agreed herein.

2.b. CUSTODY The US Army will retain custody of the nuclear and training warhead sections, except "Type X" training warhead sections, at all times. Upon receipt of appropriate instructions from SACEUR/USCINCEUR, US Army custodians will make US nuclear warhead sections available for use by the supported Canadian Army delivery forces.

2.c. EXPENDITURE Canadian Army forces will fire missiles with attached nuclear warhead sections in accordance with SACEUR approved NATO defense plans and SACEUR directives only.

2.d. MAINTENANCE AND ASSEMBLY Canadian Army delivery units will assume all responsibilities, that can be assumed without violation of US atomic energy law or regulations, that fall within the normal functions of personnel in a similar US Army delivery unit. United States Army personnel will be responsible for the maintenance, surveillance, and assembly of nuclear warhead sections.

2.e. SECURITY OF TRAINING ITEMS Security, custodial, and operational procedures for training warhead sections, except "Type X" training warhead sections, will be the same as for nuclear warhead sections.

2.f. COMMAND AUTHORITY The presence of US Army personal at Canadian Army bases will not alter the command responsibility and authority of the designated Canadian station commander, but with respect to US Army units, personnel, equipment and material, all functions of command, control, administration, training and tactical actions will be the sole responsibility of the US Army commander. The US Army commander, however, will make every effort to conform with existing procedures and regulations of the supported Canadian commander.

2.g. "TYPE X" TRAINING WARHEAD SECTIONS Canadian Army delivery forces will, upon receipt, make available to US custodial detachments or support units the Canadian "Type X" training warhead sections for the training of US personnel. The commanding officer of the US custodial detachment or support unit will make technical personnel available to the Canadian Army delivery unit commander for instruction of Canadian personnel on the "Type X" training warhead section.

2.h. TRAINING GENERAL

(1) The US Army will be responsible for providing the necessary and authorized information for the training of the Canadian Army. The US Army will be responsible for providing authorized equipment and technical publications, etc., to the Canadian Army.

(2) Training of the Canadian Army delivery units is the responsibility of the Canadian Army. US Army participation in the training of Canadian Army delivery units will be limited to monitoring tasks and service as instructors in the scheduled training programme of the Canadian Army units when specifically requested. The US Army will maintain the maximum condition of readiness to render full operational support to these forces. The US Army schedules will be compatible with those of the supported units, where applicable.

(3) The US Army will provide for travel and other expenses incurred by US Army personnel in normal support of training and operation of Canadian Army forces.

2.i. COMBINED TRAINING Combined training of US Army and the Canadian Army will begin at the earliest practicable time. US Army units will participate fully in the training activities of these units. The appropriate commanders may submit recommendations to improve this training support.

2.j. US ARMY TRAINING INSPECTIONS Appropriate US Army authorities will conduct routine, periodic training inspections of the US Army units and Canadian units as mutually agreed stationed within the area of responsibility of the Canadian authorities signatory to this agreement. The scheduling of such inspections will be coordinated by designated US Army commands with the appropriate NATO/Canadian command.

2.k. MANEUVERS Training warhead sections mat be connected to the missiles of Canadian Army delivery forces for training exercises. The operational and security procedures to be utilized during the course of field training with training warhead sections, except "Type X" training warhead sections, will be the same as that employed with atomic warhead sections.

2.l. SAFETY AND HANDLING CRITERIA

(1) The US Army and Canadian Army forces will be responsible for compliance with nuclear safety rules and safety procedures which have been provided by the US Army for operations with nuclear weapons. In the event of differences of interpretation, the US interpretation will prevail.

(2) The Canadian Army forces will perform, on a timely basis, all US required modifications which affect nuclear safety of nuclear weapons delivery systems. The Canadian Army forces will advise USAREUR of all country-developed modifications to be performed on the nuclear weapon delivery system to insure that nuclear safety is not adversely affected.

(3) USAREUR will conduct an annual nuclear safety inspection of applicable Canadian nuclear delivery units and participate, as required, in NATO directed operational readiness inspections to insure that concerned units comply with US safety rules and safety procedures. The safety rules and procedures established and disseminated by the US Army to the Canadian forces will be the basis for inspection. The conduct of these inspections will be coordinated between USAREUR and the Canadian Army Europe.

2.m. PUBLIC RELEASES Because of the sensitivity of the whole subject of US Army atomic warhead section support to the delivery units of the Canadian Army, no public release of information regarding this agreement or its implementation will be made by the forces of the United Kingdom or Canada or of the United States except by mutual agreement.

3. DIFFERENCES OF OPINION If in the implementation of this arrangement differences of opinion should arise which cannot be solved at the local level, the point in controversy will be submitted, as appropriate, to the Commander in Chief, United States Army,

Europe, the Ministry of Defence, London, and Army Headquarters, Ottawa, for resolution.

4. REVIEW Any of the parties signatory to this arrangement may at any time request the other parties to enter into renegotiation of any provision of this arrangement.

Signatories:

Major General G.R.D. Fitzpatrick, Chief of Staff, British Army of the Rhine.

Brigadier M.R. Dare, Commander, Canadian Army National Force, Europe.

General P.L. Freeman, Commander in Chief, United States Army, Europe.

Date 18 June 1964

6 pages

154 copies

SECRET

COMMANDING OFFICERS

The following are the names and command dates for those who commanded Canadian nuclear weapons units, and for US warhead custodial units serving Canadians. The lists are restricted to the duration of the nuclear deployments and do not reflect the entire lifetime of the unit itself.

Air Defence Command Commanding Officers

A/V/M MM Hendrick	Sep 62–Aug 64
A/V/M MD Lister	Aug 64–Mar 66
A/V/M ME Pollard	Apr 66–

446 SAM Sqdn Commanding Officers:

W/C A.G. Lawrence	Dec 61–Jul 64
W/C F.G. Fellows	Jul 64–Oct 68
Maj J.B. Randall.	Oct 68–c. 70
Maj R.W. Fraser	c. 70–Spt 72

447 SAM Sqdn Commanding Officers

W/C JEA Laflamme	Spt 62–May 63
W/C JLA Roussell	May 63–Jul 66
W/C PJ Roy	Jul 66–c. 67
Major Red Scanlon	c. 67–Oct 68
LtCol R Banville	Oct 68–Jul 71
LtCol JE Dardier	Jul 71–Sep 72

409 AW(F) Sqdn Commanding Officers

W/C G Inglis	1962–1965
W/C WH Vincent	1965–1967
W/C GW Patterson	1967–1968
LCol GF Hammond	1968–1970
LCol SJ Telford	1970–1972
LCol LC Price	1972–1974
LCol AE McKay	1974–1976
LCol GH Herbert	1976–1978
LCol G McAffer	1978–1980
LCol LG Lott	1980–1984

416 AW(F) Sqdn Commanding Officers

W/C JC Henry	1964–1967
W/C SA Miller	1967–1969
LCol D MacCaul	1969–1971
LCol JL Twambley	1971–1973
LCol S Popham	1973–1975
LCol A Sundvall	1975–1977
LCol M Rudderham	1977–1979
LCol J Partington	1979–1981
LCol WJC Ross	1981–1983
LCol WA Kalbfleisch	1983–1984

425 AW(F) Sqdn Commanding Officers

W/C MJ Dooher	1964–1966
W/C WJ Marsh	1966–1967
LtCol RHI Pike	1967–1969
LtCol JGC Couillard	1969–1971
LtCol R Hayman	1971–1973
LtCol D Broadbent	1973–1974
LtCol J Deacon	1974–1976
LtCol J Sosnkowski	1976–1978
LtCol R Koehn	1978–1981
LtCol R Maltais	1981–1984

425 Munitions Maintenance Squadron (USAF) Commanding Officers

Lt Colonel Borton	1963–196_
Lt Colonel James P. Huffman	196_–1970
Lt Colonel Roy W. Wampler	1970–1975
Lt Colonel Samuel R. Fowler	1975–197_
Lt Colonel David Hollenbaugh	197_–1978
Major Joseph P. West	1978–198_

Detachment 1, 425 Sqdn, Commanders

Major WD Pickett.	1963–1966
Major GF Graham.	1966–1967
Major Leroy C. Kronvall	1967–1972

Detachment 2, 425 Sqdn, Commanders

Major Daniel Chisa	1963–1966
Lt Col John Barth	1966
Capt Deryl Duncan	1967–1970
Captain Arthur K. Bryden	1970–1972

Detachment 3, 425 Sqdn, Commanders

Major Roy W. Wampler	1964–196_
Captain Arthur R. Miller	196_–1971
Captain Gordon L. Moog	1971–197_
Major Thomas W. Wadzinski	197_–1981
Major P.R. Ray	1981–1984
Major Jordan	1984.

Detachment 4, 425 Sqdn, Commanders

commanders unknown	1964–196_
Captain James H. Grey	196_–1970
Captain Clyde H. Roberts	1970–1972
Captain William Stavisky	1972–1974
Captain Ernest H. Daniels	1974–1975

Detachment 5, 425 Sqdn, Commanders

Major R.L. Crutchfield	1964–196_
Captain Seth H. Stephens	196_–1970
Captain Charles B. Stutts	1970–1971
Captain Eugene S. Chaney	1971–197_
commanders unknown	197_–197_
Major William Wright	197_–1981
Major Ronald Carlson	1981–1984

Detachment 6, 425 Sqdn, Commanders

Captain Don Cushing	1964–1965
Major J.J. Vogl	1965–1966
Captain Nading	1966–1968
Captain Tom Jones	1968–1970
Captain Larry T. Doyle	1970–1972
Captain Herbert W. Wessell	1972–1974

1 SSM Bty Commanding Officers

Maj J McGregor	1960–1961
Maj CR Davidson	1961–1962
Maj DB Crowe	1962–1964
Maj AC Moffat	1964–1966
Maj JE Crosman	1966–1969
Maj GNR Olson	1969–1970

2 SSM Trg Bty Commanding Officers

Maj JN Robertson	1960–1963
Maj JG Henderson	1963–1965
Maj JP Stickley	1965

Maj JL Mantin	1965–1967
Maj GNR Olson	1967–1968

69 Missile Warhead Support Detachment, US Army

commnders unknown	1964–1969
Capt Glossmeyer	19__–1970

1 Air Division Commanding Officers

A/V/M DAR Bradshaw	Jul 63–Jul 66
A/V/M RJ Lane	Aug 66–Jul 69
LGen DC Laubman	Jul 69–Aug 70

1 Canadian Air Group Commanding Officers

BGen MF Doyle	Aug 70–Oct 71
BGen KE Lewis	Oct 71–Jul 73

1 WING Commanding Officers

G/C AF Avant	Aug 63–Aug 66
G/C RG Christie	Spt 66–Dec 68
Col AJ Pudsey	Dec 68–Jun 70

3 Wing Commanding Officers

G/C DC Laubman	Aug 63–Aug 66
G/C KE Lewis	Aug 66–Jan 68
Col WJ Marsh	Feb 68–Jul 69
LCol RK Trumley	Jul 69–Aug 69

4 Wing Commanding Officers

G/C JJ Jordan	Sep 61–Jul 65
G/C C Allison	Aug 65–Oct 68
Col FG Kaufman	Oct 68–Jun 71
Col AJ Bauer	Jul 71–May 74

421 S/A Sqdn Commanding Officers

W/C JB Lawrence	Feb 64–May 67
W/C RH Annis	Apr 67–?

422 S/A Sqdn Commanding Officers

W/C WHF Bliss	Jul 63–Jul 66
W/C WJ Stacy	Aug 66–Jul 67
W/C RK Scott	Aug 67–?

427 S/A Sqdn Commanding Officers

W/C WR Knight	Feb 64–Jul 65
W/C JF Dunlop	Jul 65–Sep 65
W/C PJS Higgs	May 66–Sep 67
W/C RE Carruthers	Sep 67–?

430 S/A Sqdn Commanding Officers

W/C HR Knight	Spt 67–Jan 64

W/C AJ Bauer   Feb 64–Jul 66
W/C WG Paisley   Jul 66–Oct 66
W/C JW Whitley   Nov 66–?

434 S/A Sqdn Commanding Officers
W/C OB Philp   Apr 63–Dec 65
W/C JAGF Villeneuve   Dec 65–Mar 67

439 S/A Sqdn Commanding Officers
W/C RM Edwards   Jan 64–Sep 65
W/C JF Dunlop   Sep 65–Feb 68

444 S/A Sqdn Commanding Officers
W/C KJ Thornycroft   Apr 63–Jun 66
W/C RH Annis   Aug 66–Apr 67

7232 Munitions Maintenance Group Commanding Officers, USAFE
Colonel Francis A. Kelly   1963–1965
Colonel Virgil R. Epperson   1965–1967

306 Munitions Maintenance Sqdn Commanding Officers
commanders unknown   1964–1968

26 Tactical Reconnaissance Wing Commanding Officers
commanders unknown   1967–1972

326 Munitions Maintenance Sqdn Commanding Officers
commanders unknown   1967–1972

Detachment 1900, 2100, 3, 4, Commanders
commanders unknown for all USAFE Detachments
                                   1964–1972

DIRECTORATE OF NUCLEAR WEAPONS
Director of Nuclear Weapons
G/C C.F. Phripp (first DNW)   1963–1965
G/C (Col) E.N. Henderson   1965–1972
LCol D.C. Manion   1973–1974
LCol R.S Dziver   1975–1977
LCol G.F. D'Eon (last DNW)   1978–1981
                               Section Head, Nuclear Weapons
Major J.M. Aucoin   1982
LCol G.L. Untereiner   1983–1984
(section closed)

BIBLIOGRAPHIC NOTES
SOURCES, FILES, ARCHIVES, LIBRARIES AND AGENCIES

Any serious researcher in the field of Canadian nuclear weapons will have to look in varied, and sometimes far-flung places to find useful material. This section discusses the principal research sites, offices, agencies and archives which hold materials dealing with this curious period in the life of the Canadian government and military. The documentation is both political and military; it is both historical and current; it is held in both Canada and the US; and it is both organizational and personal.

THE NATIONAL ARCHIVES OF CANADA
The National Archives on Wellington Street, Ottawa, has the greatest collection of material on Canadian nuclear weapons in Canada. However, the collection is not a homogenous mass, and the researcher will spend weeks looking in disparate places for various scraps of information in various unrelated files.

The Government Archives Division of the National Archives is the unit best equipped to help. Within the GAD there are archivists who specialize in the RCAF, the Canadian Army, Cabinet Documents, and External Affairs. Each will be able to guide the researcher through various and massive finding aides.

Through the efforts of the author, many of the National Archives files dealing with nuclear weapons have been opened for public viewing, or are under review by one or more government departments in Canada and the US.

THE DIRECTOR OF NUCLEAR WEAPONS
Probably the single greatest wealth of nuclear weapons information in Canada is contained in the partial records of the Director of Nuclear Weapons files held in only three file boxes at the National Archives of Canada. Although some pages have been removed, the author has been successful in having the vast bulk of this material opened for public inspection. These central files cover deployments, inspections, operational orders, safety, accidents, deliveries, arrangements, storage, Canadian and US military units, and all four nuclear weapons systems. Researchers are

encouraged to seek the files under the following heading:
RG24 Accession # 1986-87/165, Box 16, Box 17, Box 18. "Plans,
Operations, & Readiness. Nuclear Weapons:"

EXTERNAL AFFAIRS CANADA
At the Department of External Affairs, now known as Foreign Affairs and
International Trade Canada, in the Lester Pearson Building on Sussex Drive
in Ottawa, there is a considerable body of political history available to
qualified researchers. Through their academic historian programme, the staff
at the External Affairs Historical Section will grant certain academics the
privilege of inspecting original files generated by that department. The most
important of these files regarding nuclear weapons for the Canadian military
have been transferred to the National Archives.

CABINET DOCUMENTS
The Prime Ministers Office and the Privy Council Office (PMO and PCO)
in Ottawa are the primary source for documents generated by or for the
Cabinet and the Cabinet Defence Committee (CDC). The Access to
Information Office at the PCO provided virtually all of the Cabinet and
CDC documents and minutes used in this study. The remaining documents,
generally older than 1963, came from the National Archives.

NATIONAL DEFENCE HEADQUARTERS
None of the material used in this study came directly from National Defence
Headquarters. However, the Access to Information Office at NDHQ was
instrumental in declassifying a vast amount of documentation given them on
referral from the National Archives, DHist, External Affairs, and PCO. They
were both helpful and always forthcoming. It is the unofficial policy of DND
to consider that all material of the Canadian nuclear age is fit for
declassification due to its age. They will therefore generally allow for the
opening of files which do not have political or third-party information, such as
foreign relations documentation and comments on Germany or France: such
materials having to be referred to External Affairs for further declassification.

DIRECTORATE OF HISTORY
The DND Directorate of History (DHist) in Ottawa holds the records of all
of the military units in Canada. Although the records are often not complete
for various bureaucratic reasons, they are second to none. There seems to
have been what could be termed an administrative mutiny following the
unification of the Canadian forces during the mid- to late-1960s, and many
units did not send reports and records to NDHQ. This situation degrades
the collection at DHist, but does nothing to diminish its value to the
nuclear researcher. Without the input of staff at DHist and their provision

of files, this study would have been impossible. Sadly, due to government spending cuts, the office is now only open two days per week. Documents from this book are being donated to DHist.

CFB SHILO
The Royal Canadian Artillery Museum at CFB Shilo maintains a small but rather fine archives and library. They have a collection of photographs of both 1 and 2 SSM Bty, as well as copies of the book *Surface-to-Surface Missile, Royal Canadian Artillery, 25th Anniversary Reunion, 20–22 September 1985*. The book is a fine collection of photos, documents and clippings from and about the only Army unit to operate a nuclear weapons system.

CFS LA MACAZA
Although the old shelter-launcher facilities are still in place, there is nothing at the old La Macaza site which would be of much interest to the researcher. This is especially true as the site is now used by Corrections Canada as a federal prison. However, I did not know this until I approached it and was cut off by a person armed with an automatic weapon and no knowledge of the English language. Do not visit this place for the purpose of research.

PHOTOGRAPHS, FILMS AND VIDEOS
The Canadian Forces Photographic unit in Ottawa is the repository for all important negatives, films, and videos in the military. The collection is arranged with a cross-referenced index, and photographs of nuclear weapons can be found under the name or number of the user unit, the base or station, or the name of the weapon.

The facility also has great number of films and videos covering all of Canada's nuclear weapons systems. Although many of them run from only a few seconds to a few minutes, they are of historical interest. The head of video services did manage to find the ignored negative of the film showing the first warhead delivery in Canada.

U.S. NATIONAL ARCHIVES
The National Archives at College Park, Maryland, just outside of Washington, D.C., have tremendous holding of both military and civilian documentation. State Department files for the 1963–1964 period dealing with nuclear weapons for Canada, although heavily censored, recently became available to the public. The State Department Decimal Files and Central Files on CANUS Defense Relations are the researcher's best friend.

NARA also has an extensive military photo and film collection on the fifth floor, including many of nuclear weapons, bases, and Canadian aircraft. This was used for research, but none of the images have been reproduced in this work.

US AIR FORCE

The US Air Force maintains a large historical section at Maxwell Air Force Base, Montgomery, Alabama. Most of the records of the USAF units which supported nuclear weapons in Canada are on file at this facility. The records of the 425th Munitions Maintenance Squadron and its Detachments are only partially declassified, as are the records of USAF flying units which operated in Canada from time-to-time.

While some of the records of the USAFE are in Alabama, much of the material remains in Europe. Further research in this area will have to be done through FOI requests to the USAFE HQ. However, the files of the units which had custody of the nuclear weapons in Europe fall under the partial jurisdiction of the US Department of Energy, and cannot be released without a formal declassification process outside of the USAF.

US ARMY

The daily logs of the US Army Custodial Detachment which cared for the Honest John rocket warheads are kept in St. Louis at a federal records centre. They can be viewed with prior clearance and permission of the facility administrator.

NATIONAL SECURITY ARCHIVE

The National Security Archive, a private research and publication organization in Washington, D.C., has one of the single largest private collections of US government documents on the history of nuclear weapons and nuclear weapons policy in North America. The collection, by its very nature, includes material dealing with NORAD and therefore with Canada.

CHUCK HANSEN

Another specialist in nuclear weapons from the United States who has been especially important to the completion of this work is Chuck Hansen of Sunnyvale, California. His seminal work, *U.S. Nuclear Weapons* in 1988, and his recent CD-ROM and microfiche collection *Swords of Armageddon*[1] are probably the most important sources of information on United States' nuclear warhead design and history from sources opened under the US Freedom of Information Act.

ENDNOTES

INTRODUCTION

1 Haydon, P. *The Cuban Missile Crisis: Canadian Involvement Reconsidered.* CISS, Toronto, 1993. P. 78.
2 Haydon, p. 197.
3 Haydon, p. 127, 149 (fn).
4 08 November 1963, S0029-106-6(AMTS) secret, Memorandum, from AMTS A/V/M WW Bean, to CAS, re: 446 SAM Squadron North Bay Delivery of Warheads. (and satisfactory ICI).
5 RCAF Stn North Bay, Annual Historical Report 1963.
6 Historical Summary 446 SAM Squadron, 01 Jan to 31 Dec 1964.
7 24 February 1964, RCAF/ORI Inspection Team and US AFHQ ADC Inspection Team arrived at Stn North Bay.
8 Historical Summary 446 SAM Squadron, (February)01 Jan to 31 Dec 1964.
9 02 March 1964 "The ORI/CI (Operational Readiness Inspection/Capability Inspection) team arrived to examine and inspect the operational capability of the BOMARC Site during 2–6 March." 447 Annual Report.
10 06 March 1964, CI/ORI of 2–6 March 1964. DNW File S964-106-3(DNW) Secret. 447 SAM Sqdn classified as "Marginally Satisfactory".
11 Telephone interview (source anonymous by request), NDHQ, 14 November 1984.
12 Hansard, 23 October 1963. p.3912.

CHAPTER 1: PEARSON'S CABINET AND THE POLITICAL AGREEMENT TO ACQUIRE NUCLEAR WEAPONS FOR THE CANADIAN MILITARY

1 The Memo to Pearson from Hellyer appears courtesy of Paul Hellyer and can also be found in Peter Newman's book, *The Distemper of Our Times*, 1968.
2 14 May 1963, Cabinet Conclusions, #9-63. "Nuclear Weapons Agreement with the United States"
3 07 May 1963, Cabinet Defence Committee, #139. "I. Nuclear Policy"
4 25 July 1963, Cabinet Conclusions, #37-63. "Nuclear Weapons for the Canadian Armed Forces"
5 25 April 1963, Cabinet Defence Committee, #138. "III. Nuclear Weapons"
6 Paul Martin, *A Very Public Life.* p.384–387.
7 25 April 1963, Cabinet Defence Committee, #138. "III. Nuclear Weapons"
8 25 April 1963, Cabinet Defence Committee, #138. "III. Nuclear Weapons"
9 25 April 1963, Cabinet Defence Committee, #138. "III. Nuclear Weapons"
10 25 April 1963, Cabinet Defence Committee, #138. "III. Nuclear Weapons"
11 25 April 1963, Cabinet Defence Committee, #138. "III. Nuclear Weapons"
12 25 April 1963, Cabinet Defence Committee, #138. "III. Nuclear Weapons"
13 07 May 1963, Cabinet Defence Committee, #139. "I. Nuclear Policy"
14 07 May 1963, Cabinet Defence Committee, #139. "I. Nuclear Policy"
15 07 May 1963, Cabinet Defence Committee, #139. "I. Nuclear Policy"
16 07 May 1963, Cabinet Defence Committee, #139. "I. Nuclear Policy"
17 07 May 1963, Cabinet Defence Committee, #139. "I. Nuclear Policy"
18 07 May 1963, Cabinet Defence Committee, #139. "I. Nuclear Policy"
19 07 May 1963, Cabinet Defence Committee, #139. "I. Nuclear Policy"
20 07 May 1963, Cabinet Defence Committee, #139. "I. Nuclear Policy"
21 09 May 1963, Cabinet Conclusions, #7-63. "Report of Cabinet Defence Committee; nuclear weapons agreements"
22 09 May 1963, Cabinet Conclusions, #7-63. "Report of Cabinet Defence Committee; nuclear weapons agreements"

23 09 May 1963, Cabinet Conclusions, #7-63. "Report of Cabinet Defence Committee; nuclear weapons agreements"

24 09 May 1963, Cabinet Conclusions, #7-63. "Report of Cabinet Defence Committee; nuclear weapons agreements". Please see Chapter 7 for a full discussion of the political and military side of the ASW issue.

25 09 May 1963, Cabinet Conclusions, #7-63. "Report of Cabinet Defence Committee; nuclear weapons agreements"

26 09 May 1963, Cabinet Conclusions, #7-63. "Subjects for Discussion with President Kennedy"

27 13 May 1963, Cabinet Conclusions, #8-63. Report on Pearson visit with Kennedy.

28 15 May 1963, Meeting between President John F. Kennedy and Prime Minister Lester B. Pearson at Hyannis Port, Mass. USA, May 10–11 1963. Summary Report.

29 15 May 1963, Cabinet Conclusions, #10-63. "Draft Agreement on Nuclear Weapons"

30 20 May 1963, Cabinet Conclusions, #12-63.

31 23 May 1963, MEMCON, US State Department, US/MC/6. Pearson, Rusk, McNamara, Butterworth. Ottawa. This conversation took place during the NATO Ministerial meeting in Ottawa 22–24 May 1963.

32 16 July 1963, Cabinet Defence Committee, #140. "I. Draft General Agreement Concerning Nuclear Weapons Required for Canadian Forces and Accompanying Letter of Understanding"

33 Hansard, 15 July 1963. p.2179–2180.

34 16 July 1963, Cabinet Defence Committee, #140. "I. Draft General Agreement Concerning Nuclear Weapons Required for Canadian Forces and Accompanying Letter of Understanding"

35 16 July 1963, Cabinet Defence Committee, #140. "III. Public Announcement Concerning Stockpile Agreement"

36 14 August 1963, Cabinet Conclusions, #44-63. "Nuclear Warheads for the Canadian Forces"

37 18 July 1963, Cabinet Conclusions, #35-63. "Nuclear weapons; draft agreement with U.S. and public announcement"

38 25 July 1963, Cabinet Conclusions, #37-63. "Nuclear Weapons for the Canadian Armed Forces"

39 07 August 1963, Cabinet Conclusions, #43-63. "Nuclear weapons agreement"

40 Hansard, 29 July 1963, p.2730.

41 02 August 1963, Cabinet Conclusions, #41-63. "Nuclear weapons agreement"

42 18 July 1963, Cabinet Conclusions, #35-63. "Nuclear weapons; draft agreement with U.S. and public announcement"

43 14 August 1963, Cabinet Conclusions, #44-63. "Nuclear Warheads for the Canadian Forces"

44 16 August 1963, Cabinet Minutes, #45-63. "Nuclear Weapons for the Canadian Forces"

45 16 August 1963, Cabinet Minutes, #45-63. "Nuclear Weapons for the Canadian Forces"

46 16 August 1963, Cabinet Minutes, #45-63. "Nuclear Weapons for the Canadian Forces"

47 23 August 1963, Draft message to Canadian Embassy Bonn, from External Affairs, re Agreement between Canada and USA concerning nuclear weapons for Cdn Forces, Priority, Secret.

48 Hansard, 30 September 1963. p.3028.

49 Hansard, 03 October 1963. p.3167.

50 23 August 1963, secret, to A/C/M Miller, Chairman, Chiefs of Staff Ottawa, from N.A. Robertson, Under Secretary of State for External Affairs.

51 21 August 1963, secret telex, to External Affairs Ottawa from Canadian Embassy Bonn, re: Agreement between Canada and USA concerning nuclear weapons for Cdn Forces.

52 23 August 1963, priority, to Canadian Embassy Bonn, from External Affairs, #DL-1107, re: Agreement between Canada and USA concerning nuclear weapons for Cdn Forces. Secret.

53 23 August 1963, priority, to Canadian Embassy Bonn, from External Affairs, DRAFT, re: Agreement between Canada and USA concerning nuclear weapons for Cdn Forces. Secret.

54 NATO Military Committee, MC48, 18 November 1954, Cosmic – Top Secret.

55 NATO MC 14/3 (Final), 16 January 1968. NATO Secret.

56 NATO MC 14/3 (Final), 16 January 1968. NATO Secret.

57 06 November 1962, Memorandum for the Ambassador of Canada to Washington, re: Agreements Relating to Canada-United States Consultations. Top Secret. File 4-12.

58 08 January 1964, Secret, Letter to PM Pearson from SSEA Martin, re: Authorization for the Operational Use of Nuclear Weapons.

59 06 December 1963, Letter to the SSEA from the MND, re: answers to question on control and custody of nuclear weapons for the BOMARC (includes attachment).

60 Hansard, 06 December 1963. p.5575. SAGE was the Semi-Automatic Ground Environment, a computerized control system to guide interceptors and missiles to bombers.

61 22 January 1964, Memo for SSEA from Ross Campbell, Secret, re: Nuclear Weapons for the CF104 Aircraft – Service to Service Agreement.

62 Paul Martin, *A Very Public Life*. p.387.

63 Paul Martin, *A Very Public Life.* p.384–387.

64 08 January 1964, Memo to the Prime Minister from the SSEA, re: Authorization for the Operational Use of Nuclear Weapons.

65 08 January 1864, letter to A/C/M F.R. Miller, Chairman, Chiefs of Staff, from Ross Campbell, Ass't Under-Secretary of State, re: authorization for the operational use of nuclear weapons.

66 23 March 1965, Cabinet Minutes, #22-65. "Authorization For Use of Nuclear Weapons by NORAD Forces"

67 01 April 1965, Order in Council, PC 1965-595. signed by Watson MacNaught, Allan MacEachern, LB Pearson, and Judy LaMarsh.

68 27 July 1967, Top Secret, memo for PM Pearson from SSEA, re: Agreement between Canada and the USA for the storage of nuclear weapons at a US leased base in NFLD for US forces (Argentia).

69 11 July 1966, Secret Memo for the SSEA re: "US Requirement for storage of nuclear ASW weapons at Argentia".

70 US State Department, Foreign Relations of the United States, Europe and Canada, 1960–1963.

CHAPTER 2: BOMARC

1 01 January 1968, BOMARC, unclassified Briefing, 446 SAM Sqdn, (DHist R S7 446)

2 01 January 1968, BOMARC, unclassified Briefing, 446 SAM Sqdn, (DHist R S7 446)

3 North Bay Nugget. "BOMARC Missile Available at Command or NORAD". 31 May 1971. p.14.

4 16 August 1963 letter to SoD McNamara from MND Hellyer, transmitted in External Affairs telegram DL-1111 of 23 August 1963.

5 19 November 1963, letter to A.R. Menzies at External Affairs from Basil Robinson in Canadian Embassy Washington, re: BOMARC-B life span.

6 All of the technical information on the W40 nuclear warhead is taken from the following works: Hansen, U.S. Nuclear Weapons. **p.151, 187; Hansen, Swords of Amageddon; Gibson, The History of the US Nuclear Arsenal. p.166–167.**

7 09 February 1965, S55-08-01(ONCDR), to CDS from Senior RCAF Officer A/C Pollard, re Operational Review Briefing RCAF CIM-10B Nuclear Weapon System. Ottawa NORAD Sector briefing summary by ADCHQ: BOMARC Operational Review.

8 29 September 1969, 1618z, secret, to CANFORCEHED from CANDEFCOM, CFADC Operational History of BUIC III/CIM-10B Weapon System. "Neither of the adjacent SAGE Divisions (in the USA) can launch the Canadian BOMARCs but they can

of course accept handover of airborne BOMARCs."

9 01 January 1964. S0030-101. Message Form. To CANAIRDEF from CANAIRHED, re: Interim Procedures for Employment of RCAF CIM-10B. Secret.

10 02 June 1964, 2228z, S1100-105-8. to CANAIRHED from CINCNORAD, re: Interim Procedures for Employment of Canadian BOMARC. Secret.

11 02 June 1964, 2228z, to CANAIRHED from CINCNORAD, re: Interim Procedures for Employment of Canadian BOMARC. Secret.

12 21 October 1969, Annex A to V 3312-20(DNW), secret, Canadian BUIC III/CIM10B (BOMARC) Operational History.

13 09 February 1965, S55-08-01(ONCDR), to CDS from Senior RCAF Officer A/C Pollard, re Operational Review Briefing RCAF CIM-10B Nuclear Weapon System. Ottawa NORAD Sector briefing summary by ADCHQ: BOMARC Operational Review.

14 Hansard, 20 November 1963. p.4961.

15 Hansard, 04 December 1963. p.5427.

16 Hansard, 16 December 1963. p.5932.

17 Hansard, 06 December 1963. p.5524.

18 30 December 1963, Top Secret, Memo from the President to the Secretary of Defense, regarding nuclear weapons for Canada. LBJ Library, NSF Subject File, "Nuclear Weapons – Canada, Vol. 1, 1963–65". Doc #28.

19 USAF Military Airlift Command Logistic Support Squadron

20 RCAF Stn North Bay, Annual Historical Report 1963.

21 08 January 1964, Letter to Prime Minister Pearson from Secretary of SSEA Paul Martin, re: authorization for the operational use of nuclear weapons. Secret.

22 08 January 1964, Letter to COS A/C/M Miller from Ross Campbell, External Affairs.

23 29 October 1963 memorandum, secret, S0069-106-6(DADSI). also History of the 62nd TCW 1 Jan–30 Jun 64, Chapter I. USAF Historical Agency.

24 History of the 62nd Troop Carrier Wing, 1 Jan–30 Jun 64, Chapter I. Paragraph 5. USAF Historical Agency.

25 17 January 1966, secret, memorandum, V3312-3059/4(DNW), by DNW-NW5

26 Arkin & Fieldhouse, Nuclear Battlefields. 1985. p.199.

27 The Montgomery Advertizer. p.1. "Royal CAF Launches First Interceptor" 15 Dec 61

28 North Bay Nugget. "First BOMARC-B in North Bay Next Thursday", Orma McNaughton. c. October 1962.

29 446 Scrapbook held in Directorate of History, Ottawa, News item by Harold Morrison,

Washington, CP. "First BOMARC for Canada being Shipped in Secret".

30 08 November 1963, S0029-106-6(AMTS) secret, Memorandum, from AMTS A/V/M WW Bean, to CAS, re: 446 SAM Squadron North Bay Delivery of Warheads.

31 North Bay Annual Historical report, 1964.

32 Historical Summary 446 SAM Squadron, 1 Jan to 31 Dec 1964.

33 Third test, 2 March 1965. Fourth test, 26 April 1966.

34 446 SAM Sqdn Historical Summary Jan 68–31 Dec 71. Combat Evaluation Launches.

35 19 February 1970, Service-to-Service Agreement between the United States Air Force and the Canadian Armed Forces on a Supplementary Arrangement for the Canadian CIM-10B... Secret. Section II, 1.(a)(1–6).

36 425 MMS Report for Oct–Dec 1969.

37 USAF ADC Movement Order 5, 15 May 1972.

38 425 MMS Report for Jan–Mar 1969.

39 425 MMS Report for 30 June 1972

40 425 MSS History Report for July–Sept 1978, Attachment 3. See also 425 MSS Report for Oct–Dec 1978.

41 425 MMS Report for Jan–Mar 1973

42 425 MMS Report for July–Sept 1973

43 Treasury Board Meeting, 07 April 1959, Minute #542000 as amended, for La Macaza construction costs.

44 Hansard, 21 May 1963. p.134.

45 21 January 1964, memorandum 0030-1(AMTS) to VCAS from AMTS A/V/M WW Bean, re: BOMARC Implementation.

46 09 February 1965, S55-08-01(ONCDR), to CDS from Senior RCAF Officer, re: Operational Review Briefing RCAF CIM-10B Nuclear Weapons System. Secret and Confidential. "A Brief History" section.

47 CFS La Macaza Monthly Historical Report, January 1964. and 16 January 1964 2110z, telex from NNRHQ North Bay to 446 SAM Sqn La Macaza, secret.

48 6 March 1964, Capability Inspection/Operational Readiness Inspection (CI/ORI) at CFS La Macaza on 2–6 March 1964. DNW File S964-106-3(DNW) Secret.

49 11 March 1965, S0030-105(AMTS) Memorandum for the CAS from AMTS, re: Nuclear Weapons – Inspections – Results of CI/ORI – 447 SAM Sqn LA Macaza. Secret.

50 11 March 1964, quick reading copy, message from AOC CANAIRDEF to CAS CANAIRHED, A5 11 Mar (signal in five parts) 3312-20. Telex. Secret. Para. 4.

51 20–24 July 1964, Joint RCAF/USAF Spot Inspection of safety, armament, and Broken Arrow procedures found 447 SAM Sqdn to be satisfactory.

52 24 January 1964, 1430z, to CANAIRHED from CANAIRDEF. La Macaza Dull Sword Report.

53 26 November 1968, 1935z, La Macaza Dull Sword Report.

54 RCMP Memo for File, Ottawa, 09 July 1964. Re: protests and demonstrations – BOMARC Missile Base La Macaza, Quebec. Ottawa SIB, re: 41 pages of photographs of protesters for identification.

55 RCMP Memo for File, Ottawa, 18 September 1964. Re: protests and demonstrations – BOMARC Missile Base La Macaza, Quebec. Ottawa SIB.

56 RCMP "A" Division Ottawa,, North Bay Sub-division, Detachment Timmins, 7/8 September 1965. RE: Communism, report by Inspector HF Law. (film forwarded to Ottawa)

57 RCMP Memo for File, Ottawa, 30 September 1965. Re: protests and demonstrations – BOMARC Missile Base La Macaza, Quebec. Confidential.

58 RCMP Memo for File, Ottawa, 19 November 1964. Re: protests and demonstrations – BOMARC Missile Base La Macaza, Quebec. Memo to Kingston, Toronto, Montreal, and Ottawa, re: license plates at La Macaza. See also RCMP Memo for File, Ottawa, 18 September 1964. Re: protests and demonstrations – BOMARC Missile Base La Macaza, Quebec. list of Ontario license plates, 2 pages. See also RCMP Memo for File, Ottawa, 25 June 1964. Re: protests and demonstrations – BOMARC Missile Base La Macaza, Quebec. re: license plates from Quebec, Ontario, British columbia and New York, USA.

59 RCMP Memo for File, Ottawa, 11 September 1964. Re: protests and demonstrations – BOMARC Missile Base La Macaza, Quebec. Secret. "O" Division Toronto, re: Sandy and Rita Cline of Niagra Falls.

60 RCMP Memo for File, Ottawa, 23 July 1964. Re: protests and demonstrations – BOMARC Missile Base La Macaza, Quebec. Secret. "F" Division infiltration of Univ. of Saskatchewan to seek records.

61 RCMP Priority Secret Encrypted Message from La Macaza to "A" division Ottawa, 3 September 1964, 14:05, re: La Macaza vigil.

62 21 October 1969, Annex A to V 3312-20(DNW), secret, Canadian BUIC III/CIM10B (BOMARC) Operational History.

63 29 September 1969, 1618z, secret, to CANFORCEHED from CANDEFCOM.

64 25 January 1966, V3313-20 DNW, secret, memorandum, to DNW from DNW/NW4, re, BUIC III.

65 21 October 1969, Annex A to V 3312-

20(DNW), secret, Canadian BUIC III/CIM10B (BOMARC) Operational History.

66 31 December 1968, 1530Z, from CANDEFCOM to CANFORCEHED, secret, V3312-2367.

67 07 January 1969, 1345Z from CANFORCEHED to CFLO Kirtland AFB NMex, secret, V3312-2367.

68 07 January 1969, 1345Z from CANFORCEHED to CFLO Kirtland AFB NMex, secret, V3312-2367.

69 DND, Defence 1972. p.51.

70 "The History of the Aerospace Defense Command, FY 1972", ADCHO 73-1-1. p.243.

71 Secret Priority message from 22NRHQ, info to CANDEFSAM North Bay. 29 2055Z Mar 72. Subject: BOMARC Closure.

72 The talks and note are referred to in the Secret message from CANDEFCOM to CANDEFSAM La Macaza and CANDEFSAM North Bay. 29 1625Z Feb 72.

73 Secret Priority message from CANDEFCOM to CANDEFSAM La Macaza and CANDEFSAM North Bay. 19 1510Z OCT 71.

74 24 August 1971 "Announcement for all Personnel of 446 (SAM) Sqdn." from CO Major Randall.

75 DND Message form, 25 May 1972, 1220z, file 1920-3. from Major Fraser, re: document destruction.

76 05 April 1972, 1651z, V3313-20, from CANDEFCOM to CANDEFSAM North Bay and CANDEFSAM La Macaza.

77 DND Message form, 15 Apr 1972, 1615Z, file 1920-3. From Major Fraser, re: Weapons Techs needed at 446.

78 Secret Priority message from 22NRHQ, info to CANDEFSAM, North Bay. 2055Z 29 March 1972. Subject: BOMARC Closure.

79 13 March 1972, 2019z, to CANDEFSAM North Bay from CANDEFCOM.

80 15 December 1971, to CANDEFSAM La Macaza and CANDEFSAM North Bay from CANDEFCOM, re: Closure SAM sites. Telex, Secret.

CHAPTER 3: STARFIGHTER NUCLEAR WEAPONS

1 Hellyer, *Damn the Torpedoes*. p.75.

2 Hellyer statement to the Special Committee on Defence, 27 June 1963.

3 Hansard, 28 June 1963. p.1684.

4 Hansard, 30 May 1963. p.465.

5 Air Marshal CR Dunlap. Chief of the Air Staff testimony before the Special Committee on Defence, 16 July 1963.

6 Air Vice Marshal DAR Bradshaw, Air Officer Commanding 1 Air Division testimony before the Special Committee on Defence, 14 November 1963.

7 21 January 1965, 2130Z, to CAFORCEHED from CANAIRWASH, Nuclear Safety Rules for the CF-104/Mk28/Mk43 Weapon System. Restricted.

8 14 May 1964, S1100-104-5(DNW), Royal Canadian Air Force Nuclear Weapons Instruction, NWI 64-202, "CF104 Weapon System Safety Rules (T-1517 AMAC). Secret. This document specifically refers to both the Mk 28 RE and the Mk 28 EX as used on the RCAF CF-104.

9 The technical information on the Mk28 is taken from the following works: Arkin. *Nuclear Weapons Databook*. 1984. p.42–44; National Atomic Museum Factsheet, Weapon History Exhibits. p.30–31.; Gibson, *The History of the US Nuclear Arsenal*. p.92.; Hansen, *US Nuclear Weapons*. p.150–154.; and Hansen, *Swords of Armageddon*.

10 1 Air Division Historical Narrative, May 1964, referred to "the introduction of permissive action link (PAL) equipped weapons".

11 Senate Armed Services Committee, DoD FY 1983, pt.7, p.4172. as noted in Arkin, U.S. Nuclear Weapons Databook.

12 11 May 1967, V3312-22(DNW) Annex B, secret, Summaries of Briefings Presented to Joint RCAF/USAF Operational Review Board - CF104/Mk57 NWS.

13 The technical information on the Mk28 is taken from the following works: Arkin. *Nuclear Weapons Databook*. 1984. p.42–44; National Atomic Museum Factsheet, Weapon History Exhibits. p.30–31.; Gibson, *The History of the US Nuclear Arsenal*. p.92.; Hansen, *US Nuclear Weapons*. p.150–154.; and Hansen, *Swords of Armageddon*.

14 1 Air Division Historical Narrative, May 1964, referred to "the introduction of permissive action link (PAL) equipped weapons". This was a ground or aircraft operated 4 digit coded switch.

15 Senate Armed Services Committee, DoD FY 1983, pt.7, p.4172. as noted in Arkin, U.S. Nuclear Weapons Databook.

16 421 Squadron History. Canada's Wings, 1982.

17 Negative #CF66-576-7. This is a series of photos around the same neg.#. DND photo by Thomas.

18 1 July 1968, 0837z, secret, telex from CINCUSAFE to CANFORCEHQ.

19 11 September 1968 Special Capability Inspection at 4 Wing for CF104/Mk 43 Weapon System "Satisfactory". V3312-3059/4.

20 11 July 1968, 0837z, secret, telex from CINCUSAFE to CANFORCEHQ.

21 The technical information on the Mk43 was taken from the following works: Arkin. *Nuclear Weapons Databook.* 1984. p.49–50; National Atomic Museum Factsheet, Weapon History Exhibits. p.33.; Gibson, *The History of the US Nuclear Arsenal.* p.96.; Hansen, *US Nuclear Weapons.* p.158–162.; and Hansen, *Swords of Armageddon.*

22 20 September 1968, V3312-2453, Minutes of a Meeting on the Capability Inspection of 4 Wing CAF Held at CFHQ/DNW 0900 Hrs 18 Sep 1968. Secret. Item #2, Decision.

23 1 Air Division Historical Narrative, May 1964, referred to "the introduction of permissive action link (PAL) equipped weapons".

24 RCAF S-000-115-62 Vol 1. 27 April 1962, RCAF Defence Programme 62–63. Ballistic Shape: BDU8B.

25 11 September 1968, secret, to CDS from USAFE Inspector General, USAFE/CF Baden Soellingen Pre-Atomic Capability Inspection.

26 11 July 1969, 0837z secret telex from CINCUSAFE to CANFORCEHQ. and 11 September 1968 Special Capability Inspection at 4 Wing for CF104/Mk 43 Weapon System "Satisfactory". V3312-3059/4.

27 11 September 1968, secret, to CDS from USAFE Inspector General, USAFE/CF Baden-Soellingen Pre-Atomic Capability Inspection.

28 20 September 1968, V3312-2453, Minutes of a Meeting on the CI of 4 Wing CAF Held at CFHQ/DNW 0900 hrs 18 Sep 1968.

39 21 February 1969, V3312-20DNW, Memorandum to NW 2-2 and NW 2-2-2, from A/NW2, re: DNW Actions Pursuant to DNW/DNS Conference. Unclassified.

30 11 May 1967, V3312-22(DNW) Annex B, Summaries of Briefings Presented to Joint RCAF/USAF Operational Review Board – CF104/Mk57 NWS. Secret. Section 5.b.

31 28 February 1966, 0928z, V3312-22, to CANFORCEHED from USAFE, re: Mk 57 Weapon. Secret. "USAFE has requested shipment of weapons from CONUS to Zweibrucken for week of 14 March 1966 and week of 21 March 1966 for Soellingen."

32 11 May 1967, V3312-22(DNW) Annex B, Summaries of Briefings Presented to Joint RCAF/USAF Operational Review Board – CF104/Mk57 NWS. Secret. Section 5.b.

33 The technical information on the W57 is taken from the following works: Arkin. *Nuclear Weapons Databook.* 1984. p.63–64.; Gibson, *The History of the US Nuclear Arsenal.* p.95; Hansen, *US Nuclear Weapons.* p.164–166.; Hansen, *Swords of Armageddon*, and a data sheet from the US National Atomic Museum.

34 1 Air Division Historical Narrative, May 1964, referred to "the introduction of permissive action link (PAL) equipped weapons".

35 14 February 1966, 1500z, V3312-22, secret, to CONFORCEHED from CANAIRDIV.

36 1 Air Division Historical Narrative 1965, Appendix B, Technical., Armament, Nuclear Weapon Systems.

37 11 May 1967, V3312-22(DNW) Annex B, secret, Summaries of Briefings Presented to Joint RCAF/USAF Operational Review Board – CF104/Mk57 NWS.

38 11 May 1967, V3312-22(DNW) Annex B, secret, Summaries of Briefings Presented to Joint RCAF/USAF Operational Review Board – CF104/Mk57 NWS.

39 1 Air Division Historical Narrative 1965, Appendix B, Technical., Armament, Nuclear Weapon Systems.

40 12 July 1965, 0-3313-22 DNW, report on Mk57 clearance tests on a fully loaded CF104.

41 17 December 1965, to CANFORCEHED from RCAF LO Kirtland AFB NMEX, re: Mk 57 Delivery Restrictions. Secret.

42 1964, 005-64/___(CAE), draft, RCAF/AFHQ, Test and Development Instructions 64/72, Evaluation of the CF-104D Special Weapon Delivery Capability (Project Abalone).

43 14 February 1966, 1500z, V3312-22, secret, to CONFORCEHED from CANAIRDIV.

44 1 Air Division Historical Narrative 1965, Appendix B, Technical., Armament, Nuclear Weapon Systems.

45 1 Air Division Historical Narrative 1965, Appendix B, Technical., Armament, Nuclear Weapon Systems.

46 1 Air Division Historical Narrative 1966, Annex B, Technical, Armament.

47 11 May 1967, V3312-22(DNW), Annex B. Summaries of Briefings Presented to Joint RCAF/USAF Operational Review Board – CF104/Mk57 NWS. Secret. Section 5.c., 5.c.(3).

48 Hellyer testimony before the Special Committee on Defence, 27 June 1963.

49 Air Marshal CR Dunlap. Chief of the Air Staff testimony before the Special Committee on Defence, 16 July 1963.

50 14 November 1963, 1630Hrs. Briefing by A/V/M DAR Bradshaw, Air Officer Commanding 1 Air Division, RCAF, at 3 Wing RCAF. National Archives Acc. 87-88/146. Box 96.

51 Hellyer, *Damn the Torpedoes.* p.117.

52 CF-104 General Study Material, Rev. January 1963.

53 427 (F) Sqdn Diary written for Sqdn interest, finished March 1973. pages 231–232. DHist 78/475.

54 RCAF file S-000-115-63. (RG24, Vol 17541). Security Personnel Requirements.

55 1 Air Division Historical Narrative 1965 Appendix J. Nuclear Safety.

56 October 1964, USAFE, CF-104 IP, Joint Munitions Inspection Plan. 3312-22.

57 01 September 1964, O 3312-5-22, to CDS and DNW from USAFE Inspector General, re USAFE-RCAF CF104 Joint Munitions Inspection Plan. and 15 June 1964, USAFE-RCAF JOINT MUNITIONS INSPECTION PLAN. attached to above letter.

58 FILM of CF104 Loading: Bomb Loading on CF014. DND D651048Z1.AC, (7 min. 49 sec.) Ottawa.

CHAPTER 4: CF-104 STARFIGHTER AIR DIVISION, WINGS, AND SQUADRONS

1 2 December 1966 Memo to Cabinet from MND Paul Hellyer (written October 1966).

2 1 Air Div. 1964 Historical Report, January–March 1964.

3 1 Air Division Historical Narrative, 1964. Appendix F. Operations/Tactical Evaluations.

4 23 August 1963, priority, secret, to Canadian Embassy Bonn, from External Affairs, DRAFT, re Agreement between Canada and USA concerning nuclear weapons for Canadian Forces.

5 "The Stewardship Briefing, 30 November 1967" by A/V/M R.J. Lane, CO 1 Air Division. Top Secret.

6 "The Stewardship Briefing, 30 November 1967" by A/V/M R.J. Lane, CO 1 Air Division. Top Secret.

7 24 March 1964, Cabinet Conclusions, #27-64, "White Paper on Defence".

8 1 Air Division Historical Narrative, 1964. Appendix F.

9 1 Air Division Historical Narrative 1966 Annex H.

10 "The Stewardship Briefing, 30 November 1967" by A/V/M R.J. Lane, CO 1 Air Division. Top Secret.

11 1968 Historical Report, Decimomannu.

12 19 February 1965, 1342Z, to CANFORCEHQ from USAFE. re: Custodial shelter requirements.

13 USAF Historical records note that files of July 1967 through January 1968 contain final report of 7232 MMG. This file includes special orders. (USAF Historical Office, IRIS 00442350, K-GP-MS-7232-HI, 01/07/67 - 31/01/68.)

14 04 August 1964, secret, to USAFE (DS-MN) from USAF HQ Inspector General AFINSW Kirtland AFB NMex, re Nuclear Safety Survey of Non-US NATO.

15 In this case I have said that the US war was against the population of South Viet Nam, as the vast bulk of the bombing, political killing,

defoliation, and detention was targetted against that country and its population rather than against North Viet Nam and its people.

16 26 June 1969, Joint Nuclear Safety Inspection, USAF/CAF, Lahr, Germany, Secret, V3312-2467.

17 05 May 1969, 0840z, DND Minute Sheet, file V3312-2467(DNW) to VCDS.

18 26 June 1969, V3312-2467, secret, TacEval/CI Narrative Report. Minute Sheet, to VCDS from DNS.

19 24 March 1969, 1440z, secret, to CANFORCEHED from CANAIRDIV.

20 26 June 1969, V3312-2467, Joint Nuclear Safety Inspection, USAF/CAF, Lahr, Germany. Secret.

21 11 May 1967, V3312-22(DNW) Annex B, Summary of Briefings Presented to Joint RCAF/USAF Operational Review Board – CF104/Mk57 NWS. Secret.

22 430 Squadron. Les Presses Lithographiques Inc. Quebec, 1981.

23 26 June 1969, V3312-2467, secret, USAFE/CAF, Lahr, Germany, Joint Nuclear Safety Inspection Report.

24 3 Wing Historical Narrative, 31 January 1964

25 USAFE 160R 196 17 April 1964

26 29 April 1964, S1100-105-5(DNW), secret, minute sheet (8), to DNW from DNW/NW2, W/C DT Bain.

27 20 September 1968, V3312-2453. Minutes of a Meeting on the Capability Inspection of 4 Wing CAF held at CFHQ/DNW 0900 Hrs 18 Sep 1968. Secret

28 427 (F) Sqdn Diary written for Sqdn interest, finished March 1973. pages 231–232. DHist 78/475.

29 Restricted DND 3009/444 CFHQ Ottawa "Effective 1 April 67 434 Strike/Attach (sic) Squadron, Zweibrucken Germany, will be reduced to nil strength and made dormant." RL Hennessy Vice Adm, for CDS.

30 11 May 1967, V3312-22(DNW) Annex B, Summary of Briefings Presented to Joint RCAF/USAF Operational Review Board – CF104/Mk57 NWS. Secret.

31 Strike Swift Strike Sure by Capts D. Harrison and T. Edwards, c. 1982. p.77.

32 1964 Annual Historical Report, 4 Wing Soellingen, 01 Jan 64–31 Dec 64. Technical Summary. Secret.

33 9–13 March 1970 Capability Inspections of special weapons #1 (Mk 28) and #3 (Mk 57).

34 20 September 1968, V3312-2453. Minutes of a Meeting on the Capability Inspection of 4 Wing CAF held at CFHQ/DNW 0900 Hrs 18 Sep 1968. Secret

35 11 September 1968, secret, to CDS from USAFE Inspector General, USAFE/CF Baden Soellingen Pre-Atomic Capability Inspection.

36 11 September 1968, USAFE/CF Baden Soellingen, Pre-Atomic Capability Inspection. Secret.

37 03 March 1970, V3313-22(DNW), Visit Report to HQ USAFE Weisbaden 3 Feb 70, 4 Wing Baden 4 Feb 70, and 1 Air Div Lahr 5 and 6 Feb 70. Secret. This document states that only #1 & #3 weapons remained in use at 4 Wing. para. 4.

38 24 March 1969, 1440z, V3312-2453, to CANFORCEHED from CANAIRDIV, re: Capability Inspection Date – 4WG Baden Soellingen. Secret No Unclassified Reply or Reference.

39 18 November 1971, V3313-22(DNW), to DGAF from DNW, re: DNW Field Activity – 1 CAG Final Visit. Restricted.

40 421 Squadron History. Canada's Wings, 1982.

41 1964 Annual Historical Report, 4 Wing Soellingen, 01 Jan 64–31 Dec 64. Operations Section. Secret.

42 421 Squadron History. Canada's Wings, 1982.

43 11 May 1967, V3312-22(DNW) Annex B, Summary of Briefings Presented to Joint RCAF/USAF Operational Review Board – CF104/Mk57 NWS. Secret.

44 19 March 1963, first CF104 delivered to 4 Wing.

45 11 May 1967, V3312-22(DNW) Annex B, Summary of Briefings Presented to Joint RCAF/USAF Operational Review Board – CF104/Mk57 NWS. Secret.

46 Strike Swift Strike Sure (1947–1982) book by Capts D. Harrison and T. Edwards, c. 1982. Dhist, Ottawa.

47 Restricted DND 3009/444 CFHQ Ottawa RL Hennessy Vice Adm, for CDS.

48 15 March 1967. 895-59/1 (COS), Organizational Instructions. 4.5.3/1 "it has been decided to stand down 444 Strike/Attack Sqn." (as of 01 April 1967)

CHAPTER 5: HONEST JOHN

1 Cabinet Minutes, 01 October 1958. Procurement of Lacrosse missile for Canadian Army.

2 15 January 1957, CAS(W) 8931-4-1-P1 Vol 2(AR), Canadian Joint Staff Washington, re: Canadian Army Headquarters, re: "Purchase of Honest John Rocket, Unserviceable Condition". The $4000.00 price tag was called "exorbitant", and it was said that a mockup could be locally built for less.

3 28 May 1959, HQS 8931-4-1-P1 DQMG(D&D), Memorandum, "Procurement of Honest John Guided missile System".

4 02 October 1959 Memorandum to the CGS from the VCGS, re: Honest John versus Lacrosse.

5 25 February 1960, Letter to the Prime Minister from the Minister of National Defence, re: Honest John purchase.

6 04 March 1960, HQS 6001-MISSILES/H2(CGS) Secret, Memorandum to the MND from the CGS, re: Procurement of 762mm Rocket (Honest John) in Lieu of Lacrosse".

7 11 March 1960, HQS 6001-MISSILES/H2(CGS) Secret, Memorandum to the MND from the CGS, re: Procurement of 762mm Rocket (Honest John) in Lieu of Lacrosse".

8 15 July 1960, HQC 3460-1 TD 0061 DMT, Organization and Training Directive. 762mm SSM Batteries RCA.

9 11 March 1060, HQS 6001-MISSILES/H2(CGS), to MND from CGS, re: Procurement of 762mm rocket. Secret.

10 05 December 1960, Memorandum to the Chief of the General Staff, re: Army Honest John Rocket.

11 Canadian Army, SD 1, Letter 60/29 of 5 July 1960, authorizing formation of 1 SSM Bty and 2 SSM (Training) Bty.

12 16 December 1960, DND Message #30236B/237.

13 "Firepower: Honest John Rocket", Canadian Army Journal. Winter 1962, Vol. XVI, #1.p.72–76.

14 NATO stock number 1055-00-601-6900.

15 All technical information on the W31 nuclear warhead comes from the following works: Arkin. Nuclear Weapons Databook. p.45–46, 282–283; National Atomic Museum Factsheet, Weapon History Exhibits. p.19–20.; Gibson, The History of the US Nuclear Arsenal. p.68–69.; Hansen, U.S. Nuclear Weapons. p.193.; Hansen, Swords of Armamgeddon.

16 Report of a DNW Visit to Various Army Formations in Europe in Connection with the Canadian Army Honest John Programme – 20 to 29 October 1964." file 0 3313-25 (DNW) 16 November 1964. by Group Captain C.F. Phripp DNW.

17 01 May 1965, 8931-4-1-_1 DMP(ARMY)7, 6211-064902. Confidential Memorandum, to DEE(Army) through DNW, from DMP(Army). "Warhead Section, Atomic Training, Honest John System".

18 Note to Minister of National Defence's aide from the Chief of the General Staff, 19 February 1964, in 1 SSM historical file, DND/DHist.

19 Letter to Chief of the General Staff from the Chairman of Chiefs of Staff, 3 Jun 64, re: service-to-service technical agreement for Honest John.

20 Letter from CO 50 Msl Regiment (RA), to

HQ 4 Division, 31 January 1966, re: Damage Control – SAS Site.

21 06 June 1964, 4 CIBG S2190-1 TD 260, from Commander, Canadian Army National Force Europe, Brigadier Dare, to CINC US Army Europe, re: US/UK Service-to-Service Technical Arrangement.

22 Restricted, Army HQ Letter HQC 1452-80/3P, Ottawa, 5 July 1960., Reorganizations – CA(R), 1 SSM Bty and 2 SSM Trg Bty.

23 Letter to MND from CGS, HQS 6001-Missiles/H2 (CGS) 30/6/61

24 20 May 1960, to the Chairman Chiefs of Staff from the CGS, re: Special Ammunition Storage Site, 4 CIBG. Secret – Canadian Eyes Only.

25 24 ___ 1961, Support of Atomic Delivery for Northern Army Group. Prepared by DMO&P. Top Secreet. The only copy available at DHist is so faded and gutted by censors that most identifying information has been obscured.

26 20 April 1966, V 3312-3059/5(DNW) "A Report on Items Noted While Observing a Nuclear Safety Inspection of the 1 SSM Honest John Battery, RCA 21–22 March 1966." by CFHQ/DNW. (Cdn Army file 4500-NSI. 20 Apr 66 NSI Report.)

27 1 SSM Bty Historical Report, 1962, 5 July 62 entry.

28 The records of the US Army Custodial Detachment are kept in a storage facility in St. Louis, MO, and are currently unavailable for research.

29 HQ, US Army Europe, 30 September 1964. to CINC USAEUR, thru OC 1 SSM Bty and CO 4 CIBG. subject: "Nuclear Safety Inspection of the 1 SSM Battery, Royal Canadian Artillery (Trip No 10C)(FY 65)(C)". Confidential, War Room Registration #1330.

30 16 November 1964, "Report of a DNW Visit to Various Army Formations in Europe in Connection with the Canadian Army Honest John Programme – 20 to 29 October 1964." Secret, O 3313-25(DNW).

31 US Army USEUCOM Directive 60-10, Dispersal, Storage and Peacetime Utilization of Nuclear Weapons, Annex C, Para 5d.

32 20 April 1966, V 3312-3059/5(DNW) "A Report on Items Noted While Observing a Nuclear Safety Inspection of the 1 SSM Honest John Battery, RCA 21–22 March 1966." by CFHQ/DNW. (Cdn Army file 4500-NSI. 20 Apr 1966 NSI Report.)

33 29 September 1965, 1 SSM: S/6001-H2, from CO 1 SSM Bty to HQ 4 CIBG, re: "Employment of Nuclear Weapons".

34 Report of a DNW Visit to Various Army Formations in Europe in Connection with the Canadian Army Honest John Programme – 20 to 29 October 1964." file 0 3313-25 (DNW) 16 November 1964. by Group Captain C.F. Phripp DNW.

35 13 1628Z December 1968 from CANLANEUR to CANFORCEHED Secret.

36 13 0750Z December 1968 from CANLANEUR to CANFORCEHED Secret.

37 US Army Europe Regulation 702-190, 6 May 1965, NUCLEAR WEAPONS. Evacuation and Destruction of Nuclear Weapons.

38 US Army Europe, USAEUR Regulation 702-190, Nuclear Weapons, Evacuation and Destruction of Nuclear Weapons. 06 May 1965. Secret. Canadian Army copy #281. p.3.

39 03 November 1965, 1 SSM: S/6001-H2. to HQ 4 CIBG from CO 1 SSM Bty, re: Employment of US Perrsonnel. Secret.

40 US Army Europe, USAEUR Regulation 702-190, Nuclear Weapons, Evacuation and Destruction of Nuclear Weapons. 06 May 1965. Secret.

41 Commanding Officer, Major AC Moffat, 1 SSM Bty, to the Editor of CF Nuclear Safety Bulletin, NDHQ, 17 May 1966. V3313-25 DNW.

42 17 May 1966, 1SSM: 1580-1 from 1 SSM to Editor CF Nuclear Safety Bulletin.

43 13 May 1968, 2001-10 TD 340/67(G), to Commander 1 British Corps, from Commander 4 CIBG, re: "Implementation New Field Force Structure Reduction – 1 SSM Bty, RCA".

44 13 May 1968, 2001-10 TD 340/67(G), to Commander 1 (British) corps, from Commander 4 CIBG, re: Implementation New Field Force structure reduction – 1 SSM Bty, RCA. Secret, UK/Canadian Eyes Only.

45 19 May 1970, V3312-1765 (DNW). "A Report on Items Noted While Observing a Nuclear Surety Inspection of the 1 SSM (Honest John) Battery RCA on 11, 13 May, 1970." by Major J.E. Goodine, CFHQ/VCDS/DNW.

46 13 May 1970, "Observations of USAEUR Nuclear Surety Inspection Team" to CO 1 SSM Bty. RCA, Iserlohn, Germany. by Lt Col. Donald G. Manring, Inspector General.

47 24 March 1964, Cabinet Conclusions, #27-64, "White Paper on Defence".

48 16 November 1964, 0 3313-25(DNW), Report of a DNW Visit to Various Army formations in Europe in Connection with the Canadian Army Honest John Programme – 20 to 29 October 1964. Secret.

49 Restricted, Army HQ Letter HQC 1452-80/3P, Ottawa, 5 July 1960., Reorganizations – CA(R), 1 SSM Bty and 2 SSM Trg Bty.

50 16 November 1964, "Report of a DNW Visit to Various Army Formations in Europe in

Connection with the Canadian Army Honest John Programme – 20 to 29 October 1964." Secret, O 3313-25(DNW).

51 19 May 1963, 1 SSM fired HJ 22 247m at Shilo.

CHAPTER 6: THE CF-101B VOODOO AND GENIE ROCKET

1 14 March 1961, letter to the Canadian Ambassador to the USA from the Department of Defence Production, J.A. Teeter, re: F-101B reciprocal procurement. J.A. Teeter mistakenly referes to the VooDoo as the "F10B" four time in the letter. Canadian Embassy in Washington files, Canada-US Defence Relations, 1961–1964.

2 03 July 1958, S1929-104 (VCAS/EA), Secret, to COR from VCAS/EA, re: Requirement for Atomic Warheads in Canada. (Note that the nuclearized USN weapon, the Sparrow-N-9, was cancelled on 13 January 1958.)

3 05 December 1960, Memorandum for Cabinet Defence Committee, "Nuclear Weapons for NATO and NORAD Forces". Top Secret, Document #_7-60.

4 05 December 1960, Memorandum for Cabinet Defence Committee, "Nuclear Weapons for NATO and NORAD Forces". Top Secret, Document #_7-60.

5 02 December 1959, Memorandum to the Cabinet Defence Commitee from the MND, re: Acquisition and Storage of Defensive Nuclear Weapons and Warheads for Canadian Forces.

6 ADCHQ/SASO Monthly Record of Activities, Appendix B to 1965 Annual Historical Report, 01 Jan 65–31 Dec 65.

7 Standing Committee on External Affairs and National Defence. 75:32, 25/5/82.

8 14 March 1961, letter to the Canadian Ambassador to the USA from the Department of Defence Production, J.A. Teeter, re: F-101B reciprocal procurement. Attached to the letter was the "Notes Made After Oral Review of Proposed Gilpatric Letter to Ambassador Heeny" which refers to 330 MB-1 missiles.

9 13 March 1961, "Notes Made After Oral Review of Proposed Gilpatric Letter to Ambassador Heeny". $36.7 million total cost to be shared 2/3 by USA, and 1/3 by Canada.

10 The technical information for the W25 is taken from the following works: Arkin. US Nuclear Weapons Databook. p.41.; Gibson, The History of the US Nuclear Arsenal. p.78.; Hansen, US Nuclear Weapons. p.176–178.; and Hansen, Swords of Armageddon.

11 15 September 1959, to the MND from the Chairman Chiefs of Staff, re: Storage of Defensive Nuclear Weapons at Goose Bay and Harmon Air Force Base. Top Secret. Section 4(b)(ii).

12 USAF, History of Continental Air Defense Command and Aerospace Defense Command. 01 January 1973, 30 June 1974. Secret. p.87.

13 CFB Bagotville Annual Historical Report, 1982.

14 24 June 1974, Val d'Or Combat Air Control log book, DHist, Ottawa.

15 Hansard, 21 May 1963. p.110.

16 See Cabinet Document 578-74, and annex A to 578-74/673-74RD, 28 November 1974.

17 1965 ADC Historical Report, Appendix B. (STSO/ ADCHQ), January 1964, "CF101B/AIR2A Weapon System"

18 1965 ADC Historical Report, Appendix B. (SASO/ADCHQ)

19 1966 ADC Historical Report, Appendix B.

20 Department of Energy (Albuquerque Operations Office) letter to the author, 29 July 1997, regarding W25 retirement date confirmation.

21 History of Continental Air Defense Command and Aerospace Defense Command, 01 January 1973–30 June 1974. USAF, ADC Headquarters. Secret. p.70.

22 01 June 1965, 1300z, O 3312-3036/2, secret, memorandum to CDS, VCDS, Minister's Military Secretary, from DNW, re Acquisition of Nuclear Warheads at RCAF ADC CF101 Units. Reference: Memorandum O 1550-3310 TD5145(DNW), 25 May 65.

23 Hansard, 03 June 1965. p.1925.

24 Val d'Or Historical Summary, 01 Dec 64–31 Dec 65.

25 ADCHQ/STSO Monthly Record of Activities, Appendix B to the 1964 Annual Historical Report, 01 Jan64–31 Dec 64. Secret.

26 Comox Annual Historical Report, 1965. Press clipping, 28–29 August 1965, "Peace Marchers Demonstration"

27 "Sailors Dump Sign into Drink at Comox", Daily Colonist. Vistoria, B.C., 22 August 1965. p.19.

28 Annual Historical Report 1984, CFB Comox, Base Security Section, A/B Secur O, 16 January 1985.

29 409 Sqdn Annual Historical Report, 1970; 26–30 October 1970, William Tell 70.

30 USAF History of Continental Air Defense Command and Aerospace Defense Command, 01 July 1974, 30 June 1975. Secret. p.56.

31 1984 Annual Historical Report, CFB Comox, Security Section.

32 Totem Times. 28 June 1984. back cover.

33 Detachment 5, 425 MMS, Report for July–Sept 1965.

34 Colonel AM Lee, Chatham, An airfield History. 1989, Unipress, NB. p.47.

35 Operation Starlifter: 31 March–03 April 1975.

36 416 Squadron History. The Hangar Bookshelf, 1984. 28 July 1962 scramble of 1 minute, 30 seconds.

37 Chatair. April 1974. p.13.

38 USAF History of Continental Air Defense Command and Aerospace Defense Command, 01 January 1973, 30 June 1974. Secret. p.77–78.

39 Confirmed Mass Loads at Bagotville by 416 occurred on 17 November 1980, and 21 September 1981.

40 Chatair. May 1974 Insert. p.11.

41 Detachment 4, 425 MMS, Report for April–June 1965.

42 Chatair. April 1975. front page and centre-section.

43 Chatair. March 1975. p.2.

44 Bagotville 1964 Historical Report, Appendix B. CE Section.

45 1300hrs, 01 June 1965, 0 3312-3036/2(DNW) Memorandum to the CDS & VCDS from the Secretary of the Defence Staff, re: Acquisition of Nuclear Warheads at RCAF ADC CF101 Units. Secret.

46 Annual Hist Report 1984, CFB Bagotville, Base Operations Officer, 25 March 1985; and Military Police Section, 26 February 1985.

47 Annual Hist Report 1984, CFB Bagotville, Military Police Section, 26 February 1985.

48 425 Squadron. Ottawa, c.1985. p.64.

49 February 1967, PM LB Pearson visits Bagotville/425.

50 USAF History of Continental Air Defense Command and Aerospace Defense Command, 01 January 1973, 30 June 1974. Secret. p.77–78.

51 425 Annual Historical Report 1979.

52 CF101 VooDoo. SMS Publishers. p.40.

53 1965, Val d'Or Historical Summary 01 Dec 64–31 Dec 65.

54 1965 Val d'Or Historical Summary 01 Dec 64–31 Dec 65,

55 Hansard, 29 October 1963. p.4128.

56 Hansard, 11 December 1963. p.5686.

57 05 November 1965, V3312-3036/2, secret, to CFHQ/ RCAF Ottawa, from USAF ADC Inspector General, re: Initial Capability Inspection of Station Val d'Or/Det 6, 425th Munitions Maintenance Squadron, conducted 31 October–05 November 1965.

58 Val d'Or Historical Summary, 01 Dec 64–31 Dec 65.

59 05 November 1965, V3312-3036/2(DNW), Initial Capability Inspection Narrative Report RCAF Station Val d'Or Que 01–05 Nov 65.

60 17 June 1965, O 3312-3036/2(DNW) secret, memorandum to COPR, from DNW, re Acquisition of Nuclear Warheads – RCAF Station Val d'Or. Reference: Min(2) to O 3312-3036/2(DNW, 09 June 65.

61 Memo, DNW 18 Feb 66, V3312-3036/2(DNBW), – August 1965, secret.

62 07 October 1965, secret, ADC message T168, re limited primary weapons capability at Val d'Or.

63 13 May 1970, V 3312-2419(DNW), Minute Sheet from DNW Col. EN Henderson, re: Val d'Or Message CO 15. Secret.

64 01 June 1965, 1300z, O 3312-3036/2, secret, memorandum to CDS, VCDS, Minister's Military Secretary, from DNW, re Acquisition of Nuclear Warheads at RCAF ADC CF101 Units.

65 Val d'Or Historical Summary, Dec 64–31 Dec 65.

66 Weapons acquisition by USAF flight. Val d'Or 1966 Annual Historical Report.

67 "C-124 Globemaster (USAF) arrrives at 2100 local for munitions acquisition. Departs 2200 local." Val d'Or 1968 Annual Historical Report.

68 "Weapons acquisition", Val d'Or 1969 Annual Historical Report.

69 13 May 1966, V 3312-3036/2(DAFOR), secret, memorandum, to DGAF, re Val d'Or Concept of Operations.

70 15 May 1970, USAF ADC HQ, Inspector General Report, V3312-2419, secret. Report of a combined capability and general inspection at CFB Val D'Or, 10–15 May 1970.

71 13 May 1970, 1900z, secret, minute sheet, V3312-2419, Val d'Or Message CO 15, by DNW.

72 Val d'Or Combat Air Control log book, 05 July 1974. DHist, Ottawa.

73 22 June 1967, priority, secret, from D/Security CANFORCEHED, to CANDEFCOM.

74 31 January 1969, FMC 350-1 OPS, 3312-2419 Vol 2. OPERATION RIVET, OPERATIONAL INSTRUCTION NO 2.

75 Jan 75, 1901-2414(VCDS), Annex A, Guidelines – Cloba Val d'Or.

76 23 March 1975, Val d'Or Combat Air Control log book, DHist, Ottawa.

77 Standing Committee of External Affairs and National Defence. 65:13, 25/2/82.

78 Standing Committee of External Affairs and National Defence. 65:38, 25/2/82.

79 Standing Committee of External Affairs and National Defence. 65:51, 25/2/82.

80 Standing Committee of External Affairs and National Defence. 4:12, 14/2/85.

CHAPTER 7: ANTI-SUBMARINE WARFARE

1 02 December 1959, Memorandum for the Cabinet Defence Committee from the MND, re: Acquisition and Storage of Defensive Nuclear Weapons and Warheads for Canadian

Forces. Top Secret.

2   15 December 1958, Extract from Canada-United States Committee on Joint Defence – Record of Meeting. Appendix A. "Problems Connected with the Acquisition and Control of Defensive Nuclear Weapons in Canada. Secret.

3   07 December 1959, "Draft of Proposed Agreement with the United States on the Acquisition of Nuclear Warheads for Canadian Forces", Cabinet Defence Committee Document # 6-60. Top Secret.

4   06 March 1964, Top Secret, "Acquisition of Nuclear Anti-Submarine Weapons for Canadian Maritime Forces", NSTS 1240-21-4 (Staff), originally dated 27 Feb 64.

5   17 April 1963, NATO Standing Group, NATO Document IR(63) Canada-D/1.

6   09 May 1963, Cabinet Conclusions, #7-63. "Report of Cabinet Defence Committee; nuclear weapons agreements"

7   09 May 1963, Cabinet Conclusions, #7-63. "Report of Cabinet Defence Committee; nuclear weapons agreements"

8   09 May 1963, Cabinet Conclusions, #7-63. "Report of Cabinet Defence Committee; nuclear weapons agreements"

9   Anti-Submarine Weapons System Requirements for the RCN. Report prepared by Directorate of Naval Fighting Equipment Requirements, March 1964. Secret. p.25.

10 14 August 1962, Letter to SSEA from MND, re: nuclear warheads for Canadian forces, schedule B.

11 HMCS Assiniboine, Fraser, Margaree, Ottawa, Saguenay, St. Lauent, Skeena.

12 Probably HMCS Qu'Appelle and Yukon; but possibly either Mackenzie or Saskatchewan.

13 06 March 1964, Top Secret, "Methods of Providing Nuclear Weapons to Canadian Maritime Forces", NSTS 1240-21-4 (Staff), originally dated 27 Feb 64.

14 13 May 1963, Cabinet Conclusions, #8-63. Report on Pearson visit with Kennedy.

15 13 May 1963, Memorandum to the Cabinet, #34/63, "Nuclear Weapons Policy", by the Secretary of State for External Affairs, Paul Martin.

16 14 May 1963, Cabinet Conclusions, #9-63. "Nuclear Weapons Agreement with the United States"

17 14 May 1963, Cabinet Conclusions, #9-63. "Nuclear Weapons Agreement with the United States"

18 13 May 1963, Memorandum to the Cabinet, #34/63. from the Secretary of State for External Affairs, Paul Martin.

19 13 May 1963, Cabinet Conclusions.

20 14 May 1963, Cabinet Conclusions, #9-63. Nuclear Weapons Agreement with the United States.

21 16 August 1963, Cabinet Minutes, #45-63.

22 12 September 1963, Cabinet Minutes. Storage of nuclear warheads in Canada for United States Forces. p.18–19.

23 06 March 1964, Top Secret, "Acquisition of Nuclear Anti-Submarine Weapons for Canadian Maritime Forces", NSTS 1240-21-4 (Staff), originally dated 27 Feb 64.

24 06 March 1964, Top Secret, "Methods of Providing Nuclear Weapons to Canadian Maritime Forces", NSTS 1240-21-4 (Staff), originally dated 27 Feb 64.

25 10 March 1964, Top Secret, Memorandum to Secretary, Naval Board – for Naval Board Consideration, from VCNS, re: Nuclear Weapons for anti-Submarine Warfare. NSTS 1240-21-4 (Staff).

26 Please see the full discussion of the 09 May 1963 Cabinet meeting regarding nuclear ASW weapons for Canada.

27 Anti-Submarine Weapons System Requirements for the RCN. Report prepared by Directorate of Naval Fighting Equipment Requirements, March 1964. Secret. p.7, 25.

28 05 April 1963, S1929-106-1 TD3093 (DIPM), Secret, to D/VCAS from DIPM, RCAF Minute Sheet. (Argus and Neptune nuclear modification/training costs.)

29 Argus Operating Instructions, 01 June 1973, EO 05-120A-1, Part 9, figure 9-5.; and Argus Armament and Armament Systems, 12 May 1980, C-12-107-OHO/MF-000, Part 3, figures 3-6, 3-7.

30 Argus Operating Instructions, 01 June 1973, EO 05-120A-1, Part 9, figure 9-5.; and Argus Armament and Armament Systems, 12 May 1980, C-12-107-OHO/MF-000, Part 3, figures 3-6, 3-7.

31 15 Nov 62 Memorandum S1924-104(D/AMTS) Confidential, to VCAS from D/AMTS re: Visit to USN HQ Regarding Maritime Special Ammunition Storage and Maintenance.

32 Anti-Submarine Weapons System Requirements for the RCN. Report prepared by Directorate of Naval Fighting Equipment Requirements, March 1964. Secret. p.7.

33 05 April 1963, S1929-106-1 TD3093 (DIPM), Secret, to D/VCAS from DIPM, RCAF Minute Sheet. (Argus and Neptune nuclear modification/training costs.)

34 RCAF P2V7 NEPTUNE Special Weapons Loading Procedures. EO 05-110A-2HAB. Issued on authority of the Chief of the Air Staff. 30 August 1963.

35 24 March 1961, Memorandum, S1929-106-1(DMTR) TD 0349A, Secret, to COR, from DMTR, re: Nuclear Capability in Maritime Air Command.

36 05 April 1963, S1929-106-1 TD3093

(DIPM), Secret, to D/VCAS from DIPM, RCAF Minute Sheet. (Argus and Neptune nuclear modification/training costs.)

37 Gibson, The History of the US Nuclear Arsenal. p.95., Hansen, U.S. Nuclear Weapons. p.207–208.

38 05 April 1963, S1929-106-1 TD3093 (DIPM), Secret, to D/VCAS from DIPM, RCAF Minute Sheet. (Argus and Neptune nuclear modification/training costs.)

39 Gibson, The History of the US Nuclear Arsenal. p.88., Hansen, U.S. Nuclear Weapons. p.154–155.

40 Arkin. Nuclear Weapons Databook. 1984. p.63–64.; Gibson, The History of the US Nuclear Arsenal. p.95.; Hansen, U.S. Nuclear Weapons. p.164–166.

41 05 April 1963, S1929-106-1 TD3093 (DIPM), Secret, to D/VCAS from DIPM, RCAF Minute Sheet. (Argus and Neptune nuclear modification/training costs.)

42 Anti-Submarine Weapons System Requirements for the RCN. Report prepared by Directorate of Naval Fighting Equipment Requirements, March 1964. Secret. p.34–35, 56–57.

43 19 September 1961, NSS 1240-21-2 (DGA), Secret, Memorandum to AMTS from CNTS, RAdm Caldwell, re: CS2F-2 Nuclear Weapon Carrying Capability.

44 06 March 1964, Top Secret, "Acquisition of Nuclear Anti-Submarine Weapons for Canadian Maritime Forces", NSTS 1240-21-4 (Staff), originally dated 27 Feb 64.

45 RCN file NSS 1240-21-2 (DGA). National Archives, RG24, Acc. 1983-84/167, boxes 1–4.

46 Soward, Hands to Flying Stations. p.260–261.

47 15 Nov 62 Memorandum S1924-104(D/AMTS) Confidential, to VCAS from D/AMTS re: Visit to USN HQ Regarding Maritime Special Ammunition Storage and Maintenance. Also see: Soward, Hands to Flying Stations. p.260–261. The Tracker arrived at Kirtland the week of 03 December 1962.

48 06 March 1964, Top Secret, "Acquisition of Nuclear Anti-Submarine Weapons for Canadian Maritime Forces", NSTS 1240-21-4 (Staff), originally dated 27 Feb 64.

49 10 April 1962, NSS 1240-21-4, SECRET, DND, Royal Canadian Navy letter to RCAF A/C E.M. Reyno, Joint Special Weapons Policy Committee, from RCN Cmdre R.P. Welland, JSWPC. "Stowage of Special Weapons – West Coast".

50 17–18 July 1962, Secret, 245th Meeting, Naval Policy Co-ordinating Committee, re: Ammunition Stowage Facilities at HMCS Shearwater.

BIBLIOGRAPHIC NOTES

1 Hansen, C., Swords of Armageddon. California, Chukelea Publications, 1995–96. hansenc@attmail.com